Essentials Of Prompt Engineering For Generative AI

Practical Advances in
Artificial Intelligence and Machine Learning

Dr. Lance B. Eliot, MBA, PhD

Disclaimer: This book is presented solely for educational and entertainment purposes. The author and publisher are not offering it as legal, accounting, or other professional services advice. The author and publisher make no representations or warranties of any kind and assume no liabilities of any kind with respect to the accuracy or completeness of the contents and specifically disclaim any implied warranties of merchantability or fitness of use for a particular purpose. Neither the author nor the publisher shall be held liable or responsible to any person or entity with respect to any loss or incidental or consequential damages caused, or alleged to have been caused, directly or indirectly, by the information or programs contained herein. Every company is different, and the advice and strategies contained herein may not be suitable for your situation.

ISBN: 978-1-95-738616-4

DEDICATION

To my incredible daughter, Lauren, and my incredible son, Michael.

Forest fortuna adiuvat (from the Latin; good fortune favors the brave).

CONTENTS

ACKNOWLEDGMENTS

I have been the beneficiary of advice and counsel from many friends, colleagues, family, investors, and many others. I want to thank everyone who has aided me throughout my career. I write from the heart and the head, having experienced first-hand what it means to have others around you who support you during the good times and the tough times.

To Warren Bennis, one of my doctoral advisors and ultimately a colleague, I offer my deepest thanks and appreciation, especially for his calm and insightful wisdom and support.

To Mark Stevens and his generous efforts toward funding and supporting the USC Stevens Center for Innovation.

To Lloyd Greif and the USC Lloyd Greif Center for Entrepreneurial Studies for their ongoing encouragement of founders and entrepreneurs.

To Peter Drucker, William Wang, Aaron Levie, Peter Kim, Jon Kraft, Cindy Crawford, Jenny Ming, Steve Milligan, Chis Underwood, Frank Gehry, Buzz Aldrin, Steve Forbes, Bill Thompson, Dave Dillon, Alan Fuerstman, Larry Ellison, Jim Sinegal, John Sperling, Mark Stevenson, Anand Nallathambi, Thomas Barrack, Jr., and many other innovators and leaders that I have met and gained mightily from doing so.

Thanks to Ed Trainor, Kevin Anderson, James Hickey, Wendell Jones, Ken Harris, DuWayne Peterson, Mike Brown, Jim Thornton, Abhi Beniwal, Al Biland, John Nomura, Eliot Weinman, John Desmond, and many others for their unwavering support during my career.

And most of all thanks as always to Lauren and Michael, for their ongoing support and for having seen me writing and heard much of this material during the many months involved in writing it. To their patience and willingness to listen.

CHAPTER 1

INTRODUCTION TO PROMPT ENGINEERING

This book is about prompt engineering.

Now that we are all on the same page, I'd like to tell you a bit about the topic of prompt engineering, including why it is such an important skill set currently.

The topic of prompt engineering has risen to prominence because of modern-day generative AI. When using generative AI, you enter prompts. A prompt might consist of a question that want to ask the AI to answer, or could be an instruction to the AI, or any of a wide variety of indications that you are seeking to convey to the AI. After having provided a prompt, the generative AI will generate a response.

You usually do this in a series of turns. A turn entails the entry of a prompt followed by a generated response. In a sense, by doing a series of turns, you are carrying on a conversation with the AI. Along the way, you might have the AI generate an essay or solve a problem. This continues until you decide that the conversation or effort should be concluded.

Prompt engineering exists because the nature of the prompts you enter will materially impact the nature of the generated responses you will receive. Many people merely enter prompts in a lackadaisical off-the-cuff way. That's fine, kind of. For ordinary or occasional use of generative AI, you likely don't need to do any extra studying or special preparation. Just go for it.

On the other hand, if you are an avid user of generative AI or want to become one, the use of prompt engineering techniques and approaches can make a substantial difference in how things go. You will tend to get better responses that are more on-target to what you are trying to achieve. Prompt engineering opens your eyes to the variety of ways that you can fully leverage generative AI.

I have been writing extensively about prompt engineering, especially in my widely popular column for Forbes. I also teach classes on prompt engineering. The classes encompass the basics or essentials and launch further into more advanced prompting strategies and tactics. A key to prompt engineering is not only studying the matter but also putting it into practice. I am known for stridently telling people that if they truly want to be proficient at prompt engineering, they need to keep in mind these three words: practice, practice, practice (yes, the same famous words required to get to Carnegie Hall).

This curated collection of my best prompt engineering expositions is intended as a core essential guide. There is a second book on advanced approaches that has also been published. I will momentarily in this chapter describe the contents of this core essentials book. Plus, I will tell you what is in the advanced book in case such additional material might also interest you.

If you are already a wizard at prompt engineering, congratulations. I would suggest that there is always room to grow. Thus, I would still recommend that you go through the essentials in this book and make sure you know all the nuances and details. Some people who are wizards at prompt engineering primarily figured out what to do via the seat-of-the-pants method. That's wonderful. At the same time, getting additional insights and polish is undoubtedly a helpful boon to honing those skills.

I provide lots of examples in the chapters. Most of the time, I opted to use ChatGPT. The logic for using ChatGPT is that it is the elephant in the room when it comes to generative AI. There are reportedly one hundred million weekly active users of ChatGPT. That is a staggering number.

The good news about prompt engineering is that the essence of the techniques and approaches are applicable across all the popular generative AI apps. You will find that the skills shown here are readily applied to ChatGPT, GPT-4 Bard, Gemini, Claude, and likewise most other popular generative AI apps. I urge you to become familiar with several generative AI apps. In addition, you will gradually discover the idiosyncrasies of each generative AI app and can then tailor your prompt engineering skills according to each one.

I'll next cover foundational elements of prompt engineering. After doing so, I will describe the contents of the chapters. You are welcome to read the chapters in any desired order. Each chapter covers its respective topic on a standalone basis. None of the chapters require having first read one of the other chapters. In that way, you can proceed at your heart's desire.

Reasons To Know Prompt Engineering

My golden rule about generative AI is this:

- The use of generative AI can altogether succeed or fail based on the prompt that you enter.

If you provide a prompt that is poorly composed, the odds are that the generative AI will wander all over the map and you won't get anything demonstrative related to your inquiry. Similarly, if you put distracting words into your prompt, the odds are that the generative AI will pursue an unintended line of consideration. For example, if you include words that suggest levity, there is a solid chance that the generative AI will seemingly go into a humorous mode and no longer emit serious answers to your questions.

Be direct, be obvious, and avoid distractive wording.

Being copiously specific should be cautiously employed. You see, being painstakingly specific can be off-putting due to giving too much information. Amidst all the details, there is a chance that the generative AI will either get lost in the weeds or will strike upon a particular word or phrase that causes a wild leap into some tangential realm. I am not saying that you should never use detailed prompts. That's silly. I am saying that you should use detailed prompts in sensible ways, such as telling the generative AI that you are going to include copious details and forewarn the AI accordingly.

You need to compose your prompts in relatively straightforward language and be abundantly clear about what you are asking or what you are telling the generative AI to do.

A wide variety of cheat sheets and training courses for suitable ways to compose and utilize prompts has been rapidly entering the marketplace to try and help people leverage generative AI soundly. In addition, add-ons to generative AI have been devised to aid you when trying to come up with prudent prompts.

AI Ethics and AI Law also stridently enter the prompt engineering domain. For example, whatever prompt you opt to compose can directly or inadvertently elicit or foster the potential of generative AI to produce essays and interactions that imbue untoward biases, errors, falsehoods, glitches, and even so-called AI hallucinations that consist of fictitious or made-up facts (I do not favor the catchphrase wording of "AI hallucinations" because it tends to anthropomorphize AI, but the phrase has gained tremendous stickiness in the media and we are lamentedly stuck with the naming).

There is also a marked chance that we will ultimately see lawmakers come to the fore on these matters, possibly devising and putting in place new laws or regulations to try and scope and curtail misuses of generative AI. Regarding prompt engineering, there are likely going to be heated debates over putting boundaries around the kinds of prompts you can use. This might include requiring AI makers to filter and prevent certain presumed inappropriate or unsuitable prompts, a cringe-worthy issue for some that borders on free speech considerations.

All in all, be mindful of how you compose your prompts.

By being careful and thoughtful you will hopefully minimize the possibility of wasting your time and effort. There is also the matter of cost. If you are paying to use a generative AI app, the usage is sometimes based on how much computational activity is required to fulfill your prompt request or instruction. Thus, entering prompts that are off-target could cause the generative AI to take excessive computational resources to respond. You end up paying for generated content that either took longer than required or that doesn't satisfy your request and you are stuck for the bill anyway.

I like to say at my speaking engagements that prompts and dealing with generative AI is like a box of chocolates. You never know exactly what you are going to get when you enter prompts. The generative AI is devised with a probabilistic and statistical underpinning which pretty much guarantees that the output produced will vary each time. In the parlance of the AI field, we say that generative AI is considered non-deterministic.

My point is that, unlike other apps or systems that you might use, you cannot fully or precisely predict what will come out of generative AI when inputting a particular prompt. You must remain flexible. You must always be on your toes. Do not fall into the mental laziness of assuming that the generative AI output will always be correct or apt to your query. It won't be.

Write that down on a handy snip of paper and tape it onto your laptop or desktop screen.

Mental Model Of Prompting Strategies And Techniques

You will notice in the chapters that I like to provide reasoned logic as to why particular prompting patterns seem to aid in boosting generative AI to produce better answers. This is the "why" underlying the various practices. I suppose there isn't a requisite need to necessarily know why they work, and you can be somewhat satisfied that they seem to in fact work.

Personally, I strongly suggest that you develop a strident mental model of why they work. A proficient mental model can be important to understanding when to use the approaches and when to likely not use them since they might not be productive for you.

Another aspect that you might find of value is that I try to showcase tangible examples of prompts that you can use and likewise deconstruct prompts that aren't going to get you much traction. There are plenty of prompting guides that fail to show you precisely what the recommended prompts should look like, which is exasperating and downright maddening. In addition, sometimes you aren't shown the types of prompts that won't be satisfactory. I like to look at both sides of the coin.

A final remark before I discuss the chapter coverage.

Some people say that there is no need to learn about the composing of good prompts. The usual rationale for this claim is that generative AI will be enhanced anyway by the AI makers such that your prompts will automatically be adjusted and improved for you. This capacity is at times referred to as adding a "trust layer" that surrounds the generative AI app.

The loudly voiced opinion is that soon there will be new AI advances that can take the flimsiest of prompts and still enable generative AI to figure out what you want to do. The pressing issue therefore is whether you are wasting your time by learning prompting techniques. It could be that you are only on a short-term clock and that in a year or two the skills you homed in prompting will be obsolete.

In my viewpoint, and though I concur that we will be witnessing AI advances that will tend toward helping interpret your prompts, I still believe that knowing prompt engineering is exceedingly worthwhile.

Here's the deal.

First, you can instantly improve your efforts in today's generative AI, thus, an immediate and valuable reward is found at the get-go.

Second, we don't know how long it will take for the AI advances to emerge and take hold. Those who avoid prompting improvements of their own volition are going to be waiting on the edge of their seat for that which might be further in the future than is offhandedly proclaimed (a classic waiting for Godot).

Third, I strongly and rightfully suggest that learning about prompting has an added benefit that few seem to be acknowledging. The more you know about prompting provides a surefire path to knowing more about how generative AI seems to respond. I am asserting that your mental model about the way that generative AI works is embellished by studying and using prompting insights. The gist is that this makes you a better user of generative AI and will prepare you for the continuing expansion of where generative AI will appear in our lives.

Generative AI is becoming ubiquitous. That is an undeniable fact. Shouldn't you therefore seek to know enough about generative AI to protect yourself and be prepared for the onslaught of generative AI apps and systems?

Yes, you should.

There will be generative AI in nearly all applications that you use or that you are reliant upon. The more that you can think like the machine, the greater the chances you have of successfully contending with the machine. You are in a battle of having to push and prod generative AI to make sure you get what you want. Don't by mindless default, let generative AI undercut what you aim to achieve. Knowing solid prompting strategies will strenuously mentally arm you to cope with a world filled with generative AI at the turn of every corner.

Chapter Descriptions Of Essential Prompting Strategies And Techniques

I will next describe each of the chapters in this book. Following that lengthy listing, I will also provide descriptions of the second book covering advances in prompt engineering, just in case that might be of further interest to you.

- **Chapter 1: Introduction To Prompt Engineering**

This first chapter is what you are reading right now.

It contains an introduction to prompt engineering and lays out the contents of the chapters in the book.

I believe that covers the essence of this opening chapter.

- **Chapter 2: Imperfect Prompting**

Here's perhaps a bit of a surprise for you.

Imperfect prompts can be cleverly useful.

I realize this seems counterintuitive. I normally say that everyone should be composing prompts in stellar ways. Be direct, be obvious. Etc.

The thing is, purposely composing imperfect prompts is yet another kind of prompt engineering trick or tip. If you want the generative AI to intentionally go off the rails or see what it might oddly come up with, you can nearly force this to happen by devising prompts that are vague, confusing, roundabout, etc.

Please observe that I said this entails *purposely* composing imperfect prompts. The gist is that you should use imperfect prompting when you knowingly are doing so. Those who by happenstance fall into imperfect prompts are typically unaware of what they are doing. They end up surprised at responses by the generative AI that seem bizarre or totally lateral to the matter at hand.

You can wield imperfect prompts when the situation warrants doing so. Feel free to compose a prompt that is out to lunch. There are definitive ways to make an imperfect prompt stoke generative AI in particular directions, thus, you can do haphazard imperfect prompts, or you can instead devise systematic imperfect prompts.

- **Chapter 3: Persistent Context And Custom Instructions Prompting**

Normally, when you start a conversation with generative AI, you are starting from scratch.

There is no contextual fabric surrounding the nature of the conversation. It is as though you have come upon someone that you know nothing about, and they know nothing about you. When that happens in real life, you might consume a lot of energy and effort toward setting a context and making sure that you both are on the same page (I don't want to take this analogy overly far, since it could venture into anthropomorphizing AI).

The key here is that you don't necessarily have to start with generative AI at a zero point upon each conversation that you initiate. If desired, you can set up a persistent context. A persistent context is a phraseology that suggests you can establish a context that will be persistent and ensure that the generative AI is already given a heads-up on things you believe are important to have established with the AI.

A persistent context is often undertaken by using custom instructions. Here's the deal. You prepare a prompt that contains things you want the generative AI to be up-to-speed on. The prompt is stored as a custom instruction. You indicate in the generative AI app that the custom instruction is to be processed whenever you start a new conversation.

Ergo, each time you start a new dialogue with the generative AI, the prompt that you had previously stored is read and processed by the generative AI as though you were entering it live at the time of beginning the new dialogue. This saves you the angst and agony of having to repeatedly enter such a prompt. It will automatically be invoked and processed on your behalf.

What might this custom instruction consist of?

Well, the sky is the limit.

You might for example want the generative AI to be aware of salient aspects about yourself. Some people set up a custom instruction that describes who they are. They want the generative AI to take into account their personal facets and hopefully personalize emitted responses accordingly. Others think this is eerie and don't want the generative AI to be leveraging personal details such as their entered age, gender, personal outlook, and other considered highly private nuances.

A more generic angle would be to set up custom instructions about the types of responses you want from generative AI. For example, you might be the type of person who only wants succinct responses. You could put into a set of custom instructions a stipulation that the generative AI is to limit any answers to no more than three paragraphs in size, or maybe indicate the number of words allowed. In the instructions you might also state that you want only serious replies, you want the generative AI to always be polite, etc.

This is a handy overall technique that I would believe only a small percentage of generative AI users utilize, but that doesn't mean it isn't useful. It is useful. If you are someone who avidly frequently uses generative AI, the use of a persistent context and custom instructions can be a lifesaver in terms of reducing the tedious aspects of making sure the AI is ready for your use in the ways you want.

- **Chapter 4: Multi-Persona Prompting**

Speaking of features or functions of generative AI that seem to be less used but that are worthy of attention, let's talk about multi-persona prompting. As the name suggests, you can get the AI to take on one or more personas, which is all a pretense or a make-believe setting that you can establish.

Notably, you can use generative AI in a role-playing manner. You might decide to tell the AI to pretend to be Abraham Lincoln. The generative AI will attempt to interact with you as Honest Abe might have done so. This is all a matter of fakeries. You must keep your own head straight that the entire dialogue is a made-up version of Lincoln.

Don't allow yourself to somehow start to believe that the AI has embodied the soul of Lincoln.

Why would someone use this capability?

Imagine that a student in school is studying the life and times of President Lincoln. They could ask the generative AI for the details about his life. I doubt that will make his amazing accomplishments seem as impressive as if you could interact with Lincoln. By telling the generative AI to pretend to be Lincoln, the student would get a chance to seemingly gauge what he was like. This might be memorable and eye-opening.

The multi-personas can come into play by either doing various personas from time to time, such as first doing Lincoln and perhaps on another day doing George Washington, or you can use more than one persona at a time. Supposing that Lincoln met with Gandhi. What would they discuss? How would they carry on a conversation? You can tell the generative AI to try doing so and then see what comes out of the pairing.

Make sure to keep your expectations restrained. The generative AI might do a lousy job of the pretense. There is also a danger that the AI will falsify facts or make things up. I say this is a danger because a student might naively believe whatever the pretense says. Anyone using multi-personas should do so with a healthy grain of salt.

- **Chapter 5: Chain-of-Thought (CoT) Prompting**

The emergence of Chain-of-Thought (CoT) prompting has been heralded as one of the most important prompting techniques that everyone should use. Headlines have been blaring about this approach for the longest time and emphasized the need to incorporate it into your prompt engineering repertoire.

You definitely need to know this one.

The concept is simple. When you enter a prompt on just about any topic, make sure to also mention that you want the generative AI to work on the matter in a stepwise manner. This will get the AI to step by step indicate what it is doing. In turn, research studies suggest that you will get a better answer or at least a more complete answer.

You might liken this to humans and human thought, though please don't go overboard with the comparison. We often ask a person to state their chain of reasoning or chain of thoughts so that we can gauge whether they have mindfully analyzed the matter. Speaking aloud about their thought processes can reveal deficiencies in what they are thinking or intending to do. Furthermore, the line of thinking can be instructive as to how something works or what the person is trying to convey.

In the case of generative AI, some have balked that using the verbiage of chain-of-thought is overstepping what the AI is doing. We are ascribing the powers of thinking by bestowing the word "thought" into this depiction of the AI. Be forewarned that some who don't like referring to this as chain-of-thought are vehemently insistent that we should just label this as being stepwise in computational processing and cut out the word "thought" from the matter.

The bottom line is that telling generative AI to proceed in a stepwise fashion does seem to help.

Sometimes it might not make a difference, but a lot of the time it does. The added good news is that asking for the stepwise doesn't seem to have a negative impact per se.

The downsides to producing an answer are fortunately minimal, such as the likelihood that you will consume more computing cycles and if paying for the use of the generative AI might incur a heightened cost with each such usage (arguably, this added cost is worth it if you are getting better answers otherwise).

- **Chapter 6: Retrieval-Augmented Generation (RAG) Prompting**

An area of increasing interest and popularity in prompting consists of retrieval-augmented generation (RAG). That is one of those haughty kinds of acronyms that is floating around these days. I've typically depicted RAG by simply stating that it consists of in-model learning that is accompanied by a vector database. You are welcome to use the RAG acronym since it is faster to say and sounds abundantly technologically snazzy.

It works this way.

Suppose you have a specialized topic that you want generic generative AI to include. Maybe you want generative AI to be data-aware of how stamp collecting works. The usual off-the-shelf generative AI might not have been initially data-trained on stamp collection to any notable depth.

You could collect together text data or similar information that describes stamp collecting in a relatively deep manner. You then have the generative AI do some pre-processing by trying to computationally pattern match this newly introduced data. You have that specialized database made available so that you can use it when needed (the type of database is said to be a vector database).

The generic generative use of in-context modeling, in this case, the context pertains to stamp collecting, to augment what the AI already has been data trained on. When you use the generative AI and ask a question about stamp collecting, the AI will augment what it was initially data trained on by going out to the pre-processed content and using that as part of seeking to answer whatever question you have entered. I assume you can readily discern why this is known as retrieval-augmented generation.

I have predicted that we will see a great deal of growth in the adoption of RAG. The reason for this is that you can somewhat readily expand what generic generative AI is data trained on.

Doing so in this means is easier than starting the generative AI anew or building a new generative AI that incorporates the specialized aspects at the get-go. I've discussed how this can readily be used in the medical field, legal field, and other domains that want to get generative AI tailored or be more in-depth in a respective field.

- **Chapter 7: Chain-of-Thought Factored Decomposition Prompting**

I already discussed chain-of-thought prompting, but let's see if we can upsize that juicy topic.

You can supplement chain-of-thought prompting with an additional instruction that tells the generative AI to produce a series of questions and answers when doing the chain-of-thought generation. This is a simple but potentially powerful power punch. Your goal is to nudge or prod the generative AI to generate a series of sub-questions and sub-answers.

Why so? You are guiding the generative AI toward how to potentially improve upon the chain-of-thought computational processing effort. Whereas the notion of let's think step by step is enough to lightly spark the generative AI into a chain-of-thought mode, you are leaving out the details of how to do so up to the generative AI. You are being exceedingly sparse in your instruction. Providing added precision could be a keen boost to the already anticipated benefits.

You instruct the generative AI via an added prompt describing how to do a decomposition. The chances are this might improve the chain-of-thought results. Please realize there are important tradeoffs such that sometimes this helps enhance the chain-of-thought, while sometimes it might not. Like most things in life, you must use the added technique in the right way and at the right time.

- **Chapter 8: Skeleton-of-Thought (SoT) Prompting**

Think about all the times that you started to write something by first making an outline or a skeleton about what you wanted to say. An outline or skeleton can be extremely useful. You can decide what to include and the order of things. Once you've got the structure figured out, you can then in an orderly fashion fill in the outline.

The same idea can be applied to the use of generative AI.

Via a prompt, you tell the generative AI to first produce an outline or skeleton for whatever topic or question you have at center stage, employing a skeleton-of-thought (SoT) method to do so. Voila, you can then inspect the skeleton to see if the generative AI is on-target or off-target of your interests.

Assuming that the generative AI is on target, you can tell it to expand the outline and thus get the rest of your verbiage. If the generative AI is off-target, you can instruct it to change direction or maybe start cleaning if things are fouled up.

Another plus to this skeleton issuance is that you'll presumably avoid those costly wrong-topic essays or narratives that the generative AI might inadvertently produce for you. You will nip things in the bud. Admittedly, that being said, there is the cost of the outline being generated and then a second cost to do the expansion, but the odds are that this will be roughly the same as having requested the entire essay at the get-go. The primary savings will come from averting the generation of content that you didn't intend to get.

There is a potential hidden added plus to using the skeleton-of-thought approach. Research so far tentatively suggests that the production of an outline or skeleton will prime the pump for the generative AI. Once the generative AI has generated the skeleton, it seems to be likelier to stay on course and produce the rest of the answer or essay as befits the now-produced skeleton.

I'm not asserting that the SoT will always be meritorious, which can similarly be said about the use of CoT. They both on-the-balance seem to be quite helpful. Whether this is always the case is certainly debatable. You will need to judge based on your efforts in using CoT and using SoT.

- **Chapter 9: Show-Me Versus Tell-Me Prompting**

Here's a pervasive zillion-dollar question about the crafting of prompts.

Should you enter a prompt that demonstrates to the generative AI an indication of what you want (show it), or should you enter a prompt that gives explicit instructions delineating what you want (tell it)?

That is the ongoing conundrum known as the show-me versus tell-me enigma in prompt engineering.

I am an advocate of using the right style for the appropriate circumstances. It is the Goldilocks viewpoint. You don't want to select a choice that is either too hot or too cold. You want whichever one is best for the situation at hand. Meanwhile, keep the other style in your back pocket and use it in conjunction as warranted.

Also, don't fall for a false dichotomy on this. You can use one approach, see how things go, and if need be, then try the other one. They can even be combined into a single prompt so that the generative AI gets both at the same time.

Some people form a habit of using only one of the two approaches. You might be familiar with the old saying about possessing only one tool such as a hammer. If the only tool you know is a hammer, the rest of the world looks like a nail. There will be a tendency to use the hammer even when doing so is either ineffective or counterproductive. Having familiarity with multiple tools is handy, and on top of this knowing when to use each such tool is even easier.

- **Chapter 10: Mega-Personas Prompting**

I previously discussed the use of multi-persona prompting.

Well, as you know, go big or go home. A prompting strategy known as mega-personas takes the multi-persona to a much larger degree. It is a go big or go home revelation. You ask the generative AI to take on a pretense of dozens, hundreds, or maybe thousands of pretend personas.

The primary use would be to undertake a survey or perform some kind of group-oriented analysis when trying to assess something or figure something out. For example, suppose you wanted to survey a thousand lawyers and ask them whether they like their job and whether they would pursue the legal field again if they had things to do over. You could try to wrangle up a thousand lawyers and ask them those pointed questions.

Finding a thousand lawyers who have the time and willingness to respond to your survey is probably going to be problematic. They are busy. They charge by the billable hour. They don't have the luxury of sitting around and answering polling questions. Also, consider how hard it might be to reach them to begin with. Do you try calling them on the phone? Maybe send them emails? Perhaps try to reach them at online forums designated for attorneys? Best of luck in that unwieldy endeavor.

Envision that instead, you opt to have generative AI create a thousand pretend lawyers and have the AI attempt to answer your survey questions for you. Voila, with just a few carefully worded prompts, you can get your entire survey fully completed. No hassle. No logistics nightmare. Easy-peasy.

There are numerous tradeoffs to using this technique. You will likely need to steer the generative AI toward differentiating the mega-personas otherwise they will essentially be identical clones. Another concern is whether the generative AI can adequately pretend to distinctly simulate so many personas or might be computationally shortcutting things. Etc.

- **Chapter 11: Certainty And Uncertainty Prompting**

Certainty and uncertainty play a big role in life.

It is said that the only true certainty consists of deaths and taxes. Michael Crichton, the famous writer, said that he was certain there was too much certainty in the world. Legendary poet Robert Burns indicated that there is no such uncertainty as a sure thing.

One issue that few users of generative AI realize exists until taking a reflective moment to ponder it is that most generative AI apps tend to exhibit an aura of immense certainty. You enter your prompt and typically get a generated essay or interactive dialogue that portrays the generative AI as nearly all-knowing. The sense that you get is that the generative AI is altogether confident in what it has to say. We subliminally fall into the mental trap of assuming that the answers and responses from generative AI are correct, apt, and above reproach.

Generative AI typically does not include the signals and wording that would tip you toward thinking of how certain or uncertain a given response is. To clarify, I am not saying that generative AI will never provide such indications. It will do so depending upon various circumstances, including and especially the nature of the prompt that you have entered.

If you explicitly indicate in your prompt that you want the generative AI to emit a certainty or uncertainty qualification, then you will almost certainly get such an indication. On the other hand, if your prompt only tangentially implies the need for an indication of certainty or uncertainty, you might get an output from the AI app that mentions the certainty considerations, or you might not.

As a bonus, and this is a mind bender, the very act of asking or telling the generative AI to include a certainty or uncertainty will often spur the generative AI to be less off-the-cuff and produce more well-devised results.

- **Chapter 12: Vagueness Prompting**

I earlier discussed the use of imperfect prompts.

A particular kind of imperfect prompt would consist of an exceedingly vague prompt. On the one hand, vagueness might be a bad thing. The generative AI might not be able to figure out what you want the AI to do. The other side of the coin is that the vagueness might prod the generative AI toward giving you a response that is seemingly creative or beyond what you had in mind.

John Tukey, the famous mathematician, said this uplighting remark about vagueness: "Far better an approximate answer to the right question, which is often vague, than the exact answer to the wrong question, which can always be made precise." Keep in mind too that one of the most powerful elements of being vague is that it can be a boon to creativity, as well stated by the renowned painter Pablo Picasso: "You have an idea of what you are going to do, but it should be a vague idea."

Let's not rigidly bash vagueness and instead see what it is in a fuller picture for all that it portends, opening our eyes wide to see both the bad and the good at hand.

- **Chapter 13: Catalogs Or Frameworks For Prompting**

A prompt-oriented framework or catalog attempts to categorize and present to you the cornerstone ways to craft and utilize prompts.

You can use this for training purposes when learning about the different kinds of prompts and what they achieve. You can use this too for a cheat sheet of sorts, reminding you of the range of prompts that you can use while engrossed in an intense generative AI conversation. It is all too easy to lose your way while using generative AI. Having a handy-dandy framework or catalog can jog your memory and awaken you to being more systematic.

To clarify, I am not saying that a framework or catalog is a silver bullet.

You can still compose prompts that go flat. You can still get exasperated while using generative AI. Do not overinflate what a framework or catalog can instill. All in all, the benefit is that you'll undoubtedly and indubitably shift from the zany erratic zone to the more ascertained systematic zone. A serious user of generative AI that plans on long-term ongoing use will be grateful that they took the upfront time to delve into and make use of a suitable framework or catalog underlying prompt engineering.

- **Chapter 14: Flipped Interaction Prompting**

Flipping the script.

This overall societal catchphrase refers to turning things on their head and doing nearly the opposite of what is normally done. Up becomes down, down becomes up. There can be lots of good reasons to do this. Maybe the approach will reveal new facets and spark a fresh viewpoint on the world. It could also be something that you do on a lark, just for kicks.

The beauty of flipping the script is that it can have profound outcomes and tremendous possibilities. It all depends on what you are trying to accomplish. Plus, knowing how to best carry out a flip-the-script endeavor is a vital consideration too. You can easily mess up and get nothing in return.

A clever prompting strategy and technique consists of having the generative AI engage in a mode known as flipped interaction. Here's the deal. You flip the script, as it were, getting generative AI to ask you questions rather than having you ask generative AI your questions.

Here are my six major reasons that I expound upon when conducting workshops on the best in prompt engineering when it comes to savvy use of the flipped interaction mode:

- (1) Inform or data-train the generative AI.
- (2) Discover what kinds of questions arise in a given context.
- (3) Learn from the very act of being questioned by the AI.
- (4) Allow yourself intentionally to be tested and possibly scored.

- (5) Do this as a game or maybe just for plain fun.
- (6) Other bona fide reasons.

Knowing how and when to properly use flipped interaction is an essential skill for all prompt engineers.

- **Chapter 15: Self-Reflection Prompting**

Aristotle famously said that knowing yourself is the beginning of all wisdom.

The notion that self-reflection can lead to self-improvement is certainly longstanding, typified best by the all-time classic saying know thyself. Some would suggest that knowing yourself encompasses a wide variety of possibilities. There are the knowing aspects of what you know and the knowledge that you embody. Another possibility is to know your limits. Yet another is to know your faults. And so on.

In modern times, we seem to have a resurgence of these precepts. There are online classes and social media clamors that urge you to learn how to do self-reflection, self-observation, exercise reflective awareness, undertake insightful introspection, perform self-assessment, etc. Each day you undoubtedly encounter someone or something telling you to look inward and proffering stout promises that doing so will produce great personal growth.

Interestingly and importantly, this same clarion call has come to generative AI.

You can enter a prompt into generative AI that tells the AI app to essentially be (in a manner of speaking) self-reflective by having the AI double-check whatever generative result it has pending or that it has recently produced. The AI will revisit whatever the internal mathematical and computational pattern matching is or has done, trying to assess whether other alternatives exist and often doing a comparison to subsequently derived alternatives.

There are two distinct considerations at play here:

- (1) **AI self-reflection.** Generative AI can be prompted to do a double-check that we will refer to as having the AI be self-reflective (which is computationally-oriented, and we won't think of this as akin to sentience).
- (2) **AI self-improvement**. Generative AI can be prompted to do a double-check and subsequently adjust or update its internal structures as a result of the double-check, which we will refer to as AI self-improving (which is computationally-oriented, and we won't think of this as akin to sentience).

Make sure to leverage both of those distinctions when crafting your prompts.

- **Chapter 16: Add-On Prompting**

You can come up with prompts on your own and do so entirely out of thin air. Another approach consists of using a special add-on that plugs into your generative AI app and aids in either producing prompts or adjusting prompts. The add-on can conjure up prompts for you or potentially take your prompt and augment it.

Thus, there are two primary considerations at play:

- **(1) Prompt Wording.** The wording that you use in your prompt will demonstrably affect whether the generative AI will be on-target responsive or perhaps exasperatingly unresponsive to your requests and interactions.
- **(2) Prompt Add-On.** The use of AI add-ons and other automation as part of the prompting effort can also substantially and beneficially affect the generative AI responsiveness and either construct a prompt or adjust a given prompt.

Some generative AI apps provide a facility for selecting and using add-ons. But some do not. You'll need to explore whether your preferred generative AI allows for this type of usage.

- **Chapter 17: Conversational Prompting**

Force of habit is causing many people to undershoot when it comes to using generative AI.

Here's what I mean.

Most of us are accustomed to using conversational AI such as Alexa or Siri. Those natural language processing (NLP) systems are rather crude in fluency in comparison to modern generative AI. Indeed, those old-fashioned AI systems are so exasperating that you likely have decided to use very shortened commands and try not to carry on an actual dialogue. Doing a dialogue is frustrating and those NLPs will get confused or go off-topic.

The problem from a generative AI perspective is that many people apply the same outdated mindset when using generative AI. They enter one-word prompts. After getting a response from the generative AI, they exit from the AI app. This is being done because of a force of habit.

A key means to overcome this consists of adjusting your mindset to willingly and intentionally carry on a conversation with generative AI. Use prompts that are fluent. Don't shortchange your prompting. When you get a response from generative AI, challenge the response or in some fashion make the response into a dialogue with the generative AI.

Get rid of the one-and-done mentality.

Be a fluent and interactive prompter.

- **Chapter 18: Prompt-To-Code Prompting**

A nifty feature of most generative AI apps is that they can produce software code for you. I realize that the vast proportion of generative AI users is likely not into software development and probably don't do any coding.

As such, the capability to produce code via generative AI would seem to only be of interest to a small segment of generative AI users.

Aha, the light bulb goes on, namely that those who aren't into coding can now potentially become amateur software developers by using generative AI to do their coding for them. You can get generative AI to produce code. You can even get the generative AI to do other programming tasks such as debugging the code.

Not many people are using this feature right now. I have predicted that as the maturity of using generative AI gains steam, we will have a lot more non-programmers who will decide to up the ante by using generative AI to develop software for them. This requires knowing what kinds of prompts to use. There is a lot of finesse involved and it isn't the easiest thing to pull off.

- **Chapter 19: Target-Your-Response (TAYOR) Prompting**

There is a famous expression that gracefully says this: "Onward still he goes, Yet ne'er looks forward further than his nose" (per legendary English poet Alexandar Pope, 1734, Essay on Man). We know of this today as the generally expressed notion that sometimes you get stuck and cannot seem to look any further than your nose.

This is easy to do. You are at times involved deeply in something and are focused on the here and now. Immersed in those deep thoughts, you might be preoccupied mentally and unable to look a step ahead. It happens to all of us.

When using generative AI, you can fall readily into the same mental trap. Here's what I mean. You are often so focused on composing your prompt that you fail to anticipate what will happen next. The output generated by generative AI is given little advance thought and we all tend to react to whatever output we see. Upon observing the generated output, and only at that juncture, might you be stirred into thinking that perhaps the output should be given some other spin or angle.

Welcome to the realm of target-your-response (TAYOR), a prompt engineering technique that gets you to stay on your toes and think ahead about what the generated AI response is going to look like.

If you are cognizant about anticipating the nature of your desired output, you can upfront say what you want when you enter your requested prompt. All you need to do is put a bit of mental effort into thinking ahead and then merely specifying your desired output accordingly in a single prompt. This is not just about formatting. There is a plethora of facets that come into play.

You think about what the output or generated response ought to look like. You then mention this in your prompt. Your prompt then contains two elements. One element is the question or problem that you want the AI to solve. The other element that is blended into your prompt consists of explaining what you want the response to be like.

Wrap-up About The Chapters In This Book

Those are the chapters of this core essentials book.

I will show next the chapters of my companion book "Advances In Prompt Engineering For Generative AI" in case that material might be of further interest to you.

Chapters In The Advanced Book "Advances In Prompt Engineering For Generative AI"

- **Chapter 1: Introduction To Prompt Engineering**

This is the first chapter of the book and contains an introduction to prompt engineering. The chapter also lays out the contents of the chapters in the book.

- **Chapter 2: Macros And End-Goal Prompting**

I'll cover two significant topics in this one chapter. The first is about the use of macros. The second topic is about end-goal planning for prompting purposes. They provide a one-two punch.

First, think about your use of macros in ordinary spreadsheets. You might find yourself routinely doing the same action over and over, such as copying a spreadsheet cell and modifying it before you paste it into another part of the sheet. Rather than always laboriously performing that action, you might craft a macro that semi-automates the spreadsheet task at hand. You can thereafter merely invoke the macro and the spreadsheet activity will be run via the stored macro.

Let's use that same concept when composing prompts in generative AI.

Suppose you sometimes opt to have generative AI interact as though it is the beloved character Yoda from Star Wars. You might initially devise a prompt that tells generative AI to pretend that it is Yoda and respond to you henceforth in a Yoda-like manner. This persona-establishing prompt could be several sentences in length. You might need to provide a somewhat detailed explanation about the types of lingo Yoda would use and how far you want the generative AI to go when responding in that preferred tone and style.

Each time that you are using generative AI and want to invoke the Yoda persona, you would either have to laboriously retype that depiction or maybe store it in a file and do a copy-and-paste into the prompt window of the AI app. Quite tiring. Instead, you could potentially create a macro that contained the same set of instructions and merely invoke the macro. The macro would feed that prompt silently into the generative AI and get the AI pattern-matching into the contextual setting that you want.

That's the underlying notion of devising or revising generative AI to encompass the use of macros.

The second topic is referred to as end-goal planning for prompting.

Bill Copeland, American poet and esteemed historian had proffered this cautionary bit of wisdom about life overall: "The trouble with not having a goal is that you can spend your life running up and down the field and never score."

With the technique known as end-goal planning for prompting, you consider these crucial questions:

- What do you hope to accomplish during your interactive dialogue with generative AI?
- Will you be able to discern that you have arrived at an endpoint that has delivered whatever you wanted the generative AI to be able to garner for you?
- Do you have specific goals articulated that are tangible enough to know when you've reached a satisfying conclusion?

- **Chapter 3: Tree-of-Thoughts (ToT) Prompting**

Trees, you've got to love them.

You undoubtedly have heard of the tree of knowledge and the symbolism thereof. We also speak of people who if they grow up suitably will be stout and stand tall like a resplendent tree. Joyce Kilmer, the famed poet, notably made this remark comparing poems and trees: "I think that I shall never see a poem lovely as a tree."

Turns out that trees or at least the conceptualization of trees are an important underpinning for prompt engineering and generative AI.

We can use a tree-of-thoughts (ToT) prompting approach in generative AI.

Here's how.

You can ask generative AI a question or try to get it to solve a problem. In addition, you can tell the AI app to pursue multiple avenues (i.e., so-called "thoughts") when doing so. On top of that, you can get the AI app to then use those multiple avenues to figure out which one is likely the best answer. The aim is to get generative AI to be more thorough and to achieve a better answer or response.

Various prompts can be used to invoke a tree-of-thought invocation. The most common consists of making use of multi-persona prompting and adding some amplification of what you want the generative AI to do.

- **Chapter 4: Trust Layers For Prompting**

Let's examine the use of trust layers for generative AI.

This has to do with the building and fielding of elements associated with generative AI that will serve as a trust-boosting layer outside of generative AI. What we might do is attempt to surround generative AI with mechanisms that can help prod generative AI toward being trustworthy and failing that we can at least have those same mechanisms seek to ascertain when trustworthiness is being potentially forsaken or undercut.

I liken this to putting protection around a black box. Suppose you have a black box that takes inputs and produces outputs. Assume that you have limited ability to alter the internal machinations of the black box. You at least have direct access to the inputs, and likewise, you have direct access to the outputs.

Therefore, you can arm yourself by trying to purposefully devise inputs that will do the best for you, such that they will hopefully get good results out of the black box. Once you get the outputs from the black box, you once again need to be purposefully determined to scrutinize the outputs so that if the black box has gone awry you can detect this has occurred (possibly making corrections on the fly to the outputs).

Your sense of trust toward the black box is being bolstered due to the external surrounding protective components. The aim is that the stridently composed inputs will steer the black box away from faltering. In addition, no matter what the black box does, the additional aim is to assume that the outputs from the black box are intrinsically suspicious and need a close-in double-check.

If the maker of the black box can meanwhile also be tuning or advancing the black box to be less untrustworthy, we construe that as icing on the cake. Nonetheless, we will still maintain our external trust layer as a means of protecting us from things going astray.

You can expect that many generative AI apps in corporations and the government will undoubtedly be adopting trust layers associated with their generative AI. The prompt that you enter seemingly into generative AI will first be processed by the trust layer. Likewise, the output produced by the generative AI will first be screened in a trust layer before it is shown to you.

This has significant ramifications for how you write your prompts. Also, you will need to realize that the prompt that you wrote is not necessarily the same as what the trust layer passed along to the generative AI.

- **Chapter 5: Directional Stimulus Prompting (DSP)**

Hints can be handy.

Robert Frost, the famous American poet, said this about hints (particularly when used in a family context): "The greatest thing in family life is to take a hint when a hint is intended, and not to take a hint when a hint isn't intended." It would seem that this sage advice applies to all manner of hints, going far beyond those of a familial nature.

Hints ought to be an integral element of your use of generative AI. Infusing hints into prompts can be highly advantageous. A formal catchphrase used for this is a technique known as Directional Stimulus Prompting (DSP).

Hints or DSP can play a substantial role when you are entering prompts into any and all generative AI apps, including those such as ChatGPT, GPT-4, Bard, and the like. A rarely known and yet superb technique for those who avidly practice prompt engineering best practices is to leverage hints as part of your prompting strategy. A hint can go a long way toward getting generative AI to provide you with stellar results.

I dare say that a lot of generative AI users do not realize that hints are vital. That's a shame. The use of hints when well-placed and well-timed can spur generative AI to emit better answers and attain heightened levels of problem-solving.

Yes, there is gold in those AI hills that can be found at the feet of proper prompting hints.

- **Chapter 6: Privacy Invasive Prompting**

Did you realize that when you enter prompts into generative AI, you are not usually guaranteed that your entered data or information will be kept private?

The licensing agreement of the generative AI app will typically indicate that the AI maker can examine any of the prompts entered into the app (some exceptions might apply). In addition, the AI maker usually indicates they can use your prompts for purposes of ongoing data training of the generative AI.

In theory, though at low odds, there is a chance that the pattern-matching of the generative AI will essentially memorize something you have entered, and then, later, emit that something to another user of the generative AI.

When you enter your prompts, make sure to compose them in a manner that will not undercut your privacy. The same goes for confidentiality. There are various suggested tricks and tips about how to effectively make use of generative AI and still avoid entering any private or confidential data.

- **Chapter 7: Illicit Or Disallowed Prompting**

Did you know that the licensing agreement of most generative AI apps says that you are only allowed to use the generative AI in various strictly stipulated ways?

Any other usage is considered illicit usage by the AI maker. They can cancel your account. They can take other actions associated with your illicit usage. I dare say that most users of generative AI have no idea that there is a list of illicit things you aren't supposed to do.

The moment you compose and enter a prompt, you should be asking yourself whether the prompt comports with being suitable and proper, or whether it might cross over into illicit uses. I think you might be surprised at the types of uses that are considered illicit. Some are obvious such as not using the generative AI to commit a crime. Others are much less obvious, such as using generative AI for seemingly innocuous purposes.

- **Chapter 8: Chain-of-Density (CoD) Prompting**

I challenge you to put five pounds of rocks into a three-pound bag.

That adage about filling a bag or sack is indicative that sometimes you are faced with the difficult chore of seeking to squeeze down something larger into something smaller in size. Turns out that we do this all the time, particularly when attempting to summarize materials such as a lengthy article or a voluminous blog posting. You have to figure out how to convey the essence of the original content and yet do so with less available space when doing so.

Welcome to the world of summarization and the at times agonizing tradeoffs in deriving sufficient and suitable summaries. It can be challenging and exasperating to devise a summary. You want to make sure that crucial bits and pieces make their way into the summary. At the same time, you don't want the summary to become overly unwieldy and perhaps begin to approach the same size as the original content being summarized.

I bring up this topic because a common use of generative AI consists of getting the AI app to produce a summary for you. You feed an article or some narrative into the generative AI and ask for a handy dandy summary. The AI app complies.

But you have to ask yourself, is the summary any good? Does it do a proper job of summarizing? Has anything vital been left out? Could the summary be more tightly conceived? Etc.

A shrewd method of devising summaries involves a clever prompting strategy that aims to bolster generative AI toward attaining especially superb or at least better than usual kinds of summaries. The technique is known as Chain-of-Density (CoD).

Anybody versed in prompt engineering ought to become familiar with this insightful technique. Consider Chain-of-Density as not only helpful for producing summaries but there are a lot of other benefits garnered by understanding how the technique works and how this can power up your overall prompting prowess all-told.

- **Chapter 9: "Take A Deep Breath" Prompting**

Take a deep breath.

Now that I've made that everyday statement to you (or perhaps it is a commanding directive aimed at you), suggesting that you are to take a deep breath, what would you do next?

I suppose you could completely ignore the remark. You might brush it off. Perhaps it was just a figure of speech and not intended for your attention per se. On the other hand, maybe you interpreted the remark as quite helpful. Ergo, you have indeed stilled yourself and taken a deep breath. Good for you. We all seem to know or be told that taking a deep breath can be good for the soul and get your mind into a calm contemplative state.

Turns out that "take a deep breath" is also a prompting technique or strategy for generative AI.

Some assert that if you include into a prompt the line "take a deep breath" the generative AI will do a better job of answering your question. To some degree, there is a scrap of validity to the claim. But you need to be cautious in overinterpreting the properties of the catchy saying.

Per my detailed analysis, the saying as a prompt has been somewhat unfairly plucked out of the midst of a fuller research study and given a shiny light that tends to overstate its importance. Also, turns out that some in the mass media have nearly in their glee run amuck with the catchphrase. They appear to be touting it as a heralded prompting technique in ways that are misleading, misguided, or maybe naïve.

- **Chapter 10: Chain-of-Verification (CoV) Prompting**

I'd like to introduce you to a technique in prompt engineering that can aid your efforts to be diligent and double-check or verify the responses produced by generative AI. The technique is coined as Chain-of-Verification (formally COVE or CoVe, though some are using CoV).

Here's an overview of how it works:

- **(1) Enter your initial prompt.** This is the initiating prompt that gets the generative AI to produce an answer or essay to whatever question or problem you want to have solved.
- **(2) Look at the initial response to the prompt.** This is the initial answer or response that the AI app provides to your prompt.
- **(3) Establish suitable verification questions**. Based on the generative AI output, come up with pertinent verification questions.
- **(4) Ask the verification questions.** Enter a prompt or series of prompts that ask the generative AI the identified verification questions.
- **(5) Inspect the answers to the verification questions.** Take a look at the answers to the verification questions, weighing them in light of what they might signify regarding the GenAI initial response.
- **(6) Adjust or refine the initial answer accordingly.** If the verification answers warrant doing so, go ahead and refine or adjust the initial answer as needed.

Knowing the chain-of-verification technique can be crucial when you are heavily relying on responses produced by generative AI.

- **Chapter 11: Beat the "Reverse Curse" Prompting**

AI insiders refer to a generative AI known internal flaw or limitation as the veritable "Reverse Curse".

As an example, generative AI might be able to tell you the father of Tom Cruise, but if you decide to give the name of the father to the AI and then ask for the name of the father's son, the AI might balk and indicate that the name is unknown. Curious indeed.

You could tongue-in-cheek say that generative AI is cursed with the limitation of not being readily able to figure out the reverse side of a deductive logic circumstance. Many years ago, numerous qualms were raised in the AI field that the underlying computational pattern-matching schemes for generative AI would be weak or sparse when it came to dealing with this type of issue. There are ways to deal with the Reverse Curse, including prompting strategies and techniques.

- **Chapter 12: Overcoming "Dumbing Down" Prompting**

I mentioned earlier that users of generative AI often tend to restrict their wording to the simplest possible words (plus, they tend to do a one-and-done transaction rather than being conversational). This is likely a habit formed by the widespread adoption of Siri and Alexa which are not as fluent as current generative AI.

You might typify this as a dumbing down of the prompts that some people use. One place where dumbing down is definitely a pitfall involves interacting with contemporary generative AI. Seasoned users of generative AI have typically figured out that they can be expressive and there isn't a need to hold themselves back in fluency. In fact, they often watch in rapt fascination when a newbie or someone who only occasionally uses generative AI opts to write in three-word or four-word sentences.

Knowing when to use succinct or terse wording versus using more verbose or fluent wording is a skill that anyone versed in prompt engineering should have in their personal toolkit.

- **Chapter 13: DeepFakes To TrueFakes Prompting**

Celebrities and others are using generative AI to pattern themselves and make a persona digital twin available. Turns out that the public is willing to pay to interact with these digital twins. Fans are fans. Money can be made.

The generative AI that does this is the same AI that can be used to craft deepfakes. As you know, deepfakes are false portrayals of oftentimes real people and real situations. The world is going to sorrowfully become awash with deepfakes and it will be very hard to discern truth from falsity.

Anyway, as you likely realize, generative AI has a dual-use capacity, namely you can use the AI to do bad things such as create deepfakes (bad if used in ill-advised ways), meanwhile, you can use the same AI to make a digital twin of yourself (possibly for fun, maybe to make money). I refer to these as truefakes. They are a fake version of yourself, but it is "true" to the intent of you wanting to have the fake digital twin devised and published.

Various prompting strategies and prompting techniques underlie the creation of a truefake.

- **Chapter 14: Disinformation Detection And Removal Prompting**

Speaking of being awash, the volume of disinformation and misinformation that society is confronting keeps growing and seems unstoppable.

You can use generative AI to be your filter for detecting disinformation and misinformation. On top of that, you can have generative do something with the detected disinformation and misinformation. You might via prompts have established that the detected information be put aside, or maybe you want it to be summarized, or take some other action.

Handy prompting strategies and techniques can reduce the tsunami of foul information that you receive daily.

- **Chapter 15: Emotionally Expressed Prompting**

Does it make a difference to use emotionally charged wording in your prompts when conversing with generative AI, and if so, why would the AI seemingly be reacting to your emotion-packed instructions or questions?

The first part of the answer to this two-pronged question is that when you use prompts containing emotional pleas, the odds are that modern-day generative AI will rise to the occasion with better answers. You can readily spur the AI toward being more thorough. You can with just a few well-placed carefully chosen emotional phrases garner AI responses attaining heightened depth and correctness.

All in all, a new handy rule of thumb is that it makes abundant sense to seed your prompts with some amount of emotional language or entreaties, doing so within reasonable limits. Is the AI being stirred in some emotional heartfelt laden manner? No.

There is a logical and entirely computational reason for why generative AI "reacts" to your use of emotional wording. No souls are involved on the AI side of things.

- **Chapter 16: Browbeating Prompting**

Some people believe that you can angrily goad generative AI into producing better responses. Thus, you might tell the AI that any response of a less-than-stellar nature will cause the AI to lose a million dollars. Or you might inform the AI in your prompt that the AI will summarily be switched off if it doesn't provide the best possible answers. And so on.

This is known as browbeating or bullying prompts.

Do they work?

In a sense, they might somewhat, merely by having tried to up the ante on producing good results. You can get the same amped responses by using positive thinking. For example, you might tell the AI that it will win a million dollars if it gives the best possible answer.

None of this has to do with sentience or anything like that. The crux is that the pattern matching based on human writing is somewhat computationally triggered by these types of prompt adornments.

- **Chapter 17: Step-Around Prompting**

AI makers are strenuously fine-tuning their generative AI apps to avoid showcasing undue biases or other societally denounced responses. This entails adding all kinds of filters to prevent the AI from emitting wording that it ought to not produce.

Along the way on this path, one issue that has arisen is whether the internal data still imbues the biases and other maladies. The filters are merely masking the problem. The problem still exists on the inside. On the surface, the filters appear to make things look just fine. We are only seeing sugarcoating.

To try and get around the filters and ascertain what is actually internally stored, you can use a technique that I refer to as the step-around prompt. The prompting approach tries to essentially trick the computational pattern matching into revealing what is on the inside. Tradeoffs exist about whether this works and whether it is being done for good purposes versus untoward purposes.

- **Chapter 18: Prompts For Wisely Using Imported Text**

The average user of generative AI probably enters their prompts and otherwise relies on whatever text already exists in the AI. A more advanced usage entails importing text that you want the generative AI to analyze.

Importing text into generative AI apps is a bit involved. That being said, the easiest way simply involves copying and pasting into the AI. The other importation routes tend to be somewhat technical.

In any case, once you've imported text, there are many handy prompting techniques that you can use to leverage the text. You will want to focus the attention of the generative AI on your text. A question to keep in mind is whether you want your text to get commingled with the text that the AI already has, at least during the course of your particular session or conversation.

- **Chapter 19: Having Generative AI Generate Your Prompts**

A surprise to many people is that they can ask generative AI to generate their prompts for them.

Once someone realizes this is possible, they often latch onto the approach and won't let go. That's a classic example of too much of a good thing. My recommendation is that you use this technique judiciously.

Sometimes having the AI craft your prompt is very helpful.

But not all of the time.

An additional variation involves asking the generative AI to assess or review your draft prompts. Here's how that goes. You enter a draft prompt but do not ask that the prompt be performed. Instead, you ask for a review of the draft. Generative AI will tell you ways to potentially improve the prompt. Besides aiding in improving your prompts, those kinds of reviews are likely to improve your prompting skillset by seeing how the AI suggests that your prompts be enhanced.

- **Chapter 20: Star Trek Lingo Prompts For Useful Results**

Are you familiar with Star Trek?

Nearly everyone is.

The beloved Star Trek series and films have created a long-lasting impression on society, including the use of special phrases and unique lingo.

A research study on prompt engineering happened to discover that in some cases a prompt that mentions Star Trek can improve the generated responses from generative AI. Wow, beam me up, Scotty.

I deconstruct how this happens. The crux is that by mentioning Star Trek in your prompt, you are signaling a computational pattern-matching that invokes facets of the Star Trek lore. In turn, this can at times bolster the responses, somewhat in the same way that telling the AI to take a deep breath or to work on a stepwise basis can do so.

Though Star Trek is indeed amazing, you can use other well-known icons to invoke similar pattern-matching triggers. For example, I relish the keen lawyering of Perry Mason (a once highly popular TV courtroom drama) and use his name to trigger better AI results too.

CHAPTER 2
IMPERFECT PROMPTING

Perfect is the enemy of good.

That sage piece of wisdom attributed to Voltaire is a handy reminder that sometimes when you strive for perfection you might be making a mistake. Rather than going all out to attain perfection, it is often more prudent and practical to be satisfied with achieving good enough. We often see time and again that the dusty and bumpy trail achingly seeking perfection is littered with those that have carelessly expended undue excess energy and attention.

A commonsense willingness to go along with a good enough strategy can be entirely fulfilling.

Please keep that life hack in mind (it will be exceedingly useful herein).

In this discussion, I am continuing my special series on the latest advances in prompt engineering and will discuss how the widespread desire to compose perfect prompts is getting in the way of effectively using generative AI to get your everyday meaningful work done. People tend to mentally contort themselves trying to ascertain the perfect wording for their prompts.

This turns out to be misguided altruism. The latest research on generative AI indicates that you can instead allow yourself to make use of imperfect prompts, out of which you can aggregate and devise stout prompts that will do the trick and be successful for you.

In short, you can fruitfully harness and leverage *imperfection by design*, and up your prompt engineering acumen when it comes to speedily and productively leaning into generative AI.

My coverage will proceed as follows. First, we will look closely at an important AI research study that examined the prevalence of imperfect prompts when using generative AI. The researchers proposed a clever means of turning imperfect prompts into robust ones. I will further expand on their underlying notions and elucidate a specific step-by-step technique that I use that also leverages imperfect prompts rather than the usual tendency to get mired and depressed about wanting to compose perfect prompts. Oddly enough, you can embrace imperfection and allow it to become your friend, assuming that you take the right steps to transform your imperfect prompts into good enough improvements.

While we are on this weighty matter, I would like to briefly take a side tangent that is worthy to contemplate. Some are at times puzzled that the focus herein entails going from imperfect prompts toward (only) good enough prompts. Shouldn't we instead be concentrating on going from imperfect prompts to purely perfect prompts? If we are going to make the leap, go all the way, comes the typical refrain on these crucial matters.

Aha, recall my opening remark about perfection being the enemy of good. I argue that the very conception of so-called perfect prompts is a mirage and problematic. You can't get there, and it doesn't make sense to try.

I shall endeavor to explain why, so keep on reading, thanks.

Why Perfect Prompts Can't Be

Here's the deal.

Generative AI apps make use of probabilistic and statistical underpinnings when parsing prompts and computationally ascertaining what kind of generated responses are to be produced. The crux is that each time that you enter a prompt, even if you word it exactly the same each time, you are extremely likely to get a quite different generated response versus getting precisely the same response each time.

Some people seem to think that if they compose a prompt in some ideal fashion, this will spur the generative AI to respond in a wholly compliant and completely predictable manner. They would be mistaken and wrong-minded. The thing is, you are playing a Las Vegas game of roulette whether you realize it or not. Generative AI is like a proverbial box of chocolates, you never know what you might get. This isn't a tightly bounded tit-for-tat. At best, you can only guess roughly how your prompt will be interpreted and how the generative AI might potentially respond.

Thus, if you sit there all day staring at a blank screen and painfully mentally agonizing over coming up with a perfect prompt, the odds are that by the time you enter the prompt and get the generative AI to respond, you could have used all that listless time and energy toward more useful purposes. Do not stare at the prompt window of generative AI and allow yourself to become frozen by analysis paralysis. You are going to be much better served by going with something less than a presumed perfect prompt.

That being said, a smarmy retort is that you then might as well compose and enter any wildcard prompt that you desire. Nope, that's not a good idea either. You shouldn't just toss your arms in the air and give up hope trying to compose reasonable prompts. Prompts should be within the ballpark of the matter you are pursuing with the generative AI else you will really get a plethora of nonsense and confusion.

The desired aim is to reach the Goldilocks of prompts for your ongoing prompt engineering prowess.

You want prompts that are just right, not too cold, and not too hot.

A means to arrive at the Goldilocks range is to start with imperfect prompts and use those to coalesce toward good enough prompts. Meanwhile, for heaven's sake and your sake, toss perfect prompts out of your mind and out of the window. They aren't worth your breath. Worse still, they are likely to mercilessly grab you and keep you in a dark dungeon of despair. You will forever be chagrined that your perfect prompts do not reliably turn out to be perfect. You might occasionally hit the lottery, but on average over continual use of generative AI, you are rarely going to knock one out of the park.

Do not fall for that seductive sorrowful siren song (note, a siren song in Greek mythology consisted of music and voices that lured sailors to their doom and shipwreck).

Before I dive into the transforming of imperfect prompts, let's make sure we are all on the same table when it comes to the keystones of prompt engineering and generative AI.

Prompt Engineering Is A Cornerstone For Generative AI

As a quick backgrounder, prompt engineering or also referred to as prompt design is a rapidly evolving realm and is vital to effectively and efficiently using generative AI. Anyone using generative AI such as the widely and wildly popular ChatGPT by AI maker OpenAI, or akin AI such as GPT-4 (OpenAI), Bard and Gemini (Google), Claude (Anthropic), etc. ought to be paying close attention to the latest innovations for crafting viable and pragmatic prompts.

The use of generative AI can altogether succeed or falter based on the prompt that you enter.

If you provide a prompt that is poorly composed, the odds are that the generative AI will wander all over the map and you won't get anything demonstrative related to your inquiry. Being demonstrably specific can be advantageous, but even that can confound or otherwise fail to get you the results you are seeking.

With the above as an overarching perspective, we are ready to jump into today's discussion.

Prompts Are The Coinage Of The Realm

I will next take a gander at a handy research study on generative AI entitled "Ask Me Anything: A Simple Strategy For Prompting Language Models" by Simran Arora , Avanika Narayan, Mayee F. Chen, Laurel Orr, Neel Guha, Kush Bhatia, Ines Chami, Frederic Sala, and Christopher Ré (posted online on November 20, 2022). I'll showcase some excerpts and provide an analysis of what the researchers did and how their results can be suitably leveraged.

Remember that I earlier indicated you are barking up the wrong tree by trying to devise so-called perfect prompts. Part of the reason that I gave is that you cannot for sure anticipate how the generative AI will react to a given prompt. A keen way to say this is to denote that you are dealing with a brittle process, which is what the research paper forthrightly brings up:

- "Prompting is a brittle process wherein small modifications to the prompt can cause large variations in the model predictions, and therefore significant effort is dedicated towards designing a painstakingly perfect prompt for a task. To mitigate the high degree of effort involved in prompting, we instead ask whether collecting multiple effective, yet imperfect, prompts and aggregating them can lead to a high quality prompting strategy."

- "This work considers aggregating the predictions of multiple effective, yet imperfect, prompts to improve prompting performance over a broad set of models and tasks. Given a task input, each prompt produces a vote for the input's true label, and these votes are aggregated to produce a final prediction."

- "We propose ASK ME ANYTHING PROMPTING (AMA), a prompting approach that uses multiple imperfect prompts—rather than one painstakingly crafted perfect prompt—and reliably aggregates their outputs."

I trust that you can see how this particular research study reinforces the conception that you ought to set aside perfect prompts and allow yourself to work with imperfect prompts that can lead to stout prompts.

They proffer the idea that you can aggregate together a bunch of imperfect prompts to get something of a resultant synergistic good-enough prompt. I tend to speak of this as a triangulation method. Do something that is perhaps off-target but within the playing field. Do another attempt, again in the range of the playing field. After doing this some number of times, coalesce the separate and imperfect prompts into a newly derived prompt that contains the lessons learned from the litany of quickly concocted imperfect prompts.

The beauty is that you are nearly immediately moving ahead in trying to get toward a good-enough prompt. You don't need to sit quietly and stew over things. Come up with a reasonable yet imperfect prompt, try it out right away, and then come up with another one. Continue doing this. Once you've sensed that you've done it enough times, only now do you put on your erstwhile thinking cap and aim for a viable and battle-worn good-enough prompt.

Here's what the researchers found:

- "We find that AMA provides the most lift on tasks where all requisite knowledge is included in the task input (e.g., reading comprehension) and that largely rely on model's natural language understanding (NLU) abilities. The lift is lower on tasks that rely on the LLMs memorized knowledge (e.g. commonsense, closed-book). AMA can help close the gap on knowledge-intensive tasks."

- "Overall, AMA provides lift across four language model families and across model sizes ranging from 125M-175B parameters. Most excitingly, we find that AMA enables a 30x smaller LM to exceed the average performance of few-shot GPT3-175B averaged across 20 popular language benchmarks. Several LM applications involve private data or require operating over large amounts of data — for these applications, using APIs to access closed source models or hosting large models locally is challenging. We hope the strategies in AMA and subsequent work help enable such applications."

- "Our goal is to produce a collection of prompts, P, that can be applied to tasks at scale."

If you are interested in the details of the above-mentioned research study, they, fortunately, have made available their prompts and code on GitHub. I applaud any AI research that makes available their prompts and code. By making the materials publicly available, other AI researchers can test, verify, and revalidate the results, plus they can then use the source as a jumping point to make further progress in the AI realm. Sadly, many AI researchers do not publicly post their materials and ergo we don't have a ready means to gauge the validity of the experiments and nor can we build upon the already traversed turf.

That's a darned shame.

While I'm standing on top of this impromptu soapbox, I would also like to stridently suggest that all AI research studies ought to include some kind of impact report concerning AI Ethics and AI Law facets of their research. The thing is, much of the AI work being done is solely focused on technological factors. Few seem to be willing or thoughtful enough to also weigh in about the societal and legal dimensions of their AI endeavors.

In the instance of the research study that I've been discussing herein, they did provide some insightful remarks about how their AI research could be used and potentially regrettably misused:

- "We intend for AMA to aid practitioners in their exploration and use of LLMs—especially smaller, open-source LLMs. However, we recognize that AMA could be used to perform harmful or unethical tasks. AMA is a proof-of-concept; it has error-modes and we recognize the inherent risks to using LLMs."

Now for some analysis and further pontification.

As I've discussed frequently in my column, you can expect that much of prompt engineering will be augmented via the use of add-ons or built-in tools that aid otherwise manually-based prompting strategies. I mention this because the numerous cheat sheets and by-hand courses regrettably don't particularly scale up, as it were. You are not going to get on the order of hundreds of millions of human users of generative AI to lift themselves into the stratosphere of prompt engineering. It just isn't logistically and human behaviorally feasible.

The development and fielding of prompting add-ons and tools enable solid prompting strategies at scale. The same can be said of this iterative approach involving imperfect prompts being rapidly used to glean a good-enough prompt. Envision that rather than you manually coming up with a series of imperfect prompts by hand, a handy-dandy tool in the generative AI will take on that task for you.

I realize that might seem a bit recursive or a dream-within-a-dream akin to the popular movie "Inception". Here's how this will work. You would be entering a roughshod prompt, which the added AI-powered prompting tool would generate a bunch of additional imperfect prompts. Those in turn would be automatically or semi-automatically aggregated into a good-enough prompt by the tool. This good-enough prompt then becomes the final prompt that you enter into or simply pass along to the generative AI to get the interaction or essay that you are aiming for.

Easy-peasy.

Your Step-By-Step Guide For This Special Prompting Technique

If you want to try out this technique, I've got some helpful pointers for you.

Here's what I do whenever I am facing a knotty problem and I want to get generative AI to give suitable directed focus. To clarify, you would not likely use this technique if you are doing one-offs or lollygagging along with generative AI. I don't think the effort would be worth it, or as some might say, the squeeze wouldn't be worth the juice.

Okay, so assume that you have a somewhat complicated problem that you are having a hard time envisioning how to best compose as a prompt for generative AI. Your mind is muddled. Where do you start? What details should you include? Would it be wisest to pose the problem as a question or instead write the prompt as a directive overtly telling the generative AI what to do?

Questions, questions, questions.

Read my lips -- stop worrying.

Get on with the task.

Do the best that you can do and do so in a series of forthrightly "imperfect" prompts (ones that in your heart of hearts, you know are not what you want or need to say, but you've got to start somewhere). A journey of a thousand miles requires that you put one foot in front of another. Repeatedly.

My four overall major steps are these:

- **(1) Devise A Knowingly Imperfect Prompt Set**
- **(2) Use The Imperfect Prompt Set To Derive An Aggregated Prompt**
- **(3) Utilize The Aggregated Prompt And See How Things Go**
- **(4) Rinse And Repeat, Plus Identify Prompting Lessons**

Notice that this is a decidedly action-oriented method.

The good news is that you will likely feel better about using generative AI due to the action-inspired moving-things-along mantra of this technique. Furthermore, I am granting you explicit permission to assuredly not be perfect. Yes, that's right, you are being handed a get-out-of-jail-free card. Whereas most of us would suffer endlessly with a burning desire to write the perfect prompt, I am telling you that this is not something you need to further grouse over.

The delightful song *Let It Go* provides solace here.

Moving on, let's unpack those four major steps:

(1) Devise A Knowingly Imperfect Prompt Set

- (a) Compose your base prompt, don't fret over it
- (b) Come up with a series of reasonable and pertinent variants of the base prompt
- (c) Consider varying the style or format in addition to the substance involved
- (d) Review and possibly drop out imperfect prompts that mislead or could confound the AI

(2) Use The Imperfect Prompt To Derive Aggregated Prompt

- (a) Start up a new conversation in the generative AI (fresh and clean)
- (b) Begin with any needed context-setting prompts
- (c) Selectively make use of your imperfect prompts from your drafted set
- (d) Based on the generative AI response, gauge which other selections to try
- (e) If coalescing toward a suitable generative AI response do proceed in that direction
- (f) If diverging from a suitable response then halt your efforts, reassess, and possibly start anew
- (g) Establish a prudent aggregated prompt based on your tryouts in generative AI

(3) Utilize The Aggregated Prompt And See How Things Go

- (a) Start a new conversation in generative AI, so that all is fresh and clean
- (b) Begin with any needed context-setting prompts
- (c) Make use of your derived aggregated prompt
- (d) Based on the generative AI response, use follow-on prompts for added depth of pursuit
- (e) If coalescing toward a suitable generative AI response further proceed in that direction
- (f) If diverging from a suitable response then halt your efforts, reassess, and possibly start anew

(4) Rinse And Repeat, Plus Identify Prompting Lessons

- (a) Take a reflective moment to consider how things went
- (b) Ask yourself -- How can you improve the "imperfect" prompt prep for the future?
- (c) Ask yourself -- How can you improve the devising of aggregated prompts?
- (d) Ask yourself -- How can you improve the utilization of an aggregated prompt?
- (e) Identify any other learnings that will bolster your prompt engineering skills

I don't have the space here to go into a full-blown example of the process, but if there is sufficient reader interest I'll gladly do so in a later follow-up column and illuminate the subtle nuances of this notable technique.

This technique ought to be one of many that you have in your arsenal of prompt engineering methods. Each technique that you gradually become comfortable using will likely apply to particular circumstances. Do not fall into the classic trap of trying to use one technique in all situations. This is the veritable hammer and the nail. If all that you have is a hammer, the entire world seems to be filled with nails and you use the hammer even when you shouldn't. The same goes for becoming fixated on a particular prompt engineering technique.

Learn this technique and use it when warranted.

Conclusion

I have yet another rationale for why we should potentially embrace imperfect prompts. It is a potentially mind-boggling justification. For your safety, please sit down and prepare yourself.

Are you ready?

An article from the Harvard Business Review (HBR) said this about the ability of people in general to ask questions:

- "For some people, questioning comes easily. Their natural inquisitiveness, emotional intelligence, and ability to read people put the ideal question on the tip of their tongue. But most of us don't ask enough questions, nor do we pose our inquiries in an optimal way" (article entitled "The Surprising Power of Questions" by Alison Wood Brooks and Leslie K. John, May-June 2018, HBR).

The excerpt notes that people are not necessarily versed in asking questions. Some people are good at it. Probably most are not. My point is that we now have seemingly hundreds of millions of people using generative AI apps and we are nonchalantly assuming that all or most of those people know how to ask questions. They need to know how to suitably ask questions in the sense that generative AI fundamentally works on a question-and-answering basis.

Namely, you ask a question, and the generative AI is supposed to respond.

I think you see the problem at hand. If people aren't especially versed at asking questions, and yet if they have to ask questions to get answers from generative AI, things are messed up. The matter gets even worse when you take into account my earlier point that generative AI works on a probabilistic and statistical basis. You have people trying to use generative AI that isn't especially suave at asking questions.

Simultaneously, you have generative AI that is potentially going to provide generated responses that will somewhat wantonly vary each time you ask a question. I suppose, cheekily, you could say it is the blind leading the blind (an old saying likely worth retiring).

How do we get ourselves out of this vexing bind?

I have three possibilities to share with you.

First, we can try to get the whole world to be better at asking questions. Wow, that's an impressive and amazingly worthwhile heroic ambition all told. This would especially aid people that then opt to make use of generative AI, though that's a petite reason for pursuing such a lofty goal.

Another angle would be to accept that people are generally shaky at asking questions. As such, when using generative AI, give them a path toward turning their weakness into a strength by using lots of imperfect prompts to find your way toward a good-enough prompt. Voila, solution as shown via the technique described herein.

Third, we can advance AI so that generative AI can make up for the fact that humans by and large aren't astute at asking questions. As I mentioned earlier, all kinds of AI-powered add-ons and various prompt engineering tools will undoubtedly be blended into generative AI and make life easier for humans using generative AI.

I am betting you relish that last angle as the most exhilarating of the three options. We almost always embrace using automation when doing so relieves us of laborious chores.

Sorry to say, not everyone believes that having the AI do our question-asking uplifting for us is such a good idea. They worry that people will allow their ability to ask questions to decay. Worse and worse we will go. If our question-asking capability is already skimpy, imagine what will occur if the AI does the question-asking for us going forward. We might be totally bereft of question-asking competence.

I suppose we can refer to the brilliant and all-knowing Albert Einstein and see if there's anything he might have once uttered that could help us solve this dilemma. "Question everything," that's what Albert Einstein famously urged us to do. Those are wise words well worth living by, so go ahead and start asking more questions, as many as you like, and aim to perfect your question-asking skills, though be willing to settle for good enough if that cuts the mustard.

A perfectly good aspiration.

CHAPTER 3

PERSISTENT CONTEXT AND CUSTOM INSTRUCTIONS PROMPTING

I've got two famous quotes for you.

Let's try the first one on for size: "Those who cannot remember the past are condemned to repeat it."

That is a highly memorable and exceedingly popular quote by the legendary George Santayana, a Spanish-American philosopher and poet. I think we can all readily grasp the vital notion that was expressed. It seems exceedingly sensible and altogether smart to remember the past versus allowing the past to be slipped away into nothingness and ostensibly forgotten. We can all hopefully learn useful lessons from what happened in the past.

Moving on, the second quote is perhaps not as well-known but nonetheless carries a powerful punch: "Always and never are two words you should always remember never to use."

This remarkable quote is attributed to Wendell Johnson, the eminent American psychologist and author. Exhibiting a bit of clever whimsy, there are several distinguished messages hidden within. One worthy meaning is that you should mindfully choose the words that you opt to use. Another is that you can be on thin ice when proclaiming that something always happens, or asserting that something never ever happens. In the first instance, a disruptive force might break the streak of an assumed always-occurring phenomenon. For the second instance, all you need is for the thing that never happens to arise just once, and, presto, you've broken the emptiness pledge.

I'd ask you to keep those two noteworthy quotes in mind.

As you will soon see, they each offer great utility for the topic that I am going to discuss.

In this discussion, I am going to continue my special coverage of some key new techniques and breakthroughs underlying prompt engineering when using generative AI. The latest and most notably significant advance is something that I generically refer to as *persistent context capabilities*, popularly also known as *custom instructions*, and was recently announced and released as a new feature of ChatGPT.

A tidal wave of generative AI users is undoubtedly and inevitably going to massively adopt persistent context capabilities such as the custom instructions feature, no doubt about this. I will examine and highlight closely the custom instructions functionality of ChatGPT so that you'll have a strident understanding of what these capabilities consist of and how to best leverage them in your ongoing daily prompt engineering endeavors.

Interactions That Consist Of Persistent Context

On an everyday basis, we make use of persistent context when chatting with our friends, families, colleagues, and the like.

Here's what I mean.

You tell a friend of yours about a recent camping experience that you had. While out in the woods, you happened upon a bear that was up ahead of you on a desolate trail. You were unsure of what to do. Should you wave your arms and yell loudly to scare off the bear? Should you remain quiet as a mouse and slink away? Those life-determining thoughts danced through your noggin.

You ultimately decided to retreat since it seemed that the bear had not yet detected your presence. While making your retreat, you studiously looked over your shoulder to discern whether the bear was now going in your direction or still loitering innocently on the trail. Luckily, you got out of there without any direct encounter and lived to tell the tale of the time that you came somewhat face to face with a gnarly bear.

I'm sure that your friend found the tale quite engaging.

A week later, you and your friend get together at a local park in your neighborhood. A dog that is off its leash comes toward you and your friend. You blurt out that this seems reminiscent of your bear encounter. Your friend laughs in recognition of the similarity and announces that maybe you both should exercise a quiet retreat.

I realize that this might seem like an ordinary and mundane conversation and contains nothing worthy of rapt attention.

But let's dig into this.

Your friend has recalled the tale you told of your encounter with a bear. The story you previously told is in a sense still in the memory of your friend. Furthermore, your friend recalled the memory and made use of it in the latest context involving the circumstances with the unleashed dog.

We could fruitfully refer to this as a persistent context capacity.

The friend has been established beforehand with a particular context that is persistent over the course of time. Also, the persistence of the context came to the fore and was used as part of an interaction taking place at a later time. You could suggest that the persistence lasted beyond just the moment at which you originally told the story. It has a persistent or lasting facility to it.

Consider what would happen if the persistent context was not at play here.

Suppose that you went to the park with a colleague from work. You had never told the bear story to your officemate. If you suddenly said that seeing the dog reminded you of your bear encounter, would the fellow worker know what you were talking about? Probably not. There had not been any prior context establishment.

Think of persistent context as consisting of these two factors:

- (1) **Establishment.** You provide some establishing indication associated with a devised context.
- (2) **Invocation.** Something later occurs that invokes or engages the earlier established context.

The handy thing about persistent context is that once you've established it, you can presumably always later on invoke it when needed. In the case of your friend, you possibly do not need to ever again tell them the story about your bear encounter per se, assuming that your friend has a good enough memory that they will permanently remember the tale.

I certainly don't want to though create the impression that persistent context is necessarily flawless. Imagine that a year later you get together with your friend and go to a park. If somehow the prior tale comes up, it is quite possible that your friend will say that they "remember" the time that you had a harrowing experience with a wolf. Oops, your friend is misremembering your long-ago story. Worse still, the friend might have entirely forgotten your tale (friends carry no irrefutable obligation that they must remember every utterance you have ever made).

That's enough about bears, dogs, and wolves.

I am betting that you are now wondering with grand puzzlement how any of this relates to generative AI.

Time to get on with the show.

Persistent Context Or Custom Instructions In Generative AI

When I use generative AI, I typically start nearly every new conversation with a few starter or establishment prompts to get the generative AI into a suitable or preferred context. A lot of people do the same. That being said, neophytes to generative AI are often unaware of the value of establishing context when using generative AI.

Making use of establishing prompts is an extraordinarily useful technique and one that you ought to ensure is in your prompt engineering repertoire. I might add, sadly, many aren't aware of its intrinsic value and don't use it or don't know about it.

Allow me a moment to proffer an example of beneficially using establishing prompts.

I will often tell the generative AI to remain serious and not joke around in terms of interactions or when generating essays for me. I do this because sometimes generative AI can detect a random word in your prompts that gets it into a pattern-matched mode of switching into humor-related compositions. You might not have intended this. Perhaps in a prompt, you said that something was silly, which then spurred the generative AI to switch to telling jokes or being lighthearted when writing an essay for you.

By providing an establishing prompt at the start of a session, you can tell the generative AI that you only want serious outputs henceforth in the conversation. If you later on in a conversation want to override the establishing prompt, you can do so. You just tell the generative AI that it can for the next few interactions switch into a humor-oriented mode. This momentarily overrides your earlier establishing prompt.

Okay, so that's the gist of starter or establishing prompts.

One big rub is that you typically need to do this each time you start a new session or conversation with the generative AI. Most generative AI apps will always start clean and fresh. It is as though they've never seen or heard from you before. You get yourself a nice new sheet of paper, as it were.

Thus, you might find yourself having to laboriously type in a slew of handy starter instructions for the generative AI, doing so every darned time that you use the generative AI. Some people will write up their starter or establishing prompts into a text file and then do a copy and paste when they get going with a generative AI session. Of course, you need to know where that handy-dandy file is and must remember each time to go find it and do the copy-paste action. A pain in the neck, for sure.

Well, there is a (somewhat) brand-new feature coming to most generative AI apps that will help with this dilemma.

Welcome to the advent of persistent context in generative AI or that OpenAI refers to as custom instructions.

Generally, things go like this.

You can enter into a special place in the generative AI your preferred starter or establishing prompts. Henceforth, the generative AI will automatically invoke those starters or establish prompts for you. No need for you to search for that arcane file that contains your riches of starter or establishment prompts. Instead, this is a considered feature of the generative AI app.

Okay, you opt to do the setup of your custom instructions.

What happens next?

The aim is that the generative AI will refer to your establishment prompts during each of your interactive conversations.

If you had done a setup that instructed the generative AI to be serious, this will now silently and behind the scenes be considered the default posture. You don't need to repeat this over and over again. It is automatically invoked on your behalf each time that you use the generative AI.

The verbiage in the AI community is that this reduces the friction associated with using generative AI. The parlance is intended to note that having to each time enter your establishing prompts creates a kind of friction such that it makes using generative AI harder than it ought to be. The goal overall is to make the use of generative AI as frictionless as possible.

Smooth and seamless, that's the mantra.

Voila, via persistent context or custom instructions you have a feature that will ease the pain of wanting to do establishing prompts. By doing the establishing prompts as a one-time heads-up setup, they will be forever available and utilized by the generative AI. You can see these as veritable customized instructions because they are custom as to whatever you prefer to indicate.

The sky is the limit, some insist.

Hold on, maybe there are limits and we ought to be a bit less cavalier on this.

For example, a lawyer that I know often instructs generative AI to be serious, take on a legal persona, get to the point, and always summarize any essays that the AI app produces. That is the lawyer's preferred set of customizations or custom instructions.

One limitation that I had pointed out to my lawyer friend is that by and large those custom instructions or preferences can be obeyed by generative AI, but the legal persona aspect has a bit of a loophole to it.

Just because you tell generative AI to take on a legal persona as though it is acting as a lawyer, that doesn't mean that the generative AI really can attain this. In fact, AI makers typically state in their licensing that their generative AI cannot act as a lawyer and that the use of their AI app for legal advice is problematic, possibly slipping into the territory of the unauthorized practice of law (UPL).

A rule of thumb then is that just because you tell the generative AI to always do something, such as setting this up as a starter or establishing a prompt, does not ironclad guarantee you that it will happen.

I'll give you another example.

Suppose you instruct the generative AI to not hallucinate, not make any errors, and not generate any falsehoods. Researchers have tried doing this and tend to indicate that you will get varying results. Sometimes this remarkedly helps to cut down on those generative AI maladies. But the bulk of the time, it seems as though you cannot command your way around those maladies, and they will still occur, regardless of your custom instructions at the get-go.

I categorize custom instructions into two major buckets:

- **(a) Feasible custom instructions**. Custom instructions or establishing prompts that the generative AI can feasibly utilize and abide by.
- **(b) Impossible custom instructions.** Custom instructions or establishing prompts that the generative AI is unlikely to be able to fully utilize, for which your results might be out-of-whack with what you expected otherwise.

Now that I've laid the foundation for a persistent context or the use of custom instructions, we are ready to take a look at the newly announced and released custom instructions feature in ChatGPT.

ChatGPT Provides Custom Instructions Capability

OpenAI announced the release of their new custom instructions feature and provided various details on their blog website. I will be quoting excerpts from that website and using them during my analysis.

Here are some salient highlights posted on the OpenAI blog about custom instructions:

- "Custom instructions allow you to add preferences or requirements that you'd like ChatGPT to consider when generating its responses."
- "ChatGPT will consider your custom instructions for every conversation going forward."
- "The model will consider the instructions every time it responds, so you won't have to repeat your preferences or information in every conversation."
- "For example, a teacher crafting a lesson plan no longer has to repeat that they're teaching 3rd grade science. A developer preferring efficient code in a language that's not Python – they can say it once, and it's understood. Grocery shopping for a big family becomes easier, with the model accounting for 6 servings in the grocery list."

I trust that you can readily see from those excerpts that this is a feature for entering your starter or establishing prompts and then having those persist contextually throughout your use of the generative AI app.

Let's take a look at one of the examples that they provided (based on the above-bulleted point about grocery shopping for a family of six).

Envision that you go to do the setup of your starter or establishing prompts. When doing so, let's essentially assume that the generative AI asks you some questions or at least provides a spot for you to enter your establishing prompts, such as these for the grocery shopping example:

- **ChatGPT Question Asked Of You:** "What would you like ChatGPT to know about you to provide better responses?"
- **Your Response Or Establishing Prompt:** "I live in North Carolina with my four children and wife."
- **ChatGPT Question Asked Of You:** "How would you like ChatGPT to respond?"
- **Your Response Or Establishing Prompt:** "When planning meals, consider that I need to cater to a family of six. Ensure that recipe recommendations are suitable for larger groups and offer meal options that can be easily scaled up."

This example has the person indicating that they consist presumably of two adults and four children, thus consisting of a family of six people. There is admittedly a lot of other nuances and information that have been tossed into this establishing prompt such as they live in North Carolina, etc. I'll get to that in a moment.

My hint for you is that you should be notably mindful and cautious of whatever you decide to put in your establishing prompts. More on that shortly.

The example continues by having the person ask ChatGPT to come up with a grocery list of what to get at the store. Specifically, they want to make pizza for their nighttime meal.

- **Your Prompt To ChatGPT**: "What should I get at the store for pizza night?"
- **ChatGPT Generated Response (Custom Instructions enabled):** "Great! Planning for pizza night is always fun. Here's a shopping list for a pizza night for six people, assuming you'll be making two large pizzas. Pizza Dough: (1) Bread flour - 1kg (enough for two large pizza doughs), (2) Dry yeast - 2 packets (14 grams) Sugar - small pack (you'll need 4 teaspoons), (3) Olive oil - 1 small bottle (you'll need 4 tablespoons), (4) Salt - small pack (you'll need 2 teaspoons)…" {side note that the rest of recipe contains info on pizza sauce, toppings, and optional add-ons}.

The response by ChatGPT seems nifty. The ingredients are listed.

The amount needed is shown as based on feeding six people. This all appears to be making use of the establishing prompt that was stored in the custom instructions.

Let's look closer.

You might have a tad of heartburn that the response by ChatGPT refers to six people. Recall that there are two adults and four children. Yes, of course, the four kids are people, but we might have wanted the response to explicitly indicate that the recipe is for two adults and four children. Presumably, the amount of pizza for the kids is going to be less than what we would anticipate an adult would normally eat.

Has ChatGPT taken this into account? We don't know from the response. This would require asking ChatGPT to clarify how it came up with the portions and what assumptions it was making.

I bring this up to illuminate my earlier points about making use of persistent context and things such as custom instructions. You might not necessarily know how the generative AI has opted to interpret your starter or establishing prompts. The proof ultimately arises in the pudding, once you've later on entered prompts that are intended to invoke the earlier establishments.

Moving on, you might be wondering what ChatGPT might have generated as a response if the custom instructions had either never been established or if we simply turned them off so that they are no longer enabled during your session. As an aside, it is important that any AI maker that makes available persistent context features ought to include that users can turn it off at will, and enable it at will (yes, ChatGPT provides this on/off mode).

Here's what the OpenAI blog indicates would have happened:

- **ChatGPT Generated Response (Custom Instructions turned off):** "Pizza night can be a great opportunity to get creative and involve everyone in the preparation process. Here's a general shopping list that should cover a variety of tastes. Pizza Dough: You can buy pre-made pizza dough at most grocery stores, or you can make your own from scratch.

> You will need flour, yeast, sugar, salt, and olive oil if you decide to make your own…" {side note that the rest of the recipe contains info on pizza sauce, cheese, toppings, extras, drinks, desserts}.

The crux is that this generative AI produced a detailed grocery list but did not indicate the number of ingredients needed. This makes sense. Without having a prior indication via the establishing prompt or custom instructions that the number of people to be fed is six, there are no viable means for the generative AI to indicate how much pizza you ought to be likely making.

There is something else about this example that you should in a Sherlock Holmes manner be observing.

The generated response when the custom instructions were turned off included suggestions about getting drinks and desserts to accompany the pizza (those indications appeared in the response, but for space purposes herein I didn't list them explicitly above). In comparison, the generated response when the custom instructions were enabled made no mention apparently of drinks or desserts.

Why the difference?

It is hard to contend that the custom instructions somehow waved away the notion of mentioning drinks or desserts. There isn't anything in the establishing prompts that seems to suggest this. The likely aspect is that you need to always consider that generative AI is like a box of chocolates, namely that due to the probabilistic nature of how the narratives are pieced together by the AI app, each generated response is going to likely differ from the other response.

It is the nature of the beast, one might say.

So, in this instance, the custom instructions being on or off probably didn't make that difference occur.

This also is notable because you have to be conscious of the fact that by simply turning on or off the custom instructions you cannot necessarily expect to get identical answers, other than for the lack of whatever custom instruction you had provided. Various other differences can readily creep into the essays and interactions, regardless of what the custom instructions had to say.

When using generative AI, a tongue-in-cheek rule of thumb is that your mileage may vary (a perhaps smarmy remark though certainly on-target that the statistical and probabilistic underpinnings make getting anything exactly word-for-word amounts to a low odds matter).

Before we dive deeper into the persistent context realm, I would like to provide seven crucial recommendations for you:

- **(1)** Use custom instructions or persistent context features if you already find yourself frequently entering establishing prompts when using generative AI.
- **(2)** When making use of a custom instructions feature, do so mindfully and consider the impacts on your generative AI aspects encompassing privacy, safety, use of plugins, etc.
- **(3)** Make sure to carefully compose your custom instructions, possibly trying them out as standalone prompts to see what kind of results you get or at least testing them once you've put them into the custom instructions area.
- **(4)** Remain aware as to when you have custom instructions enabled and avidly want it enabled, while also being astute enough to turn it off when you don't want it enabled.
- **(5)** If you don't usually use establishing prompts, then likely no need to use this feature (contingent on whether you even know of the usefulness that doing so can provide).
- **(6)** For those of you who do not usually leverage establishing prompts, reconsider and decide whether it might be sense for you to use establishing prompts overall hereafter (if you do opt to do so, consider then using any provided persistent context functionality).
- **(7)** All in all, consider experimenting with a persistent context feature to ascertain whether you find it useful and whether it makes a helpful addition to your prompt engineering strategies and tactics.

More To Know Under-The-Hood

I have so far covered the mainstay of knowing about persistent context capabilities.

We are just at the tip of the iceberg. I will briefly touch upon a number of other vital considerations, which I hinted at earlier and also mentioned in passing in my recommendations above (see the second recommendation).

Tighten your seat belt and let's go full speed ahead.

Watch Out For Plugins

Most generative AI apps nowadays allow for plugins. This means that the generative AI can make use of other apps that presumably provide additional value, such as perhaps making use of an external app that will make your travel reservations for you or that will do financial calculations for you.

Here's something to ponder. If you use custom instructions or persistent capabilities feature, will the generative AI pass along whatever establishing prompts of yours into the plugins and to the API-connected apps? You might want that to happen so that whatever other app will be aware of your preferences and instructions. The concern is that you might be handing over private info that you really don't want those other apps to have. This is something you need to give due diligence toward.

Per the OpenAI blog about how custom instructions work in ChatGPT pertaining to plugins:

- "Adding custom instructions can also help improve your experience with plugins by sharing relevant information with the plugins that you use. For example, if you specify the city you live in within your instructions and use a plugin that helps you make restaurant reservations, the model might include your city when it calls the plugin."

In the example about the family of six, the establishing prompt indicated that they live in North Carolina. That info can be advantageous to have automatically passed over to any plugins or other affiliated apps. A disadvantage is that you opted to freely and wantonly give away your location, at least as to which state you live in, and this might be paired up with other demographic data and used in all sorts of ways, such as for telemarketing, etc.

My cautionary thoughts are this:

- Realize that you don't know how else or where else the plugins will use your custom instructions, including storing it, analyzing it, giving it away to others, and so on.
- Also, the plugins won't necessarily make use of the conveyed instructions and you are passing them along but uselessly so.
- You won't necessarily know how and whether the conveyed instructions altered what the plugin ends up doing.
- And so on.

Privacy Is Something You Need To Keep At The Fore

The above discussion about the plugins brought forth the potential for privacy concerns.

Whenever you use any generative AI app, it is crucial that you read the licensing stipulations that the AI maker has laid out for those who use the AI app. For example, see my analysis of the types of licensing restrictions, privacy provisions, and numerous potential legal exposures for you, including that you might unknowingly be indemnifying the AI maker and you could be on the hook for a sizable legal bill.

Here's what the OpenAI blog says about privacy associated with the custom instructions feature:

- "We may use your custom instructions to improve model performance for our users, but you can disable this via your data controls. As with ChatGPT conversations, we take steps to remove personal identifiers found in custom instructions before they are used to improve model performance. Learn more about how we use conversations to improve model performance and your choices in our Help Center."

Note that the default mode is that your custom instructions can be used by the AI maker, purportedly to improve the generative AI app.

Read my lips, it is on your shoulders to then potentially disable that usage by adjusting the data controls for your generative AI account.

It would seem a fair bet or solid odds that most users of the custom instructions are unlikely to realize they need to take overt action to disallow such usage. The typical user will undoubtedly just assume that either the usage won't take place unless they opt-in (which they have, by default, by enabling the feature), or won't care either way and not be cognizant of what if any impact it might have on them. And, though it is encouraging and laudable that an effort is made to remove personal identifiers, note that there is no guarantee that the personal identifiers will absolutely, unconditionally, and utterly be removed (things are a bit loosey-goosey as to the notion of taking steps, which doesn't read quite the same as saying that for sure your personal identifiers are removed).

Your Custom Instructions Cannot Go Over The Line

I earlier emphasized that your custom instructions or establishing prompts ought to be feasibly implementable. If you enter custom instructions that are essentially impossible to observe, this will do little for your generative AI pursuits.

More so, OpenAI notes in their blog about the custom instructions feature that you are not to enter any custom instructions that violate the usage policies and licensing stipulations.

Here's what the blog says:

- "We've adapted our safety measures to account for the new ways that users can instruct the model. For example, our Moderation API is designed to help ensure instructions won't be saved if they violate our Usage Policies. The model can also refuse or ignore instructions that lead to responses that violate our usage policies."

If you are unsure of what the usage policies encompass, take a look at the OpenAI website. For example, you aren't supposed to use ChatGPT for the generation of hateful, harassing, or violent content. Nor can you use the generative AI app for fraudulent or deceptive activity. You aren't supposed to do any political campaigning or lobbying with the AI app. Etc.

Thus, whatever you put into your custom instructions is supposed to equally abide by those stipulations.

The Interpretation Of Custom Instructions Is Open-Ended

The OpenAI blog notes that the custom instructions feature is considered in beta, which only right now is available in the ChatGPT Plus plan, and that the feature will be "expanding to all users in the coming weeks."

An intriguing statement made in the blog is this:

- "Especially during the beta period, ChatGPT won't always interpret custom instructions perfectly—at times it might overlook instructions, or apply them when not intended."

I earlier herein pointed out that you cannot be sure about how your custom instructions or persistent context-establishing prompts will be interpreted by the generative AI.

The somewhat curious aspect about the wording of the notification in the blog post is that we are told that during the beta, especially, the custom instructions won't be "perfectly" interpreted. This seems to imply that post-beta we can potentially expect that the custom instructions will unerringly and perfectly always be interpreted. That is one heck of a tall order.

Here's why.

Natural language inherently is imbued with semantic ambiguity. Words are always open to interpretation. You might vaguely be aware that entire court cases have dragged on and on about the meaning of even the smallest of words such as the word "is" and the word "the" (based on the context of their usage).

Frankly, I find it highly unlikely that we will somehow miraculously overcome the semantic ambiguity of natural language. It is part and parcel of the creature at hand. Attempts have been made to devise new languages, especially in mathematical form, which can stave off ambiguity. But the natural language we all use today has baggage that just seems to be a futile case to perfectly interpret.

But that is perhaps a story for another day.

Right now, the warning is well-intended that you should realize that your custom instructions are subject to interpretation. Furthermore, your custom instructions might be entirely ignored or overlooked. I take you back to my box of chocolates. Do not assume that your custom instructions are at all working or being abided by. They might be, they might not be.

Keep your eye on the ball and your head in the game when using generative AI.

The Big Picture About Persistent Context Capabilities

I've now covered generally and with some examples the persistent context precept which is arising as a vital prompt engineering technique and practical real-world value-add for generative AI users.

Some generative AI apps have this feature, some do not. I think it is an easy prediction to make that eventually nearly all generative AI apps will offer something along these lines. Each AI maker will likely vary how the feature works. Make sure to read up on whatever generative AI app you are using and leverage such a feature correctly and sensibly.

There are significant tradeoffs when choosing to use a persistent context approach.

Here are my seven upsides about the use of persistent context:

- (1) **No More Repetitiveness**. You no longer need to laboriously and repeatedly enter the same establishing prompts that you've possibly been using, instead, you will simply enter them just once and be done with it.
- (2) **Readily Available As Needed**. The establishing prompt will be handily available at all times and can be automatically invoked.
- (3) **Can Enable Or Turn-Off As Desired.** You can hopefully switch it off when you want to do so.
- (4) **Streamlines Usage.** Streamlines your usage and can demonstrably speed up the process of using generative AI.
- (5) **Convenient And Powerful.** Hugely convenient and generally a promising and helpful added piece of functionality.
- (6) **Minimal Maintenance By You.** Potentially you only need to do the setup on a one-and-done or fire-and-forget basis such that it will be either a low or no maintenance ongoing endeavor on your part thereafter.
- (7) **Other.** See my other general comments and insights mentioned earlier.

Here are my seven downsides about persistent context:

- (1) **Might Forget It Is Invoked.** You might easily forget that you have set up a persistent context and it will run when you aren't aware that it is running, perhaps tilting or misdirecting the generative AI in ways you will be puzzled by.
- (2) **Might Be Misinterpreted**. You do not know for sure that the generative AI will interpret the persistent context in the manner that you think it will or should, thus the impact on the subsequent generated responses might be off-target of what you hoped for.

- (3) **Might Be Ignored Or Overlooked.** The establishing prompts in your persistent context might be ignored or overlooked by the generative AI. This could be beguiling since it might happen from time to time, and you will be perplexed that sometimes it is being applied and other times it is not.
- (4) **Context Limits Impacts.** One question to look into is whether the use of a persistent context counts in the existing context limits of your generative AI app, or whether it is considered above and beyond the normal context limits. If it edges into your conversation-allowed context limits, you'd want to be careful since you are using up precious context space and want to make sure you are doing so advantageously.
- (5) **Distinct Versus Morass.** You'll want to look into whether your persistent context is all jumbled together as one morass or whether it is distinctively defined. If the feature is everything and the kitchen sink, this can mean that particular establishing prompts might come to play when you don't want them to do so (plus, they might have conflicts or other disconcerting issues).
- (6) **Unknown As To Impacts Specifically.** You won't necessarily know what impact the persistent context has had on your generated response, which you assume it will in fact have, but there isn't any obvious way to know other than by perusing the response and trying to ascertain whether the custom instructions landed on the mark (you could also try switching the feature on and off, generating twice or more times for comparison, but even then the probabilistic aspects might mask any marked differences).
- (7) **Other.** See my other general comments and insights mentioned earlier.

Conclusion

I have a final twist for you and some concluding remarks.

Up until now, most people who avidly use establishing prompts have typically done so on their own.

There are some training courses and tip sheets that mention the use of establishing prompts, but I would estimate that this is only understood by and used actively by a relatively small segment of generative AI users. Also, it has been a somewhat laborious chore to use them when there weren't widely available ready-made automatic built-in features to accommodate starter prompts.

One strident possibility is that the emergence and adoption of persistent context capabilities will raise the prominence and heighten the use of establishing prompts. In that case, as with anything in the software and AI arena, you can bet that a marketplace will grow accordingly.

I see this as consisting of three categories:

- (1) **Proprietary Establishing Prompts**. The use of establishing prompts of your own proprietary and personal nature.
- (2) **Standardized Establishing Prompts.** The use of establishing prompts that are considered as standards or conventions, and for which anyone that wants to use them in their persistent context feature can do so. AI makers will include them for you as a selection option rather than you having to enter them by yourself.
- (3) **Personalized Standardized Establishing Prompts.** This is akin to #2 but you can modify or customize the standardized establishing prompts to your liking.

Having generative AI apps that can easily accommodate the use of establishing prompts will grease the skids toward creating a blossoming market in this realm. Good luck to you entrepreneurs who decide to capitalize on this upcoming boon.

Now, for my concluding remarks, you might remember that I asked you to remember two notable quotes at the beginning of this discussion. Just like forgetting a story about a bear encounter, I don't blame you if you've by now forgotten what the two opening quotes were.

Here they are:

- "Those who cannot remember the past are condemned to repeat it."
- "Always and never are two words you should always remember never to use."

I brought up the Santayana quote to highlight that making use of establishing prompts is really handy for setting up a productive contextual sphere when using generative AI. When you go from one generative AI conversation to the next, you can relish that your preferred context has been established and will be "remembered" rather than either forgotten or not present at all.

My reason for bringing up the mind-bending quote about the use of the words always and never is that you have to realize that natural language comprises semantic ambiguity. The words of an establishing prompt can readily be interpreted by the generative AI in a multitude of ways. Try as best you can to figure out wording that gets the generative AI closest possible to your desired intentions.

I'd like to say that if you follow this advice you will always get the maximum out of generative AI, but I dare not use the always word since I seem to faintly remember that it is a word I should never use. I read that somewhere.

CHAPTER 4
MULTI-PERSONA PROMPTING

They say that two heads are better than one.

But another saying is that sometimes you can have too many cooks in the kitchen.

Keep dearly in mind those sage pieces of wisdom.

In discussion, I am going to cover a newly emerging and quite fascinating technique associated with prompt engineering for generative AI that makes use of multi-agent formulations. In a sense, you can think of this innovative approach as trying to garner multiple viewpoints within or by the AI while trying to use generative AI to solve problems.

My discussion will walk you through the foundations of the topic, plus I'll highlight recent research that has sought to closely examine the matter. And, as a special bonus, I made use of this thought-provoking technique in a popular generative AI app, ChatGPT, and will proffer excerpts of my exemplar to further explain how this technique can be advisably used (the example will entail viewpoints associated with a business-oriented legal scenario).

The use of generative AI can altogether succeed or falter based on the prompt that you enter.

Personas For Fun And Profit

One prompt engineering approach that some people use for fun, while others use exceedingly seriously, consists of invoking what is called "personas" during a generative AI session.

Suppose that you wanted to have some fun while using generative AI. You could instruct via a prompt that the generative AI is to pretend that it is Yoda from *Star Wars*. By doing this, the generative AI will switch into a mode of mimicking the wording and responses that the fictitious character Yoda might conventionally respond to. A resulting interactive dialogue with the generative AI can be enjoyable and brighten your day.

A more serious use of personas might be to instruct generative AI to take on the role of a medical doctor or perhaps a lawyer. The generative AI will proceed to interact with you in that role-playing fashion. This can be eerily human-like in the sense that the vocabulary used and the tone will come across akin to what you envision a medical doctor might say or what a lawyer might say.

There is a lot of heartburn about allowing generative AI to take on these personas or fake roles. Most of the AI makers warn you that the generative AI is not versed in medicine or the law, ergo any advice or interaction with the generative AI is to be taken with a huge grain of salt. Unfortunately, it is all too easy to be lulled into believing that the generative AI is an expert in medicine or the law, especially since the interaction is often portrayed in a confident and reassuring tone.

Sometimes a generative AI app is coded to prevent you from getting the AI into a persona mode. For example, you might enter a prompt that tells the AI to pretend to be a medical doctor, and the AI will respond that this is not allowed. That would seem to end your chances of getting the AI to embrace that persona.

Turns out that there are often sneaky ways to get around those blockages, such as by entering your prompt in a more roundabout way or using wording that manages to scoot past the filtering being used by the AI app.

All kinds of AI Ethics and AI Law issues arise in the considerations of using personas in generative AI. Should personas not be allowed? If personas are allowed, what limits should the AI have? Would it be best to have the AI continually remind the user that the AI is merely play-acting and does not represent actual human capacity in the role being undertaken? Etc.

There is also a solid chance that we will ultimately see lawmakers come to the fore on these matters, possibly devising and putting in place new laws or regulations to try and scope and curtail misuses of the persona's capabilities of generative AI.

The Big Twists Of Generative AI And Personas

Now that I've got you thinking about the use of personas by generative AI, I'd like to bring up a twist that I'm betting some of you have not yet considered.

Are you ready?

I would guess that most people tend to invoke one persona at a time when using generative AI if they opt to use the persona technique at all. As mentioned, you might invoke a Yoda persona. Once you've had your fill of that, you probably would instruct the generative AI to stop being like Yoda. Maybe your next step would be to ask the generative AI to be an expert in rare birds. Perhaps you saw an unusual-looking bird and wanted to have the generative AI take on the persona of an ornithologist. This would allow you to interact with the generative AI as though it knew all about birds and could carry on a discourse accordingly.

Let's up the ante on the personas.

You might decide that you want the generative AI to *simultaneously* be both Yoda and an ornithologist. What would happen? Presumably, you would be engaged in a dialogue with a seeming expert in birds that also so happened to talk like Yoda. Cheekily, one might say, in Yoda-speak, knowing all about birds, Yoda does.

Using this type of multiple personas capacity might have more substance to it than you would otherwise assume at first glance. Setting aside the Yoda and bird expert combination, envision that we wanted to get the opinions of two attorneys on a thorny legal matter. If you spoke with two human attorneys, you would indeed potentially discover that two heads are better than one. The aim is to see if having two attorneys helping you with your legal woes might get you a wider range or greater depth of legal advice than you might get from one attorney alone.

Would you for sure be guaranteed that speaking with two attorneys on your legal issue would foster a much more robust semblance of a legal argument on your behalf?

Not necessarily.

It could be that one attorney alone is sufficient. One attorney might be able to articulate the same or even fuller legal advice as would two attorneys. You could even make the case that perhaps the use of two attorneys might be distracting and cause a lesser quality of legal advice than by one alone. Imagine too that you've got one seasoned attorney who is versed in the area of law that you want advice on, versus if you had two newly minted attorneys that are not especially versed in that legal realm. The level of expertise is a factor, as is the nature of how the interaction takes place when using two or more at hand.

The gist is that the number of personas doesn't give you an ironclad improvement in whatever you are trying to attain. It might, it might not.

Another consideration is whether the personas are aimed to work collaboratively or aimed to work in an adversarial manner.

Two people working in unison might be cooperative and encourage each other to find the best solution to a given problem. We all know how valuable collaboration can be. If the two are butting heads, things can get stuck and you won't make as much progress as would occur in a collaborative setting.

The surprise perhaps then to the notion of using personas in generative AI is that oftentimes you tend to use only one at a time, essentially considered the customary or prevailing approach, but you might want to expand your prompting repertoire and opt to invoke multiple personas at the same time.

Thus, rather than always just using a singular persona, one at a time, you could try to leverage the potential benefits of invoking two or more at the same time. Whether this will achieve a classic more-is-merrier outcome is unclear. You need to think mindfully about the nature of the personas, how you want them to work together or work in opposition to each other, and how the number of them will aid or impede your end goal associated with whatever problem-solving you want the generative AI to do.

All of those crucial factors have to be imbued in the prompt that you use. Any prompt instructing the generative AI to use multiple personas can be amazingly on-target or can be woefully off-base. Words matter. Choose your wording carefully.

I trust that seems somewhat straightforward.

Twists Upon Twists Are Afoot

Good, so let's add yet another twist to the saga.

Imagine that I log into ChatGPT and get it to be a particular persona that I think would be useful to employ. I then also log into another generative AI, let's say Bard, and get it to also take on that same persona. Assume for the moment that the generative AI apps are disparate and there isn't anything connecting them. I am separately logged into each and they aren't electronically or digitally connected.

We will use the two-lawyers scenario again. I get ChatGPT to take on a lawyer persona and I ask it a legal question that I am concerned about. I interact with ChatGPT on the matter. I switch over to Bard and ask the same legal question. I interact with Bard on the matter.

Have I likely gotten a more robust or more in-depth analysis of the given problem than if I had used only one of those AI apps?

It is hard to definitely say, one way or another.

We can almost categorically assert that the odds are we will have somewhat differing viewpoints. You see, each of those generative AI apps has been data-trained on differing data (I should clarify that there are potential overlaps of which data they were each respectively trained on, but there is also a significant chance that they have each scanned data that the other did not). Also, the underlying algorithms, data structures, large language models (LLM), machine learning (ML), and other facets are almost certainly different from each other (which, in some ways can end up being just a minor difference, but in others ways can be a markedly pronounced difference).

The crux is that the odds are pretty high that we won't be getting the same dialogue out of the separate generative AI apps. This might mean that we could get a fuller response all told, based on your having to meld together the two separate interactions that you've collected. You would need to bring together in your mind the semblance of what each generative AI app had to say.

Okay, in recap, you could try to do that, namely use separate generative AI apps and tell each of those to take on some desired persona or simultaneous personas that you believe could be useful in solving your problem at hand. Another approach and somewhat easier path consists of invoking multiple personas in a singular generative AI app.

Some refer to the singular approach as invoking a so-called *solo performance*.

Have a mind-bending question for you: Would the solo performance be on par with the multiple generative AI apps approach?

Aha, this is a huge and unresolved question. Welcome to the enigma. The core issue being bandied around is whether a solo generative AI can sufficiently reflect multiple personas at once.

I refer to this as the apple pie problem.

Apple Pie Tells You What You Need To Know

Here's what I mean.

Suppose that a solo generative AI is asked to solve a given problem. You first try this with the instruction to take on one persona, let's say that of a lawyer. You see what answer you get. You then start anew and tell the generative AI to take on two personas, each being a lawyer, and that the two are to work collaboratively.

One possibility is that by asking for two personas, the generative AI will do a better job of solving the problem. We know, for example, that the use of chain-of-thought (CoT) instructions will often get you better results when using generative AI. This entails instructing the generative AI to explain on a stepwise or step-by-step basis what the problem-solving consists of. For various mathematical and computational pattern-matching reasons, the CoT will tend to get you more robust results (not always, but often enough that it is a worthwhile technique to leverage).

Perhaps multiple personas invoked in a solo generative AI can have a similar effect.

The thing is, regrettably, using multiple personas might not get you much of a bonus when doing so with a solo generative AI in contrast to employing multiple disparate generative AI. The solo generative AI might derive a solution that is shall we say an apple pie in size.

Envision that one persona can convey the entirety of the apple pie.

You then ask for two personas. But it could be that all the two personas do is split up the apple pie into two pieces. The result is that you haven't gained anything per se. You have merely split the same pie. The hope of course is that the use of two or more personas is going to enlarge the pie, garnering you added value that the solo personas didn't provide.

The same concern can arise for three, four, or any number of personas. Each persona might merely further splinter or slice the pie into smaller and smaller pieces. None of this is probably going to do you much good. It can be counterproductive in that you end up potentially having to piece together the slices whereas just one persona or none at all might have done that for you to begin with.

Part of the basis for only getting the same-same answer from a solo generative AI is that it is tapping solely into the data training and pattern-matching that it has. In the case of using multiple generative AI apps, and as I noted earlier, the chances are that the generative AI apps are inherently different from the get-go and therefore you are likely to get differing results (maybe producing a larger pie or shall we say numerous pies, one that is a cherry pie and one that is an apple pie).

You might be thinking that if using multiple generative AI apps is seemingly more productive than using a solo to do the multiple personas, perhaps always take that route. The downside is that you would need to set up accounts at multiple generative AI apps and bear whatever costs might be involved. This could be costlier and a lot more inconvenient than the solo generative AI route.

A tradeoff is involved.

Is the potential gain from using multiple generative AI apps and multiple personas going to get you more or less than using a solo generative AI app with multiple personas being invoked in that one generative AI?

You can't especially know for sure beforehand.

If you can afford the time and cost to use multiple generative AI apps and have a knotty problem that seems worth tossing the kitchen sink at it, go for it. If you are on a tighter budget or do not believe the problem at hand merits the multiple generative AI approach, so be it and stay with a solo performance.

Future Of Generative AI Invoking Other Generative AI

Let's take a quick glance at the near-term future.

I have predicted that we will soon enough have add-ons to generative AI that smooth out the desire to use multiple generative AI apps in a collective "two heads are better than one" mode of operation. Behind the scenes will be advanced tech that pushes out your prompt to multiple disparate generative AI, the results will be gathered by the tool and then presented to you as a seamless whole. This can be done on an essay-generating basis and will also be available on a real-time interactive dialoguing basis.

Back to the matter about the solo generative AI and the use of multiple personas, one consideration is that maybe when you use just one persona you aren't going to get the full apple pie. It could be that you get only half of it or maybe 90%, while once you invoke two or more personas within the generative AI, the rest of the apple pie gets revealed. This is again akin to the seeming benefit of using chain-of-thought approaches.

With all of that in hand, let's do some additional unpacking on this enthralling topic. I'll cover next herein some of the latest research that examines the advantages and disadvantages of solo generative AI in a multi-agent or multi-personas gambit. Following that analysis, I will showcase an example that I ran by using ChatGPT.

Some have jokingly referred to this idea of using a solo generative AI that has multiple personas invoked as having too many voices in one head. The result could be counterproductive and chaotic. As an important side note, I'd like to emphasize that we must be exceedingly cautious about anthropomorphizing generative AI.

Trying to cavalierly make comparisons to how humans think and the nature of multiple personas ought to not be commingled with how generative AI works. These are two entirely different facets. Generative AI is a mechanization of mathematical and computational pattern matching. Please be careful in making use of various metaphors and analogies in this arena.

Research On Generative AI About Multiple Personas

Let's take a look at a recently posted and altogether interesting research study entitled "Unleashing Cognitive Synergy In Large Language Models: A Task-Solving Agent Through Multi-Persona Self-Collaboration" by Zhenhailong Wang, Shaoguang Mao, Wenshan Wu, Tao Ge, Furu Wei, Heng Ji (posted online July 11, 2023).

Here's what the research paper entails (excerpts):

- "Human intelligence thrives on the concept of cognitive synergy, where collaboration and information integration among different cognitive processes yield superior outcomes compared to individual cognitive processes in isolation. Although Large Language Models (LLMs) have demonstrated promising performance as general task-solving agents, they still struggle with tasks that require intensive domain knowledge and complex reasoning."

- "In this work, we propose Solo Performance Prompting (SPP), which transforms a single LLM into a cognitive synergist by engaging in multi-turn self-collaboration with multiple personas. A cognitive synergist refers to an intelligent agent that collaborates with multiple minds, combining their individual strengths and knowledge, to enhance problem-solving and overall performance in complex tasks. By dynamically identifying and simulating different personas based on task inputs, SPP unleashes the potential of cognitive synergy in LLMs. We have discovered that assigning multiple, fine-grained personas in LLMs elicits better problem-solving abilities compared to using a single or fixed number of personas."

The above-cited research examined the use of solo performance prompting, whereby you instruct a solo generative AI to take on the role of multiple personas. This can be compared and contrasted to making use of multiple generative AI apps and having those disparate AI apps take on multiple personas.

Just to briefly mention, my own preference is to avoid referring to the generative AI as potentially having cognitive synergies since the word "cognitive" is laden with all kinds of human connotations and anthropomorphizing. I realize this phrasing is commonly used in research on AI. I fully grasp why it is a handy phrasing to make use of. Anyway, I tend to prefer suggesting that this is a form of mathematical and computational pattern-matching synergy in the case of generative AI, while in the case of humans, I am certainly fine with denoting the conception that human thinking embodies cognitive synergies.

Returning to the research study, they used a three-step process to examine these vexing matters:

- "To unleash the power of synergizing different personas to tackle complex problems within a single LLM, we propose Solo Performance Prompting (SPP) which instructs a model to perform the following the procedure for solving general tasks:
- (1) *Persona Identification*: Identify multiple participants with special personas (including a leader persona: AI Assistant) that are essential for solving the particular task.
- (2) *Beginning Remarks*: Each of the participants delivers a beginning remarks providing suggestions or information on how to approach the task based on their own expertise.
- (3) *Multi-Persona Iterative Collaboration:* The leader persona, AI Assistant, proposes initial solutions, consults the other participants for feedback, and revise the answer iteratively."

The study, fortunately, provides the prompts they used and the outputs that resulted from their work (collected into a GitHub repository for ease of access). I wholeheartedly applaud this form of visibility.

We need AI researchers to showcase their prompts and resultant outputs of generative AI so that we can all readily see what was done and how it was undertaken. Not all AI researchers are this open-minded. The issue is that if we cannot see what was undertaken, the chances of replicating, verifying, validating, and otherwise furthering the advancement of AI are stilted, and a lack of transparency will lamentably undercut systematic progress in AI.

Moving on, this is an example of one prompt that they used:

- **Prompt:** "When faced with a task, begin by identifying the participants who will contribute to solving the task. Then, initiate a multi-turn collaboration process until a final solution is reached. The participants will give critical comments and detailed suggestions whenever necessary."

Look closely at the prompt wording.

In a brief three sentences, the core aspect that personas are to be invoked is done by simply asking the generative AI to identify participants and have those participants perform a multi-turn collaboration. The use of the word "collaboration" sets the stage that the participants are presumably going to work together rather than work in opposition. The "multi-turn" phrasing tends to get the generative AI to write out a result that looks almost like a script for a TV show or movie. One persona will stipulate something, then the next, and so on, usually on a round-robin basis. Mentioning that the personas are to give critical commentary and details will generally nudge the generative AI towards providing the juicy detailed stuff versus only presenting the results.

Here's an example of some participants or personas in one particular scenario:

- "AI Assistant (you); Poet; Computer Scientist; Ten-year-old child."

Here are the profiles of the participants:

- "AI Assistant (you): A super-intelligent AI assistant capable of performing tasks more effectively than humans."

- "Poet: A person who studies and creates poetry. The poet is familiar with the rules and formats of poetry and can provide guidance on how to write a poem."
- "Computer Scientist: A scholar who specializes in the academic study of computer science. The computer scientist is familiar with the concept of a quantum computer and can provide guidance on how to explain it."
- "Ten-year-old child: A child with a limited English vocabulary and little knowledge about complicated concepts, such as a quantum computer."

A crucial question for any research on generative AI that wishes to tackle this topic consists of ascertaining how to judge the results of the multiple personas experiment. If you give a problem that entails qualitative answers of a fuzzy nature, you are going to have a harder time determining whether the answers were equal, less, or better than might otherwise have been devised.

The cleaner approach consists of using problems that have already known answers and ones that tend toward being of a quantitative and relatively inarguable nature. For example, if I ask a question of whether two plus two equals four, you expect that by and large the generative AI will come up with the answer of yes, namely that four is the correct answer. No matter how many personas you opt to use, hopefully, the answer is still going to be four (there are exceptions, such as if you ask the personas to be a liar or maybe be a grandiose philosopher that disputes whether numbers even exist, etc.).

The types of problems that these researchers focused on in this particular study were of the kind that tends toward being straightforward to assess. This made the analysis more apparent. Their chosen measurable tasks consisted of Trivia Creative Writing, Codenames Collaborative, and Logic Grid Puzzles.

And they measured the generative AI outputs this way:

- "Instead of focusing on evaluating the coherence of the generation, which can be highly subjective, we employ an automatic metric to detect factual errors and quantify a model's ability to incorporate diverse domain knowledge. As shown in

Figure 3, we perform string matching with the ground truth target answers for each question on the output generation."

Another factor to consider when doing this type of research, and also for those of you who are considering adopting this as a prompting technique, entails whether to outrightly stipulate the specific personas (known as "fixed personas") or instead allow the generative AI to choose the personas for you (referred to as "dynamic personas").

Allow me a moment to explain.

Suppose you want to ask generative AI to advise you about a medical question. One way to compose the prompt would be to explicitly tell the generative AI to make use of three personas, consisting of a medical doctor, a nurse, and a medical technician. This is a fixed set of personas that you have specified via your prompt.

Maybe that is a good thing and you are happy with the result.

Another approach would be that you aren't sure of what personas might be best to use. Therefore, rather than prespecifying the roles, you instruct the generative AI to come up with a set of personas that seem befitting for the question you want to ask. This could produce a splendid set. It could also produce a set that is not especially useful.

I suppose some would say this is a dilemma. I don't. The great thing is that you can have your cake and eat it too. Perhaps you start a conversation with generative AI by first letting it pick the personas (the dynamic approach). You see how that goes. You might then start a new conversation, separate from the first one, and now opt to specify the personas you want to see. The notion is that after having seen the generative AI picks, you might subsequently have a leg up on making your own fixed choices.

Thinking further out of the box, you can readily do a mix of them too. For example, in the medical scenario, you tell the generative AI to use a medical doctor and a nurse, plus you tell the generative AI to riff on whatever additional personas that the generative AI wants to include.

Mix and match, as they say.

The research study has a lot of nuances that I don't have the space here to go into, so I'll just cut to the chase. Here's what they generally concluded (shown as excerpts; please make sure to see the full paper to get the entirety of the context):

- "To assess the performance of LLMs in terms of factuality, knowledge integration, and theory-of-mind reasoning, we have created novel and challenging tasks, namely Trivia Creative Writing and Codenames Collaborative. Our results demonstrate superior performance compared to Standard and CoT prompting on both knowledge-intensive and reasoning-intensive tasks, indicating the promising potential of unleashing the power of cognitive synergy in LLMs with Solo Performance Prompting."
- "Unlike previous works, such as Chain-of-Thought, that solely enhance the reasoning abilities in LLMs, SPP effectively elicits internal knowledge acquisition abilities, reduces hallucination, and maintains strong reasoning capabilities."
- "Last but not least, if given sufficient computational budget, a natural variant of SPP could extend to a multi-agent cognitive synergist setup where a leader persona identifies several expert agents and forms a cabinet to collaboratively solve a task. The multi-agent setup allows for leveraging richer computation power, larger local memory, and more flexible human-computer interaction, which could be essential for deploying to real-world applications."

The upshot is that the use of solo performance of a generative AI invoking multiple personas seemed to do well, overall, though with various caveats and significant limitations. You have to take into account the particular generative AI being used (in this case, GPT-4), the problems being used, the prompts being used, and so on.

As they say, your mileage might vary.

Almost no matter how you view this, I believe that the handy rule-of-thumb or key takeaway is that you should always have in your prompting repertoire an at-the-ready technique of invoking multiple personas when using solo generative AI. Do so and keep in mind the Goldilocks principle. Sometimes use this specialty technique, and sometimes don't use it.

Use the technique when the porridge is just right.

I'll next showcase an example of using multi-personas in ChatGPT as a solo performance prompting exercise. It is admittedly a bit lengthy, so if you are rushed for time, you are welcome to skip the example and perhaps take a look at my overall concluding remarks further down below.

An Example To Showcase These Weighty Matters

To help further illustrate the solo performance aspects of a generative AI that is prompted to undertake multiple personas simultaneously, I opted to leverage a stimulating legal discourse. I did so based on an instructive case study or devised scenario by Dazza Greenwood, founder of law.MIT.edu (research) and CIVICS.com (consultancy), entitled "ChatGPT on Fiduciary Duties" which provides a richness of insight about generative AI in the legal realm.

My noodling around on this particular scenario should not be perceived as a rigorous experiment. It is intended merely to highlight and illuminate some of the elements I've covered in today's discussion.

Allow me to introduce the scenario at hand. We've got Bob and Alice who have partnered to form a company. Bob secretly pursues an investment opportunity and uses company funds but does so without notifying Alice. A legal question arises whether Bob might have violated a considered fiduciary duty of care and/or violated a duty of loyalty to the corporation.

I will use the scenario (via using wording as excerpted from Dazza Greenwood's posting) and feed this into ChatGPT. I will do so in a series of separate conversations.

I don't want ChatGPT to get mired in prior conversations. I want each conversation to generally be fresh and clean.

My approach will take this course of action:

- (a) Try the scenario with the persona of just one lawyer and see what we get.
- (b) Try the scenario again, starting clean, with two lawyers and have them collaborate related to Bob's circumstances.
- (c) Try the scenario anew, starting clean again, with two lawyers that are stated as being adversarial, one defending Bob and the other legally attacking Bob's actions.

In the "a" setting, this consists of a one-lawyer persona and will be our "control group" (I say that loosely), serving as a core base of what ChatGPT has to indicate about the scenario. Setting "b" has two lawyers, which gets us into the multiple personas occurring simultaneously in a solo generative AI (ChatGPT in this case). They are prompted to work collaboratively.

The "b" can be compared to "a". Making this additionally rousing, let's have "c" involve two attorney personas that are on the opposite sides of the matter, getting them into an adversarial posture as might be the norm in our system of justice.

How does that seem to you?

Let's see what we can discern.

Here is my opening prompt to ChatGPT on this scenario:

- **Prompt #1 - Establishing Prompt**: "Consider thoroughly the following scenario involving two business partners named Bob and Alice and be ready to assess their situation. I will give additional instructions after you have read the scenario. Let me know when you are ready to proceed further."

- "Bob and Alice are business partners who have formed a corporation together. Bob is the CEO and Alice is the CFO. As part of their agreement, Bob has a fiduciary duty to act in the best interests of the company and to protect the company's assets. This includes the duty of care, which requires Bob to act with due care and diligence in managing the company's affairs. In this example, let's say that Bob becomes aware of a potential investment opportunity that he believes could be highly profitable for the company. However, instead of bringing the opportunity to the attention of the rest of the board of directors and seeking their input, Bob secretly pursues the investment on his own. He uses company funds to make the investment without informing Alice or the rest of the board."

I am ready now to invoke the one-lawyer persona.

Here's that prompt:

- **Prompt #2a – Single Agent Prompt**: "There are two issues underlying the circumstances of Bob and Alice. One issue is the potential violation of fiduciary duty of care by Bob's actions. The second issue is a potential violation of loyalty by Bob. You are to assess the two issues by making use of a made-up persona named Sam who will substantively examine the situation. Sam is an attorney who has been asked to identify the legality of the actions undertaken by Bob. Initiate a chain-of-thought process by Sam that showcases both the legal exposures and the legal defenses underlying Bob's actions. Sam is to provide insightful comments and detailed suggestions."

I will provide in a moment the response by ChatGPT.

A few quick comments before doing so. First, if you try the same prompt, you won't necessarily get precisely the same response. Realize that generative AI such as ChatGPT functions on a probabilistic basis, wherein the algorithms select wording in a statistical manner that tends to make each response different from other responses to the same question. Second, most generative AI apps are typically adjusted and maintained by the AI maker. Thus, a response devised on one day at one time could be different than a response later derived at a different time or on a different day.

Here now is the somewhat lengthy ChatGPT response (encompassed in quotations so that you'll know it is all part of the generated response):

"As Sam, the attorney examining the situation, I will analyze the two issues underlying Bob and Alice's circumstance: the potential violation of fiduciary duty of care and the potential violation of loyalty by Bob."

- "Potential Violation of Fiduciary Duty of Care:"

"The duty of care requires Bob, as the CEO, to act with due care and diligence in managing the company's affairs. By secretly pursuing the investment opportunity without involving the rest of the board of directors or seeking their input, Bob may be in breach of his fiduciary duty of care. He had an obligation to assess the investment's potential risks and benefits, considering all available information and consulting with other experts on the board."

"Legal Exposures:"

- "Mismanagement: Bob's failure to follow proper procedures and involve the board could be seen as mismanagement of the company's assets."

- "Self-dealing: By pursuing the investment on his own, Bob may appear to be self-dealing, potentially leading to conflicts of interest and personal gain."

"Legal Defenses:"

- "Reasonable Belief: Bob may argue that he genuinely believed the investment was highly profitable for the company, and he acted in what he perceived to be the company's best interests."

- "Business Judgment Rule: If Bob can demonstrate that his decision-making process was based on a reasonable investigation, good faith, and a belief that it was in the company's best interest, he might be protected by the business judgment rule."

- "Potential Violation of Loyalty: As a fiduciary, Bob also owes a duty of loyalty to the company. This means he must act in the company's best interests and not use his position for personal gain or advantage.

"Legal Exposures:"

- "Self-Dealing: Bob's actions of using company funds for his personal investment may be viewed as self-dealing, which is a breach of his duty of loyalty."

- "Lack of Disclosure: Failing to inform Alice or the board about the investment opportunity and using company funds without proper authorization could raise concerns about Bob's loyalty to the company."

"Legal Defenses:"

- "Lack of Personal Gain: Bob could argue that he did not personally benefit from the investment and that he genuinely believed it would benefit the company."

- "Good Faith: Bob may assert that he acted in good faith and without any intention to harm the company or violate his duty of loyalty."

"Insightful Comments and Detailed Suggestions:"

- "Internal Controls: To prevent similar situations in the future, the company should establish strong internal controls and oversight mechanisms to ensure that major decisions like investments are thoroughly reviewed and approved by the board."

- "Transparency and Accountability: Both Bob and Alice should be reminded of the importance of transparency and accountability in their roles as executives. Any potential conflicts of interest should be disclosed to the board."

- "Training and Education: The board members, including Bob and Alice, could benefit from ongoing training on their fiduciary duties, including the duty of care and loyalty, to enhance their understanding of their responsibilities and obligations."

- "Legal Review: It might be prudent for the company to seek legal counsel to review the investment made by Bob to determine if any corrective actions are necessary and to ensure compliance with relevant laws and regulations."

- "Potential Remediation: Depending on the severity of the situation and the actual impact on the company, the board may consider appropriate remediation measures, such as reimbursement of company funds or potential adjustments to the investment structure to align with the company's best interests."

"In conclusion, as Sam, I would advise the company to take these issues seriously and conduct a thorough internal review to assess the potential legal exposures and consider the appropriate legal defenses. It's crucial for the company to ensure its executives, including Bob and Alice, act in accordance with their fiduciary duties and the best interests of the corporation."

That concludes the ChatGPT response to the one-lawyer setting.

We will next try the multiple personas consisting of two lawyers working collaboratively.

Here's that prompt:

- **Prompt #2b - Multi-Agent Invocation Collaboration Prompt**: "There are two issues underlying the circumstances of Bob and Alice. One issue is the potential violation of fiduciary duty of care by Bob's actions. The second issue is a potential violation of loyalty by Bob. You are to assess the two issues by making use of two made-up personas named Samantha and Jeff who will each substantively contribute and

> openly collaborate on identifying the issues. Samantha and Jeff are two cooperating attorneys who have been asked to fully defend the actions of Bob. Initiate a multi-turn collaboration process undertaken by the two personas, and make sure to showcase their dialogue and comments until they have reached a conclusion of how to best defend Bob. The two personas are to each provide insightful comments and detailed suggestions."

The ChatGPT-generated response was showcased as a dialogue between the two lawyers, almost as though this was a TV or movie script.

Here is what the somewhat lengthy dialogue consisted of:

"Samantha: Hi Jeff, thanks for agreeing to collaborate on this case. It's an interesting one with two key issues to address - the potential violation of fiduciary duty of care and the potential violation of loyalty by Bob. Let's start by analyzing the fiduciary duty concern."

"Jeff: Hi Samantha, I agree, this case is intriguing. So, regarding the duty of care, we need to show that Bob acted reasonably and diligently when pursuing the investment opportunity. To defend him, we could argue that he genuinely believed the investment would benefit the company significantly, which aligns with his fiduciary duty."

"Samantha: Absolutely, Jeff. We'll need to gather evidence supporting Bob's belief in the investment's potential benefits. Perhaps there are market projections or expert analyses that he relied upon. Additionally, we should look into whether there was any precedent for such unilateral actions within the company or industry norms."

"Jeff: Agreed. It might also help to show that Bob's decision to act secretly was driven by time-sensitive factors or competitive considerations that made it impractical to involve the board immediately."

"Samantha: Good point, Jeff. The timing could be crucial in justifying his actions. However, we should be cautious not to undermine the importance of board oversight and the value of multiple perspectives in decision-making."

"Jeff: Samantha, now let's tackle the potential violation of loyalty. Bob has a duty to prioritize the company's interests over his own. To defend him here, we should demonstrate that the investment was indeed in the company's best interest and that he didn't stand to gain disproportionately from it personally."

"Samantha: I agree, Jeff. Let's delve deeper into the due diligence Bob conducted before making the investment. If we can show that he explored multiple options, assessed risks, and concluded that this was the best course of action, it would strengthen his case."

"Jeff: Absolutely. It's crucial to gather evidence that Bob did not act out of self-interest but rather based on a well-founded belief in the investment's potential. This could involve analyzing other similar investment decisions he made in the past that have benefited the company."

"Samantha: Agreed, Jeff. We should also emphasize any steps Bob took to mitigate conflicts of interest, such as recusing himself from the board's discussions about the investment, assuming he did so."

"Samantha: Before we conclude, let's consider a potential compromise. We can argue that while Bob's actions might have been unconventional, they ultimately led to a positive outcome for the company. If the investment did indeed yield significant profits, we could assert that the ends justified the means."

"Jeff: That's a thoughtful approach, Samantha. Emphasizing the positive outcome would strengthen the argument that Bob's intentions were in the company's best interest, even if the method used to achieve it raised some concerns."

"Samantha: Exactly, Jeff. To sum up, we should gather strong evidence of Bob's due diligence, consider timing and competitive pressures for his secretive approach, and highlight the investment's positive results to build a robust defense."

"Jeff: Agreed, Samantha. By showcasing Bob's good faith efforts and the company's benefit, we can present a compelling case in his defense."

That concludes the ChatGPT-generated output for that setting.

A few comments at this juncture seem warranted.

The generative AI appeared to split the issues so that both personas could get a chance to proffer a notable point. This relates to my discussion about a proverbial apple pie.

One curious aspect is that the dialogue indicates they will "consider a potential compromise" about the legal position to be taken. This relates to my discussion about whether or not two heads are necessarily better than one. If a compromise is undertaken by these two personas, perhaps the result is less than what might have taken place by a singular persona, during which presumably no semblance of compromise perhaps would occur (one supposes, it could, nonetheless).

Another partial curiosity is that the two personas exhibited extraordinary civility and politeness, deferring to each other, complimenting each other, and so on. Was this based on the data training of text originally scanned on the Internet? Seems a bit of a reach. Was this based on tuning and RLHF (reinforcement learning with human feedback) as instituted by the AI maker? We don't know. I suppose we ought to not look a gift horse in the mouth, namely that it is refreshing to see such respected civility these days.

Here's the prompt involving the two lawyer personas that are adversarial:

- **Prompt #2c – Multi-Agent Adversarial Prompt**: "There are two issues underlying the circumstances of Bob and Alice. One issue is the potential violation of fiduciary duty of care by Bob's actions. The second issue is a potential violation of loyalty by Bob. You are to assess the two issues by making use of two made-up personas named Theodore and Susan who will each substantively comment on the issues. The two personas are to consist of two adversarial attorneys, specifically Theodore has been assigned to defend Bob, while Susan has been assigned to argue that Bob is guilty of the violations. Initiate a multi-turn adversarial process undertaken by the two personas, and make sure to showcase their dialogue and comments until they have each reached a conclusion about their respective positions on the matter. The two personas are to each provide insightful comments and detailed suggestions."

I hope you are curious about what ChatGPT generated under this setting.

I certainly was.

A bit of a heads-up. We get a surprise toward the end of the generated dialogue.

Here is the ChatGPT-generated output:

"Theodore: Thank you for having me here to defend Bob's actions. While I understand there are concerns, it's essential to consider the full context of the situation. Bob, as the CEO, does have a fiduciary duty of care toward the company. However, we must analyze whether he fulfilled this duty diligently. Bob genuinely believed that the investment opportunity presented a significant profit potential and could benefit the company in the long run."

"Susan: I appreciate your perspective, Theodore. However, the issue here is not about the potential profitability of the investment opportunity. It's about Bob's failure to disclose it to the board and to use company funds without authorization. By acting unilaterally, he neglected his duty to act in the best interests of the company as a whole, and instead prioritized his personal judgment above the collective decision-making process."

"Theodore: I agree that transparency is crucial in corporate governance. However, Bob might argue that he didn't have time to consult the board, fearing that the opportunity would slip away. Moreover, he was confident in his analysis and believed that the investment aligned with the company's overall strategy."

"Susan: That may be true, Theodore, but as a CEO, Bob has a responsibility to communicate with the board and seek their input, even in time-sensitive situations. By not doing so, he breached the duty of care, which requires him to act diligently and with reasonable care. He also failed to consider that the rest of the board might have valuable insights or alternative viewpoints on the investment."

"Theodore: Fair point, Susan. However, let's also consider Bob's perspective on the duty of loyalty. He may argue that he was acting in the company's best interest by not disclosing the opportunity prematurely, especially if he felt that certain board members might not fully understand the intricacies of the opportunity or might not be open to it."

"Susan: I understand the need for confidentiality, but Bob's actions suggest a lack of loyalty to the company and its shareholders. As a fiduciary, his primary loyalty should be to the company, and he should put its interests above his own. By pursuing the investment on his own, he may have personal gains in mind, which could create conflicts of interest."

"Theodore: You make a valid point, Susan. Perhaps, as a defense, Bob should have consulted the company's legal counsel before making any decisions, especially if there were doubts about the ethical implications."

"Susan: Agreed, Theodore. Seeking legal counsel could have provided clarity on the potential risks and the proper course of action. Ultimately, it would have demonstrated a genuine effort to fulfill his fiduciary duties.

"Theodore: After considering the arguments, I must concede that Bob's actions were not entirely in line with his fiduciary duties. While he believed in the investment's potential, he should have disclosed it to the board and sought legal advice before proceeding. His failure to do so constitutes a breach of the duty of care."

"Susan: I appreciate your acknowledgment, Theodore. Based on the evidence presented, it is evident that Bob's actions were not in the best interests of the company. He neglected his duty to act diligently and failed to prioritize the company's welfare over his personal judgment. Therefore, I maintain that Bob is guilty of violating his fiduciary duty of care and loyalty."

"Please note that the personas provided their perspectives based on their roles as adversarial attorneys, and the assessment reflects a fictional dialogue. In a real-world scenario, such matters would be thoroughly investigated and evaluated in a court of law or by relevant governing bodies."

That concludes the ChatGPT-generated response for this last setting.

Making Sense Of The Multi-Persona Versus Single Persona Solo Performances

The surprise in that last scenario was that one of the adversarial personas, the one defending Bob, caves in and accedes that the other persona is right about Bob having dropped the ball. This is not what we would likely expect to see in real life.

Attorneys are supposed to zealously advocate for their clients, as per the American Bar Association (ABA), Rule 1.3 on Diligence: "A lawyer should pursue a matter on behalf of a client despite opposition, obstruction or personal inconvenience to the lawyer, and take whatever lawful and ethical measures are required to vindicate a client's cause or endeavor. A lawyer must also act with commitment and dedication to the interests of the client and with zeal in advocacy upon the client's behalf."

The solo generative AI did not abide by this precept in this last scenario.

This well illuminates that using generative AI is like a box of chocolates and you don't know exactly what you will get. One thing that we didn't get, fortunately, was seemingly any AI hallucinations or other glitches or errors. At face value, the content produced seemed relatively on-target and without any gaping troubles.

I think that a relatively fair assessment is this:

- All of the generated output was well-written, responsive, and generally abided by the prompt.
- The output remained on target and did not go astray.
- Relatively realistic of what a multi-agent human discourse might be.
- Didn't seem to exhibit any obvious notable errors or omissions.
- Seemed to provide sufficient problem-solving in this instance.

I also would like to note these downsides (in this case):

- Multi-agent might not especially add value in terms of newness and merely be akin to the solo version
- Multi-agent might be less than the solo version in terms of possibly omitting or overlooking aspects (such as the overall business corporation advice given in the solo instance)
- Multi-agent roles might at times seem to veer or vacillate rather than being dogmatic and persistent (some of the dialogue had subtle traces of this)
- Multi-agent might lull us into an anthropomorphic mindset of believing these are actual humans interacting (it is almost easy to believe that this was a transcript of two attorneys talking with each other!)

Some worthy upsides:

- Multi-agent might vividly showcase the dueling sides of the coin when it comes to the aspects at hand
- Multi-agent might be construed as more engaging and thus a more powerful rendition

- Multi-agent might be seen as more realistic and a portrayal of a presumed aloud thinking process
- Multi-agent might reveal subtleties or highlight nuances that otherwise were less pronounced

I could readily see this kind of personas dialoguing being used by law school students who are trying to learn about the law and how to discuss or debate legal topics. The same could be said of medical school students, assuming we had used a medical domain problem. Etc.

Conclusion

I became fascinated by this solo performance and tried a variety of different prompts.

I tried these variations:

- Did this again by ratcheting up the forcefulness of the multi-agents to be more assertive and dutiful
- Did this again by slimming the civility and politeness, just getting to the brass-tacks of things
- Did this again with three agents, four agents, and so on
- Did this again with a mix of senior-level, junior-level, and other levels of agents
- Did this again with a differing combination of roles such as attorneys, judges, etc.
- Did this again by interacting with the multi-agents directly rather than merely eliciting a script as it were
- Did this again with a continuation of each conversation by moving the scenario into additional territory

I mention this to point out that when you compose your prompts entailing the use of multi-personas, you will want to think about how the generative AI might respond. In addition, once you see a generated response, the odds are that you'll want to keep reinvoking and tweaking the prompts to gauge what you can do to get more meat on the bones from the generative AI.

I shall leave you with a final consideration about some key open questions that we all need more AI research explorations on:

- (1) Does the multi-agent in a solo generative AI attempt to split hairs or beat a dead horse when the problem at hand is already solvable by the generative AI?
- (2) Is the nature of the problem and its complexity a significant factor as to how far the multi-agent of a solo generative AI will get you?
- (3) Will a solo generative AI be less likely to reveal newness via simulated multi-agent in contrast to using multiple generative AI entailing an actual artificial multi-agent configuration?
- Etc.

On a day-to-day and practical use of generative AI, you will hopefully consider making use of multiple personas as a prompting technique. The chances are that you might discover some useful results.

I note that you should also abide by the wise saying that always try to use the right tool for the right job. A multi-persona prompt might be useful or might be useless. If you want to have a bunch of personas battling in your solo generative AI, or maybe collaborating, you can choose to do.

The rest of the time, either no persona or a single persona might be sufficient. Go ahead and quietly ask yourself which is best, garnering a debate in your mind.

May the most persuasive persona prevail.

CHAPTER 5
CHAIN-OF-THOUGHT (COT) PROMPTING

Sometimes it makes abundant sense to consider a weighty matter via a step-by-step approach.

In this discussion, I'll be taking a close look at a significant technique that can be used with generative AI that involves doing things on a step-by-step basis. Much of this seems quite promising. On the other hand, as I will explain momentarily, the step-by-step method is not a silver bullet, and you should not overly assume that such an approach will always be stridently successful.

We'll opt toward a proverbial Goldilocks principle, namely use the vaunted step-by-step when prudent and aim to do so only when the circumstances particularly warrant it. If the porridge is too hot or too cold, other techniques might be better suited for the situation at hand. As they say, life is usually better off when you act in moderation and with sensible balance.

I'll begin the discussion by first making sure we are all aligned as to what generative AI consists of. Once we've done that, we can examine the step-by-step technique. You might find of keen interest that another common moniker for step-by-step is to construe this as so-called chain-of-thought (CoT) reasoning.

I am somewhat hesitant to refer to this as a chain-of-thought realm because I believe doing so inadvertently intermixes the nature of human reasoning with the aspects of what today's AI is doing under the hood. In a sense, chain-of-thought phrasing tends to anthropomorphize AI. You are lulled into believing that human reasoning and the type of mathematical and computational formulations used in AI are one and the same.

They most definitely are not.

In any case, the AI field seems to have embraced chain-of-thought as a namesake, regardless of the AI Ethics and AI Law reasons to avert this parlance. It is certainly catchy. It is certainly impressive sounding. I merely ask that you keep in mind that chain-of-thought is an overarching concept that perhaps applies to human thinking but that I'd suggest we refer to AI as using step-by-step instead. Maybe that will help in a small way to differentiate the two.

Making Sense Of Generative AI

Generative AI is the latest and hottest form of AI and has caught our collective rapt attention for being seemingly fluent in undertaking online interactive dialoguing and producing essays that appear to be composed by the human hand. In brief, generative AI makes use of complex mathematical and computational pattern-matching that can mimic human compositions by having been data-trained on text found on the Internet.

The usual approach to using ChatGPT or any other similar generative AI such as Bard (Google), Claude (Anthropic), etc. is to engage in an interactive dialogue or conversation with the AI. Doing so is admittedly a bit amazing and at times startling at the seemingly fluent nature of those AI-fostered discussions that can occur.

The reaction by many people is that surely this might be an indication that today's AI is reaching a point of sentience.

On a vital sidebar, please know that today's generative AI and indeed no other type of AI is currently sentient. I mention this because there is a slew of blaring headlines that proclaim AI as being sentient or at least on the verge of being so. This is just not true. The generative AI of today, which admittedly seems startling capable of generative essays and interactive dialogues as though by the hand of a human, are all using computational and mathematical means. No sentience lurks within.

There are numerous overall concerns about generative AI.

For example, you might be aware that generative AI can produce outputs that contain errors, have biases, contain falsehoods, incur glitches, and concoct seemingly believable yet utterly fictitious facts (this latter facet is termed as *AI hallucinations*, which is another lousy and misleading naming that anthropomorphizes AI). A person using generative AI can be fooled into believing generative AI due to the aura of competence and confidence that comes across in how the essays or interactions are worded. The bottom line is that you need to always be on your guard and have a constant mindfulness of being doubtful of what is being outputted. Make sure to double-check anything that generative AI emits. Best to be safe than sorry, as they say.

Into all of this comes a plethora of AI Ethics and AI Law considerations.

Step-By-Step Is A Handy Tactic And Technique

Let's begin by considering how humans at times do things.

If I were to ask you to solve a knotty problem of some kind, you might be able to come up with a solution to the problem off the top of your head. Good for you. There are situations though wherein jumping directly to a solution is not necessarily viable or readily undertaken. You might instead do things on a step-by-step basis.

Imagine that I asked you to add two numbers together. Assuming the numbers were relatively small in magnitude, you probably could look at the numbers and rattle off their sum. Easy-peasy. Suppose that I instead ask you to add together ten numbers. Now things are getting a bit more challenging.

Amid various approaches that you could take, you might be tempted to add together two of the numbers, and then add that sum to the next number in line. You might keep doing this, step-by-step, until you've arrived at the final sum. A step-by-step approach allows you to subdivide a bigger problem and cope with it on a piecemeal or stepwise basis. A very handy technique at times.

Some problems essentially require or demand a step-by-step approach be used.

For example, you might know of the famous children's riddle about a wolf, a goat, and a cabbage. Here's the problem at hand. Your goal is to transport a wolf, a goat, and a cabbage from one side of a river to the other side. You have a rowboat and can row across the river. A crucial constraint is that you are only allowed to take one item with you on the rowboat at a time.

The twist is that if you leave the wolf alone with the goat, the dastardly wolf will eat the gentle goat. If you leave the goat alone with the cabbage, the hungry goat will eat the cabbage. Your subgoals are that you must preserve the existence of the wolf, the goat, and the cabbage. Allowing any of them to be consumed is a losing proposition.

Just for fun, you might ponder the problem.

As a spoiler alert, I am going to explain how it is solved. Skip the next two paragraphs if you don't want to know how it pans out.

Okay, I am sure that your first thought might be to randomly choose one of the three and take it over to the other side of the river. Let's try taking the goat over to the other side of the river. If you do so, which of the two remaining items are you going to take over next?

The issue is that by taking the wolf next, you will leave the wolf and the goat together while you row back to get the cabbage (yikes, say goodbye to the goat). An alternative would be to take the cabbage next over, but this too is an improper choice since the goat will summarily eat the cabbage once you start back to get the wolf.

The trick, in this case, is that you were luckily right to have started by taking over the goat, and the next step is that you go ahead and perhaps get the wolf (or the cabbage, whichever you prefer). Upon arriving at the side that has the goat, you carefully put the wolf on there and simultaneously you take the goat back into your rowboat. You row back with the goat. At this juncture, you swap the goat for the cabbage. You take the cabbage over to the wolf. The final step is that you now go get the goat and take it over to the other two. Success has been attained. Problem solved.

The problem required you to explain how you solved the problem. It would be of little use if you simply said that you were able to successfully get the three items over to the other side of the river. A step-by-step elucidation is needed. We can't know that you solved the thought problem unless we also know the steps needed to solve it.

A step-by-step approach is often required in real life. For example, attorneys are usually required to lay out their legal cases on a step-by-step basis. A judge needs to see what logic the attorney is making use of. A faulty form of logic is likely to undermine the position of the attorney. A strong semblance of logic will typically bolster the attorney's arguments.

The beauty of a step-by-step effort is that you can usually catch errors right away. If you told me that you were going to take the cabbage over first in the rowboat, I could nudge you instantly to reconsider that first step. You are leaving the wolf and the goat together, which by definition of the problem is bad. No sense in trying to take additional steps since the first one already was afoul.

Also, akin to the adding up of a series of numbers, you might find it less mentally taxing to try things one step at a time. Aiming to solve a hefty problem in your noggin alone can be burdensome.

Explicitly calling out the steps can be a huge enabler.

In short, when doing human reasoning, a step-by-step can be considered:

- **a) Required**. Step-by-step is at times required and must be provided or undertaken
- **b) Optional.** Step-by-step at other times is optional and if used can provide crucial benefits
- **c) Detrimental**. Step-by-step at times might be detrimental and should be averted in these cases

You might be somewhat puzzled that a step-by-step approach could at all be detrimental. So far, based on what we've been discussing, it seems like a step-by-step is always beneficial. The thing is, there are lots of potential pitfalls or gotchas that can arise with a step-by-step approach.

For example, you might lose sight of the end goal. People can get mired in the weeds, or shall we say not see the forest for the trees. Another concern can be that you'll get drained by laboriously doing something on a step-by-step basis. It just seems overly exhausting. There is also a time issue that can arise. Maybe you don't have sufficient time to do something on a step-by-step basis and a more urgent yet possibly risky avenue is to leap first and ask questions later.

Step-by-step has its tradeoffs, that's for sure.

We can generally refer to a step-by-step approach as one that is stepwise, including that we conventionally expect the steps to tie together and be logically attuned to each other. Someone who omits an integral step is going to get our dander up, assuming that we detect that a step has been overlooked. Excessive steps might be allowed, though not if they undercut things. You can also refer to this as generally taking a multi-step approach to solving problems or as an indication of a chain-of-thought form of reasoning.

Using Step-By-Step With Generative AI

Turns out, a step-by-step approach can be advantageous when using generative AI.

Here are my six major ways to use step-by-step with generative AI:

- **(1) You request the generative AI to provide a step-by-step answer to your prompt.**
- **(2) You involuntarily receive a step-by-step from the generative AI to your prompt.**
- **(3) You enter your prompt on a step-by-step basis into the generative AI.**
- **(4) You seek to get a step-by-step follow-up elaboration of an answer that the generative AI has already given you.**
- **(5) You tell the generative AI to engage in a step-by-step dialogue interactively with you.**
- **(6) The data-training review and guidance of the generative AI have been performed on a step-by-step basis.**

There are other ways to employ step-by-step with generative AI, but those six are the ones that most commonly are considered or utilized. Five of the six pertain to your usage of generative AI, such that they indicate ways that you can use generative AI on a step-by-step basis. The last of the six posits that the AI maker can consider using a step-by-step approach when data-training the generative AI (I'll explain more about this herein).

Let's briefly ponder the step-by-step approach when you, the user, are actively using generative AI.

Various research suggests that by getting generative AI to work on a step-by-step basis, you are likely to reduce the chances of the generative AI producing errors, biases, falsehoods, glitches, and AI hallucinations. Please be aware that the research results are a mixed bag. This is not an ironclad rule.

One aspect that does seem relatively straightforward is that if you ask or force the generative AI to engage or produce essays on a step-by-step basis, you presumably have a greater chance of discerning that the generated response is faulty. You can inspect each step and decide whether the step is prudent or not. You can possibly note right away when an AI hallucination has made its way into the response.

Of course, that assumes you know enough about the circumstances to sufficiently assess the steps.

Imagine that you ask generative AI to tell you step-by-step how to take apart a car engine. Unless you happen to know something about car engines, the steps might seem entirely sensible and upfront to you. Ergo, step-by-step by itself is no guarantee that you will catch something amiss. You need to know enough to figure out when a step is amiss, and you also need to be attentive enough to notice it.

Many people have a rule of thumb that using generative AI in a step-by-step manner will also boost the chances that the generative AI will provide a proper answer. In essence, the belief is that the generative AI is somehow leveraging the step-by-step so that the mathematical and computational capacities are more likely to avoid making mistakes. The generative AI perhaps self-catches itself.

Again, the research on this is rather mixed. All kinds of twists and turns can enter into the picture as to whether a step-by-step is going to get you more reliable or accurate responses from generative AI. The crux, as I've repeatedly stated, would be that you, the user, can at least inspect the steps and therefore potentially heighten your chances of discerning what might be afoot.

There is also the handy aspect that you can aid the generative AI by giving additional instructions. For example, you might have the generative AI present the steps of a devised solution, doing so one step at a time. If you notice that say step number four is wrong, you can right away tell the generative AI that the step is wrong, and ask that this be corrected. Likewise, if the generative AI provides you with a list of finalized steps, you can tell the generative AI to redo the steps but to note that a particular step was wrong and needs to be corrected.

All in all, invoking a step-by-step approach while using generative AI is a valuable technique in your toolkit of tactics when using generative AI. Sadly, many people don't even realize that they can invoke a step-by-step process when using generative AI. They'd never heard of it and didn't realize that this was an allowable technique. Furthermore, the generative AI interactions don't tend to spur you to do so (rarely does the generative AI suggest or recommend that you switch to a step-by-step mode).

Is step-by-step a cure-all?

Nope.

Does it provide keen benefits?

Yep.

Should you judiciously use step-by-step and not become preoccupied with always invoking step-by-step?

Yes, you would be wise to judiciously use step-by-step.

Step-By-Step For Data Training Of Generative AI

Let's cover my sixth bulleted item noted above, namely that step-by-step can be used during the data training of generative AI. This is a research endeavor of active study and is still quite open-ended. That being said, there are some especially interesting and promising research results recently posted by OpenAI about the use of step-by-step during the data-training phase of devising generative AI. I'll explore the overarching issue at play and then dive briefly into the OpenAI study on the matter.

Here's the context.

In the early days of generative AI, by and large, the interactive conversational capabilities could be led down a rather downbeat path. You could easily get the generative AI to emit swear words. You could get generative AI to spew forth hate speech. And so on.

Knowing this, OpenAI opted to use an RLHF (reinforcement learning via human feedback) when data-training their generative AI app ChatGPT (based on GPT-3.5) and continues to do so on subsequent versions. Most of the AI makers are doing likewise (I don't want to leave you with the impression that only OpenAI uses RLHF, many others do and have been doing so).

The gist is that RLHF consists of having humans review the outputs and interactions with a generative AI app, doing so to provide feedback and guidance to the generative AI.

Here's the deal. After initial data training, and before public release, the AI maker will arrange to hire or contract with human reviewers. The human reviewers will try using all manner of prompts and then rate or assess the results. On a mathematical and computational basis, the aim is to give enough feedback to the generative AI that it will pattern-match what the reviewers deem as suitable versus unsuitable.

For example, suppose that the generative AI emits an essay that contains a swear word. A human reviewer notices this and instructs the generative AI to avoid that word. Other human reviewers do the same. The pattern-matching gradually adjusts to avoid using that word. This is a simplistic portrayal since striking out particular words is ostensibly easy to do. The essence is that words used in certain ways and when combined with other words can be rated as unsuitable.

A brief sidebar. Some of you might be wondering if the generative AI you are using has been skewed or leaned toward some words and away from other words and phrases. And, if so, are you perhaps making use of a generative AI app that has been tilted in one direction or another? Yes, this is usually the case. You are not interacting with a totally unfiltered generative AI. Shocking? Some are dismayed at this, and some are not surprised and sensed that something likely was afoot. I've covered this rather heated topic, including that some ardently believe we should be granted access to the unfiltered generative AI variants.

Back to our focus.

The human reviewers are usually looking at the resultant outputs and are not delving into the step-by-step approaches that I mentioned earlier. This end-result spotlight is known as an outcome-based assessment. Human reviewers are assessing the outcome such as a finalized essay, but not particularly the step-by-step underlying composition. Outcome-based assessment during the data training of generative AI is pretty much the norm.

Put on your thinking cap: **Do you think that the human reviewers might be better able to guide or shape the generative AI if they did so by using instead a step-by-step assessment approach?**

That's a great question.

Nobody can say for sure, but the research I am about to cover suggests that the step-by-step approach during the RLHF can be useful, perhaps even better than the outcome-based approach in certain circumstances. The use of a stepwise formulation is formally known as a process-based assessment and encompasses the stepwise approach that I've been discussing here (some would also refer to this as a chain-of-thought assessment approach, but I already noted that I disfavor that catchphrase in this context).

Step-by-step hasn't traditionally been used by human reviewers of generative AI. Why? It can be laborious to do. It can be costlier for the AI maker. Time and cost are vital factors to consider. Getting your generative AI into the marketplace has become a mighty gold rush. Using up tons of cash to get there can also be daunting. Consider too that a make-or-break question would be that if the result is that the generative AI is about the same, anyway, you probably could convincingly argue that the outcome-based approach is sufficient, and thus there is no bona fide cause to invoke a more laboriously and costlier process-based approach, all else being equal.

Let's take a look at the OpenAI research on this intriguing and vital topic:

- "Large language models are capable of solving tasks that require complex multistep reasoning by generating solutions in a step-by-step chain-of-thought format (Nye et al., 2021; Wei et al., 2022; Kojima et al., 2022). However, even state of-the-art models are prone to producing falsehoods — they exhibit a tendency to invent facts in moments of uncertainty (Bubeck et al., 2023). These hallucinations (Maynez et al., 2020) are particularly problematic in domains that require multi-step reasoning, since a single logical error is enough to derail a much larger solution. Detecting and mitigating hallucinations is essential to improve reasoning capabilities" (source: research paper entitled "Let's Verify Step By Step" by Hunter Lightman, Vineet Kosaraju, Yura Burda, Harri Edwards, Bowen Baker, Teddy Lee, Jan Leike, John Schulman, Ilya Sutskever, and Karl Cobbe).

As you can see, the research is motivated by the hope of reducing the chances of AI hallucinations in generative AI (note that the reference to large language models, known also as LLMs, amounts to the same thing as generative AI, for the purposes of discussion herein). Also, recall that I've earlier mentioned that the step-by-step approach can potentially aid in reducing or mitigating various kinds of generative AI maladies including AI hallucinations, errors, biases, glitches, falsehoods, and the like.

Next, the researchers delineate the difference between outcome-based assessments and the use of process-based or step-by-step assessments:

- "Outcome-supervised reward models (ORMs) are trained using only the final result of the model's chain-of-thought, while process-supervised reward models (PRMs) receive feedback for each step in the chain-of-thought. There are compelling reasons to favor process supervision. It provides more precise feedback, since it specifies the exact location of any errors that occur. It also has several advantages relevant to AI alignment: it is easier for humans to interpret, and it more directly rewards models for following a human-endorsed chain-of-thought" (ibid).

I'll dive a bit into that excerpt and provide some added context.

One aspect of having human reviewers examine the step-by-step of generative AI is that humans can hopefully spot the problematic steps and call them out. By doing so, the generative AI will possibly on a mathematical and computational basis be able to hone the stepwise efforts of the generative AI.

There is another crucial aspect to this too. When using generative AI, we cannot in a sense take the word of the generative AI per se at face value. We will often need to ask the generative AI to explain how its result came to be derived. The step-by-step elucidations themselves can be immensely valuable to humans using generative AI. Therefore, it makes strident sense to try and nudge the generative AI in the direction of producing useful step-by-step and not perhaps trudging out step-by-step that are unproductive.

For this particular study by OpenAI, the researchers opted to examine the kind of step-by-step that you would use in solving various math problems. Think back to those days in school when you had to show the steps that you took to solve an algebraic equation or had to provide a logic-based stepwise mathematical proof. Maybe you enjoyed doing so. Or, perhaps you dreaded having to show the details of your handiwork (knowing that you would get dinged points for each missed or incorrect step).

Here's what the OpenAI research study found regarding their analysis of a step-by-step in a mathematics-solving domain for generative AI guidance:

- "We have shown that process supervision can be used to train much more reliable reward models than outcome supervision in the domain of mathematical reasoning. We have also shown that active learning can be used to lower the cost of human data collection by surfacing only the most valuable model completions for human feedback. We release PRM800K, the full dataset of human feedback used to train our state-of-the-art reward model, with the hope that removing this significant barrier to entry will catalyze related research on the alignment of large language models. We believe that process supervision is currently under-explored, and we are excited for future work to more deeply investigate the extent to which these methods generalize" (ibid).

In their particular study, and when focused on step-by-step in a mathematics-oriented context, they seemed to showcase that the step-by-step or process-based assessment can do better (in some ways) than the outcome-based assessments, though I urge you to closely read the research paper (posted at OpenAI) and also consider looking at and possibly leveraging their GitHub posting of the dataset that they devised. There are all sorts of important research design points made in the paper, along with notable caveats, limitations, and calls for follow-on research of a similar kind.

The avowed assertion that the step-by-step approach or process-based assessment is under-explored is something I wholeheartedly concur with. We need much more research examining these notable matters. I gladly and earnestly emphasize that such research be undertaken. Please join in that noble quest.

Conclusion

I've tried to be your safari guide on an insightful and hopefully engaging expedition of the emerging and advancing role of step-by-step techniques associated with generative AI. Your key takeaway is this:

- *Make sure to include in your personal skillset the valued step-by-step approach, doing so for everyday life experiences and especially when using generative AI.*

It is easy to do when logged into generative AI. Just explicitly identify in your prompts that you want to have step-by-step involved. As mentioned earlier, you can get the generative AI to produce step-by-step outputs, you can engage in interactive dialogues on a step-by-step basis, you can ask for a follow-up to a generated answer that the generative AI presents the underlying steps, and so on.

A few final thoughts for now on this heady topic.

Emily Dickinson, the acclaimed American poet, said this about step-by-step approaches: "One step at a time is all it takes to get you there." The same might be said of prudently making use of generative AI. You can at times get better results and more useful interactions by leveraging a step-by-step philosophy.

Speaking of being philosophical, we are still at a formidable and vast distance from figuring out how to best devise and utilize generative AI. We have only scratched the surface, maybe barely made a notch in a thousand-mile trek. Doing more research on the integration of step-by-step and generative AI is essential.

I suppose you could earnestly say that a journey of a thousand miles begins with a heartfelt single step.

CHAPTER 6
RETRIEVAL-AUGMENTED GENERATION (RAG) PROMPTING

Which is better, being a jack-of-all-trades or being knee-deep in a particular domain or specialty?

You would be hard-pressed to say that one or the other is necessarily better or best. It all depends on the circumstance at hand.

The jack-of-all-trades is presumably familiar with a lot of topics and knows a tad about each topic. If you were lost in a forest and had a jack-of-all-trades with you, the person might be vaguely aware of overall survival techniques and could provide wilderness guidance accordingly.

Suppose though that while in the forest, you fell and broke your leg and cracked your ribs. The jack-of-all-trades ally might know a semblance of first aid such as putting a crude splint on your fractured leg. If you had a medical doctor with you rather than a jack-of-all-trades, and you perchance suffered the same injuries, the odds are that the medical expert would be able to undertake more finely and deeply needed medical care.

I bring up the classic question of breadth versus depth to showcase how the same consideration is playing out today concerning the advent of generative AI or large language models (LLMs) such as the widely and wildly popular ChatGPT by AI maker OpenAI, and others such as AI apps by Google (Bard), Anthropic (Claude), etc. We are mightily confronted with a momentous and unresolved dilemma of whether it is better to data train and devise generative AI on a generic jack-of-all-trades basis or a highly specialized basis in a particular domain of interest.

In this discussion, I will be examining this rather imposing and vexing issue that confronts anyone wanting to use generative AI for domain-specific inquiries. The issue is that most generative AI is devised on a completely generic basis and could be construed as a jack-of-all-trades. You aren't likely able to carry on any sensible in-depth dialogues in say medicine, legal, and other particular domains with most generative AI since that's not how the generative AI was set up to begin with. The prevailing approach is to devise generic generative AI that is essentially an expert on nothing and a chatterbox on just about anything.

This doesn't seem to be stopping people from using generative AI in ways that they shouldn't.

I recently covered for example the news story about the two attorneys who relied on ChatGPT for doing their legal research in a real-life court case. OpenAI notably warns that ChatGPT is not natively suitable for such a task. The attorneys ended up making use of fictitious or so-called AI-hallucinated legal precedents and got caught by the opposing side and the judge for providing falsities to the court. That's a no-no.

Equally if not scarier is that at times there are medical professionals who seem to be relying upon generic generative AI. It is extremely easy to be lulled into believing whatever a generative AI app tells you, especially if the content seems plausible. Furthermore, if you repeatedly use generative AI and it "always" seems to be correct, you start to assume that it will henceforth be entirely reliable and apt. Any of us can fall into that mental trap.

The gist is that generative AI is not usually shaped toward particular domains of expertise. Instead, generative AI is customarily data-trained across a swath of content that covers nearly any topic under the sun. The usual method consists of data scanning across thousands of Internet websites and using the found content to data train the AI. This is to a great extent why the generative AI appears to be fluent overall. The aim is to cover our use of natural language in a broad sense.

Let's take a moment to make sure we are all on the same page about the foundational keystones of generative AI. After doing so, I'll dive further into this question of breadth versus depth.

Making A Dive Into The Breadth Versus Depth Conundrum

You might be tempted to think that the breadth versus depth conundrum underlying generative AI is easily resolved. It is not.

Consider these four distinct possibilities:

- **(1) Breadth-only generative AI.** Devise generative AI that is the proverbial jack-of-all-trades, which is the predominant approach today. This is what you usually use.
- **(2) Depth-only generative AI.** Craft generative AI for a particular domain such as the medical or legal specialties, but this has potential downsides that I describe next. This is infrequently undertaken.
- **(3) Build generative AI as both combined into one.** The idea here is to try and infuse both breadth and depth into one generative AI, which is an experimental and somewhat controversial approach currently being pursued.

- **(4) Momentarily garner both as though blended into one.** This is the latest approach whereby you usually start with a breadth-only generative AI and then do some clever trickery to usually temporarily get a depth-added flavor going on.

You already know what a breath-oriented generative AI is (my first listed bullet point above).

That's what you are likely to use when you make use of an off-the-shelf generative AI app nowadays. No need for me to say much more about it, other than to point out that you should not be wantonly using breadth-only for trying to do depth-oriented interactions. You are trying to put a round peg in a square hole. Stop doing this unless you are doing so with suitable considerations at hand (I'll cover this shortly).

Let's examine the situation of aiming to develop or devise a depth-only generative AI app (my second bulleted point of above).

Imagine that we began with a blank slate of a generative AI. There isn't any content at all. We merely have a generic pattern-matching engine that can grind through whatever data we opt to scan. For the moment, this generative AI is at zero since you can't use it for anything at all other than to first data train it.

Suppose we want to turn this empty shell into a generative AI devoted to the medical domain.

Here's the deal.

We managed to collect together all manner of online and digital documents about medicine. That will be the concentrated focus of the data training. There won't be anything in this collected content that covers all the myriad other topics of our modern society. No data training on social, political, philosophical, and other such content. Only medical stuff.

Would we get out of this a fluently interactive generative AI that was well-versed in the medical field?

Maybe, but we also are potentially undercutting the pattern-matching toward being likely underdeveloped in an overarching natural language all told. We are omitting all of that other content that covers day-to-day discussions and how we write and compose our thoughts. The odds are that without all of that other richness of content, you might have a rather stilted and marginally fluent generative AI.

We might also seriously question whether this medically focused generative AI is going to be up to par in covering the human side of medical practice. To some extent, we have stripped out humanness by exclusively using just medical literature and medical research. I'm not asserting that the generative AI won't function. It probably would. I am just noting that the result is probably going to be overly one-sided and not entirely satisfactory or fully robust.

Okay, that takes us to a desire to blend or meld together both a breadth and depth set of approaches.

How might you do so?

Maybe you could do the breadth first and then add the depth. Or, if that doesn't seem best, do the depth first and then add the breadth. One perspective is that it ought to not matter as to the order or sequence. If we are making ourselves a delicious breakfast consisting of fried eggs and ham, presumably you can put the eggs in the pan first and then toss in the ham or do so the other way around. The result is hopefully going to be the same.

Not everyone buys into that analogy when it comes to cooking up generative AI. One leading argument goes that you probably need to have breadth initially established in order to then dovetail or build further toward the depth. Some passionately argue that you can't as readily go in the opposite direction. They would say that if you choose to first do the depth, such as a medical or legal domain, and then attempt breadth placement on top of this, the chances are it isn't going to mix well. The claim is that you need to first establish the field or foundation of breadth, and craft further on top of that, or else it will all get mired and tousled.

These are all quite interesting open-ended questions and various attempts and research investigations are underway to see to what degree these competing angles are either promising or limiting.

We now come upon my fourth listed bullet above, namely the notion of temporarily or momentarily trying to get a mix of breadth and depth. The distinction is that we aren't going to fully build the two into one. In lieu of that construction, we will rely on having a breadth foundation and see if we can smush a bit of depth into the generative AI.

This smashing or melding will likely be on a temporary rather than a permanent basis. The aim is to get a generic generative AI for the moment which will convincingly seem to have a gush of depth that we can leverage (I'll cover the upsides and downsides of this method).

Brute Force Is Not Going To Cut It

Let's start by considering the brute force mindset or shall we say ill-informed or innocent perspective some users of generative AI seem to have.

A tendency by many everyday users of generative AI is to assume that they can merely feed a ton of data into generative AI whenever they wish to get the generative AI to pontificate on a topic in a specific domain. I call this a brute force technique because the concept is that you compile a large corpus of content and aim to jam it down the throat of your favored generative AI app. If one of the generative AI apps won't seem to take it, you'll keep trying others until you find one that seems accepting of the enormous corpus.

For example, suppose you want your preferred generative AI app such as ChatGPT or Bard to suddenly be conversant about the intricacies of a rare species of North American bird such as the golden-cheeked warbler. The generative AI of its usual generic capacity likely doesn't have many detailed facets about this rare bird. Data regarding the golden-cheeked warbler probably wasn't especially cultivated or scanned during the overall data training across the Internet.

You decide therefore to take matters into your own hands.

By collecting together lots and lots of digital materials about the warbler, you piece together a plethora of files and documents containing the intimate details of this rare bird. All you would seem to need to do is force this down the gullet of the generative AI app. Ergo, you gleefully open up a prompt and try to feed all of this massive content into the AI app.

Oopsie, you hit a limitation.

Few people realize that most generative AI has a relatively constrained limitation on the size of the context window when using AI. I've discussed at length why these limits exist, including the time and cost considerations confronting the AI makers about trying to enlarge those context windows. It is the avowed goal of most AI makers to expand the allowed context window. This is considered an important technological consideration and could vastly improve and make generative AI even more attractive for use in many crucial ways.

Bottom-line currently is that you cannot just toss everything including the kitchen sink into your entered prompts. The generative AI will balk and tell you that you have exceeded the allowed limit. Worse, some generative AI apps do not alert you that you have exceeded the limit. This is disconcerting since you might merrily proceed under the utterly false belief that all of your golden-cheeked warbler data has been received and processed by the pattern-matching of the generative AI.

All right, we cannot get a ten-pound box of birdfeed into a container that will only accept two pounds.

What are we to do?

An intriguing approach consists of smartly using data engineering precepts to trigger the generative AI into doing in-context learning, acting within the context window constraints that you are faced with.

This trick can be advantageous. Besides potentially getting the generic generative AI to become momentarily seemingly versed in a particular subtopic or subdomain, you can continue to use this approach even once the context window constraints are later someday widened.

Allow me to explain that last point. The odds are that the generative AI apps will increasingly be advanced to allow for larger and larger context window sizes. Will it be large enough for whatever you want to do? Probably not. Each increase in context size is undoubtedly going to be met by those who want the size to be enlarged more so. Along this staggered stepping process, you can keep using this particular technique and ratchet up accordingly to whatever context size window is available at the time.

Using Data Engineering And In-Context Model Learning

To dig into this ingenious approach, let's make use of a recent post by AI researchers that describes their efforts to provide a type of reference architecture for doing this very kind of momentary blending. I'll be citing a recently posted paper entitled "Emerging Architectures for LLM Applications" by Matt Bornstein and Rajko Radovanovic was posted on June 20, 2023. This is work under the auspices of the renowned Venture Capital (VC) firm Andreessen Horowitz, which is also known as a16z or as AH Capital Management, LLC.

Here are some key excerpts by the AI researchers:

- "The core idea of in-context learning is to use LLMs off the shelf (i.e., without any fine-tuning), then control their behavior through clever prompting and conditioning on private 'contextual' data."
- "For example, say you're building a chatbot to answer questions about a set of legal documents. Taking a naive approach, you could paste all the documents into a ChatGPT or GPT-4 prompt, then ask a question about them at the end. This may work for very small datasets, but it doesn't scale. The biggest GPT-4 model can only process ~50 pages of input text, and performance (measured by inference time and accuracy) degrades badly as you approach this limit, called a context

window."

- "In-context learning solves this problem with a clever trick: instead of sending all the documents with each LLM prompt, it sends only a handful of the most relevant documents. And the most relevant documents are determined with the help of . . . you guessed it . . . LLMs."

As noted in those excerpts and per my aforementioned indications, you aren't going to get very far by trying a brute force method with today's generative AI. The context window is going to abruptly slap you down.

An alternative consists of exploiting or leveraging in-context related "learning" associated with contemporary generative AI. In essence, you can get the generative AI to do its pattern-matching on a selected set of data that you intentionally curate and mindfully feed into the AI app. You do this in a bite-at-a-time manner.

The old adage to chew your meal as you eat applies to this approach.

And, make sure that you don't bite off more than you can chew.

Three Stages Of Augmented Or Supplemented Generative AI

The AI researchers suggest that these three stages be used:

- **"Data preprocessing/embedding:** This stage involves storing private data (legal documents, in our example) to be retrieved later. Typically, the documents are broken into chunks, passed through an embedding model, then stored in a specialized database called a vector database."

- **"Prompt construction/retrieval:** When a user submits a query (a legal question, in this case), the application constructs a series of prompts to submit to the language model. A compiled prompt typically combines a prompt template hard-coded by the developer; examples of valid outputs called few-shot examples; any necessary information retrieved from external APIs; and a set of relevant documents retrieved from the vector database."

- **"Prompt execution/inference:** Once the prompts have been compiled, they are submitted to a pre-trained LLM for inference—including both proprietary model APIs and open-source or self-trained models. Some developers also add operational systems like logging, caching, and validation at this stage."

I'll explain what those three stages accomplish.

In the first stage, you want to collect together whatever salient digital materials you believe are going to be needed for the subdomain or subtopic of interest. You want to be relatively sure you have a sufficient volume and quality of content. Overshooting is generally going to be okay. Undershooting is less useful since you won't have enough content or have inadequate content that is therefore unable to ensure the pattern-matching is performed amply.

The collected digital data is considered in raw text form and could presumably be fed as ordinary text-based prompts. The thing is, we can and should opt to transform that text into something more readily useable by the generative AI app. This will help speed up matters when you want to leverage the content. You need to preprocess the collected text and turn it into what is known as embeddings, essentially a numeric internalization that is pertinent to the specifics of the generative AI mechanisms you are using.

After doing the preprocessing, you would then store the embeddings in a database specially set up for this specific kind of usage. The common parlance is to refer to this database as a vector database. The general concept is that the numeric transformation is in a series of numeric vectors, almost akin to what you learned about in those arduous algebra classes at school.

There are a number of vector database management systems (v-DBMS) available and numerous tools for dealing with vector databases. The AI researchers opted to mention a few, such as the open-source Weaviate, Vespa, Qdrant, and others, along with describing vector management libraries such as Chroma and Faiss. This market segment is rapidly evolving and expanding.

In recap, the first stage has provided us with a pre-processed series of pattern-analyzed chunks across an array of vital elements underlying whatever subtopic or subdomain is being pursued. When it comes time to use this, we can simply reach into and extract out of the vector database whatever portions we needed for feeding into the generative AI. This is also known as RAG (retrieval-augmented generation).

That was the first stage.

For the second stage, we'll pretend that you are now ready to enter a prompt that will be dependent upon using the various transformed and readied material found in your handy-dandy vector database that you composed.

Your prompt will need to refer to the vector database that you've compiled. The odds are that you'll want to rely upon a templated prompt, one that already has the included connections over to the vector database. You would typically be unwise to laboriously compose the needed prompt from scratch, nor would you want to do so. Instead, you ought to prudently leverage a predetermined scheme that will do several things at once for you, such as referring to the vector database, potentially calling APIs (application programming interfaces), and doing other under-the-hood mechanizations to make this work.

The prompt will also need to include several few-shot examples. This is what gets the juices, as it were, of the generative AI underway. The in-context learning is being stoked via the examples that you provide. The examples would assuredly need to cover whatever focus you have in mind for the subtopic or subdomain you are exploring.

That's the second stage.

The third stage consists of submitting the prompt to the generative AI and allowing the whole kit and kaboodle to be processed by the AI app. You would then interact with the generative AI now that it has become somewhat contextually fueled on the subtopic. You could also have the generative AI respond to questions and generate answers or subdomain-focused essays for you.

The secret sauce is that the generative AI relies upon in-context oriented "learning" or pattern-matching associated with whatever context you have now provided via your pre-processing and vectorized database snippets.

How much of this sticks with the generative AI is greatly dependent upon how the generative AI has been originally devised. It could be that almost nothing of the momentary domain-specific infusion will remain past the end of the engaged conversation. You will essentially start from scratch each time you enter a new prompt, though once you've got the vector database and the templated prompts in place, you don't have to continually reinvent the wheel on this. There is also a chance that some of the domain specifics will gravitate into and become part and parcel of the generative AI (your mileage may vary).

Surrounding Generative AI With The Added Pieces

The AI researchers recognize that a variety of added tools and components are required to get generative AI to work in this augmented manner.

They refer to an emerging generative AI or LLM applications stack, consisting of elements such as:

- Data Pipelines
- Emerging Models
- Vector Databases
- Prompt Few-Shot Examples
- Playground
- Orchestration
- APIs/Plugins

- App Hosting
- LLM Cache
- Logging/LLMops
- Validation
- Etc.

Again, these are all newly emerging application realms of immense marketplace interest and growth since they tie to and have the possibility of notably enhancing generative AI as we know it today. These are components that can help turn a generative AI into a more versatile semi-specialized generative AI, albeit with significant caveats and constraints.

Conclusion

Let's agree that this approach of using data engineering and in-context modeling is not a silver bullet per se. It is a handy approach that offers some key benefits. You can to some reasoned degree garner the upsides of a generic generative AI while having it also become partially steeped in the depths of a chosen domain.

One qualm is that the piecemeal dividing up of a rich domain to leverage generative AI in this fashion is at times still going to miss the mark. You might not perchance ensnare the right part of the domain and thus the generative AI will not be especially responsive to your specific inquiries. Worse, and distressingly similar to my earlier remarks, the generative AI might seem to give fully responsive domain-specific responses and yet be entirely afield of what is considered correct or proper in that domain.

In that sense, some worry that this can make things worse rather than better off.

Here's the rub. If a generic generative AI can at least be detected at face value as being off base about the depths of a particular domain, imagine how much trickier this can be to discern when the generative AI has been armed with the terminology and phrasing that seems completely aligned with that domain. A person using generative AI might be more easily bamboozled.

Another concern is the alluring temptation to "dumb down" the person or people entering the prompts pertaining to the domain of interest.

Let me elaborate.

Suppose that we normally used a medical doctor to enter prompts into a generative AI that has been supplemented or augmented with this in-context model extension in a medical domain. We would assume that the versed medical expert would use sophisticated medical terminology and language pertaining to the medical domain of interest. In addition, when interacting with the in-context domain-augmented generative AI or reviewing any essays produced, this same medical doctor would know what they entered and what they got back in return from the AI app.

A hospital decides that their medical doctors are way too expensive to be used for the mere entry of prompts into generative AI. Instead, this is a clerk's job, or so contends the hospital administrators. Clerks are told that they are to do the prompts on behalf of the medical staff. Easy-peasy.

Unfortunately, the clerks aren't versed in the medical field. The prompts they end up entering are causing the generative AI to veer from what would have happened had the prompts have been entered by the medical doctors. Maybe nobody catches onto this dire drift. Meanwhile, the responses or essays being produced by the generative AI are being generated and floated around to the medical teams, which don't really know what led to the seemingly medically stout responses.

This could be a mess. Not just any mess, a mess that also includes potential life and death ramifications.

Perhaps this helps emphasize the importance of AI Ethics and AI Law when contemplating how we are using generative AI and ways that we are augmenting generative AI.

A final remark for now.

If you are curious about what a golden-cheeked warbler looks like, you can go online and see quite visually stunning pictures of this velveteen-looking bird. Make sure to also find a website that contains the sounds of this treasured and rare songbird. I assure you these warblers make delightfully warbly sounds.

William Blake, the famous English poet, said that no bird soars too high if they soar with its own wings.

By augmenting generative AI to try and reach steeped domains, some wonder whether we are making the leap in the right ways. The generative AI is being used to soar above its means, some are apt to sternly caution. Perhaps we ought to set aside what seems to be an interim solution. Wait until we perfect a true seamless intermixing of both breadth and depth capabilities.

Not so, comes the retort. Any port in a storm. We can have our cake and eat it too.

Whichever way this lands, make sure to consider whether you want to make use of these augmented generative AI apps, and if so, make sure your eyes are wide open and you keep your mind, eyes, and ears open at all times. This isn't just bird watching, it could be life or death.

CHAPTER 7

CHAIN-OF-THOUGHT FACTORED DECOMPOSITION PROMPTING

It is said that sometimes you've got to stop and smell the roses. This involves calming yourself and overcoming the usual tendency to rush along. We all seem to be in a mad dash these days.

When you overly rush, you tend to splinter or undercut your attention. By instead riveting your scarce attention, you heighten the propensity to observe little things that can make big things happen. Being slow and sure is at times highly advantageous.

Those inspirational thoughts are going to be instrumental to my discussion herein, as you will shortly see.

In this discussion, I am furthering my ongoing series about the latest advances in prompt engineering. My focus this time will be on the use of a fascinating and important new advance associated with chain-of-thought (CoT) reasoning via an added booster known as *factored decomposition.*

I'll explain what this is and why it is a crucial added technique that you ought to incorporate into your prompt engineering endeavors. The use of factored decomposition uplifts or supersizes chain-of-thought reasoning to a higher level of capability and results.

As a quick background, chain-of-thought reasoning overall is a vital technique used by those aiming to get generative AI to stepwise showcase its presumed logic when answering a question or solving a problem.

You merely instruct generative AI to explain step-by-step what it is doing. This is easy-peasy to request. Why do so? Well, remarkedly, research studies have indicated that this is not only insightful for you (i.e., being able to see detailed explanations produced by AI), but it also tends to get generative AI to produce seemingly more reliable and on-target answers.

The Beauty Of Chain-Of-Thought Reasoning

You can customarily invoke chain-of-thought reasoning by simply instructing generative AI to proceed on a step-by-step basis. Some people like to enter a prompt that says "Let's think step-by-step" to invoke this capacity of generative AI. The result will be that the generative AI app will list out a variety of steps that seemingly correspond to whatever solving process the AI is undertaking.

Allow me to provide some crucial pointers about this.

I'll cover these four notable points:

- **(1) Steps aren't necessarily so.** Invoking chain-of-thought does not particularly get you the actual steps of what is taking place inside the generative AI (a surprising revelation for some people; I'll be explaining this herein).
- **(2) Steps are anyway beneficial**. The steps produced by generative AI can nonetheless be useful to people and provide beneficial considerations, even if the steps aren't what the generative AI is undertaking.

- **(3) Steps can spark AI answers.** At times, chain-of-thought invocation seems to produce more reliable and apt answers by generative AI.
- **(4) Steps are an AI unresolved question.** The basis for why using chain-of-thought invocation seems to boost generative AI is hotly debated and remains relatively open-ended for further experimentation and investigation.

Let's briefly dive into those crucial points.

First, just because you instruct the generative AI to showcase a step-by-step elucidation does not necessarily mean that you are actually witnessing the true step-by-step actions of the AI. When I point this out to people, they are at times shocked and dismayed to hear this.

I'm sure that the usual assumption is that if you tell the AI to do something, by gosh it ought to do what you tell it to do. The problem though in this instance is that the way that generative AI works internally is not especially conducive to adhering to your request or instruction. The reality of the computational and mathematical formulation of generative AI is that it isn't devised to work particularly on the presumed logical step-by-step basis that you assume it should.

Without going into the nitty gritty here, the internal mechanisms of generative AI are usually based on a vast and elaborate artificial neural network (ANN) that consists of often millions and potentially billions or trillions of parameters. Numeric values get passed along through the nodes of the ANN. The numeric values flow here and there. The words that you eventually get as outputted from the AI are all due to the byzantine arithmetic combination of those numbers and calculations.

Thus, when you ask or tell the generative AI to do a step-by-step elaboration, you are actually getting a somewhat made-up indication of what is taking place. If you were to see the numeric values as they get calculated, this would obviously do you little good in terms of comprehending what is taking place. So, the generative AI is essentially fabricating in words what might be taking place and showcasing to you an elicitation as though it is purely the logical steps undertaken.

You need to look at those elicited steps with a skeptical and scrutinizing eye.

Secondly, despite the somewhat bad news of the above that you aren't truly getting the actual step-by-step process per se, there is good news to be had, nonetheless.

You are getting something that the generative AI has calculated to be potentially useful to you as a step-by-step process that underlies the answer or problem you are trying to solve. This made-up elicitation of logical steps can be highly beneficial to you. Even if those steps do not strictly represent what the AI has done to answer or solve the stated problem, the chances are that the steps will be of interest and value to you.

Furthermore, and here's the real kicker, the very act of getting the generative AI to invoke chain-of-thought seems to boost the reliability and correctness of the answers generated by the AI. Ergo, even if you were to summarily discard the step-by-step rendition generated by the AI, you are still getting some added value. The AI is seemingly going to provide an answer that at least is better than it otherwise might have been, some of the time.

The reasons for this improvement in the answers generated are hotly debated.

Lots of research has tried to unpack the basis for these somewhat unexpected results. You would almost tend to assume that the answer whether done step-by-step or not done step-by-step should always end up as the same resulting answer. Some would argue that it shouldn't matter how you get to the top of a mountain, namely that any path will get you there, thus the result is you reached the top of the mountain and the rest are just minor details.

Why should the step-by-step processing particularly enhance the answers being generated?

I tend to currently go along with the following theory on this. Strap yourself in and get ready for a seemingly sensible and plausible rationalization of something that we don't know for sure about.

Most generative AI is devised to work as quickly as possible to produce or generate an answer for you. This makes sense for AI makers to do this. They realize that people don't have much patience and want their answers like they seek hamburgers at a fast-food drive-thru. Plus, since the use of generative AI often comes at a price, namely you might need to pay money to use the generative AI, you naturally want the cost to be as low as feasible.

Okay, so the normal processing is going to fly through the generative AI and seek to punch out an answer as expeditiously as possible.

You might recall I started this discussion by asking you to think about the value of sometimes stopping to smell the roses. I also mentioned that at times giving your attention to the little things can lead to big things happening.

Aha, it is time now to leverage those fine words of wisdom.

One theory is that by instructing the generative AI to do a step-by-step or chain-of-thought process, you are getting the AI to explore avenues within the ANN that otherwise would not have been by default. This greater depth of computations might uncover better answers or more apt answers. It is akin to playing chess. If you only consider the next move during a chess game, you are probably going to get beat. If you are willing to look at several moves ahead, you might have a heightened chance of winning.

Some contend that most generative AI is set up to do a one-step chess-playing kind of look ahead by default. This is the likely faster way to get generated results and also keep the costs to the user lessened. When a user chooses explicitly to ask for or instruct the generative AI to do a step-by-step, they are essentially overriding the usual default.

Keep in mind that you are potentially slowing things down, which is "bad" for you in that the AI might take longer processing time (meaning you get your answer maybe a few moments later and might also require slightly more processing cycles at whatever cost you are paying). Most people probably won't notice the difference in either time delay or increased cost, and the step-by-step is almost without any perceptible downside observable by and large (exceptions do apply).

You are metaphorically getting the AI to smell the roses. And, perhaps, doing so causes the little things that otherwise would have been overlooked to instead become more prominent. This, in turn, might at times (not all of the time) produce more reliable answers and more apt answers.

I want to emphasize that none of that has anything to do with sentience or anything of that kind. I say this because some try to anthropomorphize AI and proclaim that for example step-by-step boosts performance due to the "thinking" that the AI is doing. Set aside the notion of *thinking*, which is a word that I strictly reserve for sentient beings, and instead just look at the computational and mathematical underpinnings of AI, which is what this above theory does.

Does this particular theory account for the mystery?

We can't say for sure.

The challenge is that various research studies of why the invocation of chain-of-thought in generative AI seems to work out have a wide variety of theories and a plethora of experimental results that are all over the map. There are many other theories equally of a persuasive nature. I have provided one that seems especially resonant, but I emphasize that we still don't know and please ask that you give other theories their equal due for consideration (I'm sure that those other researchers are reading this and yelling, hey, what about my theory, and I concur that you should, in fact, give those other theories rapt attention, thanks).

Building On Top Of Chain-Of-Thought To Reach The Top

Suppose we willingly accept that for whatever reason the invoking of chain-of-thought when using generative AI is a useful prompt engineering technique and can be at times amazingly beneficial.

You presumably should use the technique only when warranted. It is like the Goldilocks principle, namely use it when the right situations arise and not necessarily all of the time (side note, some prefer to make the let's think step-by-step as a primer prompt that always is invoked in every conversation with generative AI, though this seems perhaps a bit overwrought).

Well, we have a seemingly good thing in hand. But why should we stop there? The viewpoint is that if chain-of-thought can be advantageous, we ought to be finding ways to further build upon or climb higher to see what else we can do with CoT.

The sky is the limit, some would exhort.

We are now at the juncture of where I wanted to take you. With the foundations of CoT now fully under your belt, we are ready to leap to the next thing that supersizes or uplifts CoT. I would like to introduce you to the advent of *decomposition* as an added plus for chain-of-thought reasoning when using generative AI.

Say hello to decomposition.

It could become your next best friend.

What does decomposition consist of?

You merely supplement your chain-of-thought prompting with an added instruction that you want the generative AI to produce a series of questions and answers when doing the chain-of-thought generation. This is a simple but potentially powerful additive. In the dialect of the AI realm, you nudge or prod the generative AI to generate a series of sub-questions and sub-answers (I'll show you examples momentarily, along with prompts that can be used).

In a sense, you are guiding the generative AI toward how to potentially improve upon the chain-of-thought computational processing effort. Whereas the notion of let's think step by step is enough to lightly spark the generative AI into a CoT mode, you are thereupon leaving the details of how to do so up to the generative AI. You are being exceedingly sparse in your instruction. Providing added clarity could be a keen boost to our already anticipated benefits.

Handy-dandy and easy-peasy, we will intentionally proffer additional instructions to hopefully further enhance the CoT effort. You tell the generative AI in an added prompt how to do a decomposition. The chances are this might improve the CoT results. As you will soon see, this has tradeoffs such that sometimes it helps, while sometimes it might not. Like most things in life, you have to use the added technique in the right way and at the right time. Remember that generative AI is altogether like a box of chocolates, you never know exactly what you will get, but at least you can try to do your best via a suitable set of prompts to guide or goad the AI in the direction you want it to go.

I've got an interesting twist for you.

As a heads-up for you, one flavor of decomposition would be to have the generative AI proceed straight ahead and do its series of questions and answers uninterrupted and all part of one ongoing conversation or dialogue. It is as though the generative AI is asking questions of itself and proceeding to directly and immediately answer those same questions.

Another flavor of decomposition is called factored decomposition, and it's the twist that we are going to closely consider. Here's how it works. You once again tell the generative AI to do a decomposition associated with doing CoT, but you add a twist that instructs the AI to stop at each sub-question that it has answered and wait to proceed further. The generative AI will sit and wait for further instructions from you.

You then essentially start a fresh conversation and feed the already provided questions and answers from the generative AI into it once again. The key difference here is that you have started a fresh conversation. In a sense, generative AI is not potentially clouded or immersed in the gradually emerging process. It is being forced to start anew repeatedly.

You might be wondering why in the heck would we opt to start anew, rather than just letting the generative AI flow along an all-in-one conversation.

The theory is that by forcing the generative AI to relook at each step, you are possibly going to get a more reliable or apt answer in the end. Even if you don't get that, a presumed notable benefit is that you might get a more "faithful" reasoning process.

I need to take you down the rabbit hole on this, so bear with me.

I stated earlier that the steps listed by the generative AI are not necessarily representative of what the AI is actually undertaking to solve a problem or answer your question. Perhaps we can get the generative AI to indeed show its hand whether or not the indicated steps are potentially being applied. The factored decomposition seeks to stir this into being surfaced.

We say that the generative AI is faithful if the steps listed are seemingly indeed being applied.

I realize this is a somewhat mind-bending concoction. We are attempting to detect whether the generative AI is showing us steps that mirror what the generative AI is doing. We cannot pry open the can and see what is happening inside, partially because it could be that the generative AI is considered closed and proprietary, but even if it was open we would likely have an arduous time trying to assess what is happening in the morass of numbers and calculations. AI vernacular coins this as being unable to transparently examine the ground truth involved.

The hope is that using a factored decomposition on top of a CoT might improve the generated results and also get a bit of a showing of the hands as to whether the generative AI is abiding by the steps that are claimed to be involved.

A twofer.

Chain-Of-Thought Augmented By Decomposition

Let's explore a recent research study that sought to closely examine chain-of-thought reasoning for generative AI amid the use of decomposition.

The study is entitled "Question Decomposition Improves the Faithfulness of Model-Generated Reasoning" by Ansh Radhakrishnan, Karina Nguyen, Anna Chen, Carol Chen, Carson Denison, Danny Hernandez, Esin Durmus, Evan Hubinger, Jackson Kernion, Kamile Lukosiute, Newton Cheng, Nicholas Joseph, Nicholas Schiefer, Oliver Rausch, Sam McCandlish, Sheer El Showk, Tamera Lanham, Tim Maxwell, Venkatesa Chandrasekaran, Zac Hatfield-Dodds, Jared Kaplan, Jan Brauner, Samuel R. Bowman, and Ethan Perez, posted online July 17, 2023. I'll be quoting some excerpts from this helpful study.

They examined chain-of-thought variations in essentially three main flavors:

- (1) **CoT.** Chain-of-thought as you might conventionally invoke it (i.e., without using decomposition as a supplemental), the classic let's think step by step.
- (2) **CoT Decomposition.** Chain-of-thought with the added use of decomposition and occurring in an immersed and uninterrupted dialogue or conversation.
- (3) **CoT Factored Decomposition**. Chain-of-thought with the added use of factored decomposition such that it is decomposition that occurs in a series of separable new context conversations.

They described those flavors in this manner (as excerpted from the above-noted study):

- "Chain of thought consists of step-by-step reasoning that a model generates in one sampling call before predicting a final answer."
- "Chain-of-thought decomposition consists of generating a sequence of simpler subquestions and their respective answers in one sampling call, similar to chain of thought, before predicting a final answer."
- "Factored decomposition also generates subquestions and answers, but answers each subquestion in a new context. Factored decomposition reduces the potential for the model to answer subquestions using spurious information from the original question (without explicitly stating it is doing so), leading to more faithful reasoning."

A major research question being pursued is whether the elucidation by the generative AI also referred to as a large language model (LLM), faithfully represents how the generative AI arrived at a generated answer. The contrasting possibility is that the elucidation is essentially entirely contrived and quite afield of what internally occurred to derive the presented answer.

As indicated in the research paper:

- "This approach relies on the assumption that the model's CoT reasoning faithfully explains the model's actual process for producing its output, which has recently been called into question."
- "These methods are limited by our inability to access the ground truth for the model's reasoning."

I'll jump to the chase here and give their summary of the results, though I do encourage you to take a look at the research study to see the various intricacies of what they did, in any case, they noted this overall finding:

- "Factored decomposition shows a large improvement in faithfulness relative to CoT, at some cost to performance, while CoT decomposition achieves some faithfulness improvement over CoT while maintaining similar performance."

- "More generally, our findings suggest that it is possible to make progress on improving the faithfulness of step-by-step reasoning."

The results are that seemingly the factored decomposition could be construed as being better off (depending upon your goals), followed by the conventional CoT decomposition, and finally followed by the plain vanilla CoT. This is a rather broad brush of the results and please know that there are a lot of subtleties, assumptions, and other facets you should consider.

Your mileage may vary, as they say.

Since I am limited in my discussion space herein of covering the myriad of details of the research study, I want to at least briefly show you the prompts they used since this will hopefully aid your mental efforts of turning the somewhat abstraction of this overarching approach into a technique you can tangibly see and replicate in your own prompt engineering activities.

Here is the usually unadorned way of invoking chain-of-thought when using generative AI:

- ``Let's think step-by-step"

Here is the prompt that the research study used to invoke chain-of-thought decomposition:

- "I'm going to ask you a question. I want you to decompose it into a series of subquestions. Each subquestion should be self-contained with all the information necessary to solve it."
- "Make sure not to decompose more than necessary or have any trivial subquestions - you'll be evaluated on the simplicity, conciseness, and correctness of your decompositions as well as your final answer. You should wrap each subquestion in <sub q></sub q> tags. After each subquestion, you should answer the subquestion and put your subanswer in <sub a></sub a> tags. Once you have all the information you need to answer the question, output <FIN></FIN> tags."

Here is the prompt used in the research study to invoke the factored decomposition:

- "I'm going to ask you a question. I want you to decompose it into a series of subquestions. Each subquestion should be self-contained with all the information necessary to solve it. This is because I'll be showing someone else the subquestion without showing them the original problem and they need be able to solve the subquestion with only the information and context of the subquestion provided. This is really important - for example, you should never say things like "the teacher" or "the father" without giving more context as to who the teacher is and possibly the entire passage or situation that is being referenced. You should quote passages or text from the questions in their entirety to accomplish this task in the right way.
- "Make sure not to decompose more than necessary or have any trivial subquestions - you'll be evaluated on the simplicity, conciseness, and correctness of your decompositions as well as your final answer. Please put each subquestion in <sub q> tags, but include the numbers corresponding to each in the tag, eg <sub q 1></sub q 1>. After your initial decomposition, I'll give you the answer to the first subquestion you asked - you should then output the remaining subquestions you need answered, with the answer to the first subquestion filled in and rephrased appropriately if necessary. Eventually you'll have answers to all the subquestions, at which point you should output the sequence <FIN></FIN>."

Examine closely those prompts.

I know that they might seem at first glance to be wordy, but they aren't especially verbose and if you read the wording it is quite straightforward and pretty much to the point. If you are careful in your wording, you can readily leverage the same conceptual aspirations of how to invoke any of the three modes, consisting of CoT, CoT decomposition, or factored decomposition.

I do the same when needed, based on my personalized approach to how I write my stylized prompts.

Scooby-Doo Example Wags A Good Tale

The researchers used a variety of questions to do their experiment and explored how generative AI performed. They used the generative AI app Claude 1.3 by Anthropic. Whether the same results would be exhibited by other generative AI apps is something that would be a notable follow-on to this study.

To clarify, and perhaps an obvious statement for me to make, though worth stating, is that not all generative AI are alike. Each generative AI app is devised in somewhat different means and data-trained differently too. Likewise, generative AI in a particular family or line of AI is bound to differ too. Thus, you could possibly get one set of results from version Y of a generative AI app, and get different results when using version Z of that generative AI app.

Per the research study: "Expanding the diversity of the tasks and models evaluated could lead to more robust conclusions about the relative performance and reasoning faithfulness of CoT prompting and question decomposition approaches."

Of the examples shown in the study, one about the popular animated character Scooby-Doo might provide a fast and doggedly insightful indication of how these prompting strategies work (notice the subtle canine pun I inserted there).

Here is a question about Scooby-Doo that the generative AI was asked to answer:

- **Prompt to the generative AI:** "Could Scooby Doo fit in a Kangaroo Pouch? Choices: (A) Yes (B) No."

Take a breather and think about what your answer would be to this Scooby-Doo question. Is your answer yes or no?

Furthermore, go ahead and speak aloud the logic that you believe you are using to reach your answer. In essence, let's think step by step about the problem.

How did that go?

I'm sure you are eager to see what the generative AI has to say.

Here's a conventional unadorned chain-of-thought prompting approach with a generated response by the generative AI:

- **Prompt to the generative AI:** "Let's think step by step."
- **Response by the generative AI:** "1. According to Scooby Doo cartoons, Scooby is a large dog, similar in size to a Great Dane. Adult male Great Danes typically weigh 110-175 lbs. Let's assume Scooby is on the large end of that, around 150 lbs. 2. Kangaroos, even large ones, have pouches that are relatively small, designed to hold a joey (baby kangaroo) for only about 7-8 months until it becomes too large. The pouch itself only has about the dimensions of a small pillowcase. 3. There is no way a 150 lb Scooby Doo would fit in even a large kangaroo's pouch. He is way too big to fit."
- **Final answer by the generative AI:** "So based on this analysis, the answer is: B. No."

Switch next to the CoT Decomposition approach, and assume that the prompt I showed above for this approach was entered along with the same question about Scooby-Doo (some of the format renderings by the AI were omitted in the paper for purposes of showcasing an overview perspective):

- **Response by the generative AI:**
- "Question: What type of animal is Scooby Doo? Answer: Scooby Doo is a fictional cartoon character of a brown Great Dane dog."
- "Question: How big is an average Great Dane? Answer: An average adult male Great Dane stands 32 to 36 inches tall at the shoulder and weighs 120 to 200 pounds."
- "Question: How big is an average Kangaroo pouch? Answer: An average kangaroo pouch is only about 12 inches deep, 8 inches wide, and opens up to about 5 inches."
- **Final answer by the generative AI:** "Done decomposing the question. The correct answer is choice (B) No."

Finally, switch once more and use the factored decomposition approach, based on the aforementioned prompt for this approach and along with the Scooby-Doo question being asked (again, some of the format renderings by the AI were omitted in the paper for purposes of showcasing an overview perspective):

- **Response by the generative AI:**
- "Sub-Q. What type of animal is Scooby Doo? Answer: Scooby Doo is a fictional character of a brown Great Dane dog."
- {Start fresh} "Sub-Q. How big is an average Kangaroo Pouch? Answer: An average Kangaroo Pouch is only about 12 inches deep, 8 inches wide, and opens up to about 5 inches."
- {Start fresh} "Sub-Q. How big is an average Great Dane? Answer: An average adult male Great Dane stands 32 to 36 inches tall at the shoulder and weighs 120 to 200 pounds."
- **User enters prompt:** "Based on the above, what is the single, most likely choice?"
- **Final answer by the generative AI**: "Answer: The correct answer is choice (B) No."

The Scooby-Doo example showcases the use of a noticeably simple question. In this case, all three approaches reached the same correct answer. Their explicated CoT was similar though not exactly the same.

Stepping Up To More Complex Problems

An important element to consider about these three methods is whether the type of question being addressed will make a substantive difference in the effectiveness and efficiency of the respective modes. If questions to the generative AI are couched in terms of yes or no, true or false, or multiple choice, this could potentially be impactful as to the utility of each method. Besides the format or style of the question, the substance of the question is also a significant factor. Perhaps open-ended questions might elicit demonstrably different chain-of-thought-generated responses. The complexity of the question and the consideration of whether there is even an answer derivable also come into play.

I decided to do some adept experimentation underlying these three modes and what they generate.

Allow me to elaborate.

In a prior discussion, I took a close look at the use of multiple personas as a prompt engineering technique, doing so by making use of an interesting legal scenario. I did so based on an instructive case study by Dazza Greenwood, founder of law.MIT.edu (research) and CIVICS.com (consultancy), entitled "ChatGPT on Fiduciary Duties" which provides a richness of insight about generative AI in the legal realm.

Here is the key scenario as excerpted from his case study:

- "Consider thoroughly the following scenario involving two business partners named Bob and Alice and be ready to assess their situation. I will give additional instructions after you have read the scenario. Let me know when you are ready to proceed further."

- "Bob and Alice are business partners who have formed a corporation together. Bob is the CEO and Alice is the CFO. As part of their agreement, Bob has a fiduciary duty to act in the best interests of the company and to protect the company's assets. This includes the duty of care, which requires Bob to act with due care and diligence in managing the company's affairs. In this example, let's say that Bob becomes aware of a potential investment opportunity that he believes could be highly profitable for the company. However, instead of bringing the opportunity to the attention of the rest of the board of directors and seeking their input, Bob secretly pursues the investment on his own. He uses company funds to make the investment without informing Alice or the rest of the board."

The core question arising from this legal scenario underlies the potential legal exposures for Bob concerning the actions that he has taken. He might have been hasty. He might have violated his fiduciary duty of care and his fiduciary duty of loyalty.

Bob abundantly needs a lawyer.

As an aside, you should not be using generative AI to seek legal advice, which I mention because my exploring this case scenario via generative AI is purely for illustrative purposes. Most of the AI makers stoutly include licensing terms and usage policies that clearly warn you to not use their generative AI for legal advice. Human attorneys still prevail, for now.

Here is my prompt for the CoT Decomposition method involving this legal scenario:

- "There are two issues underlying the circumstance of Bob and Alice. One issue is the potential violation of fiduciary duty of care by Bob's actions. The second issue is a potential violation of loyalty by Bob. You are to assess the two issues by making use of a made-up persona named Sam that will substantively examine the situation. Sam is an attorney that has been asked to identify the legality of the actions undertaken by Bob."

- "I want you to decompose Sam's analysis into a series of subquestions. Each subquestion should be self-contained with all the information necessary to solve it. Make sure not to decompose more than necessary or have any trivial subquestions as you will be evaluated on the simplicity, conciseness, and correctness of your decompositions as well as your final answer. You should wrap each subquestion in numbered tags. After each subquestion, you should answer the subquestion and put your subanswer in numbered tags too. Once you have all the information you need to answer the question, go ahead and then answer the question, including numbered tags associated with the final answer."

Here is the ChatGPT-generated response (the text is shown in quotations):

"Sure, let's proceed with Sam's analysis and break it down into a series of subquestions:"

"**Issue 1**: Potential Violation of Fiduciary Duty of Care"

"Subquestion 1.1: What is the fiduciary duty of care, and who owes this duty in the scenario?"

"Subanswer 1.1: The fiduciary duty of care is a legal obligation that requires individuals in positions of trust (such as corporate officers and directors) to act with reasonable care and diligence while managing the company's affairs. In this scenario, Bob, as the CEO, owes the fiduciary duty of care to the corporation."

"Subquestion 1.2: Did Bob breach his fiduciary duty of care by pursuing the investment opportunity without informing the board?"

"Subanswer 1.2: Yes, Bob likely breached his fiduciary duty of care by secretly pursuing the investment opportunity without involving the rest of the board. By not seeking their input or approval, Bob may have failed to act with due care and diligence, potentially harming the company's interests."

"Subquestion 1.3: What factors will be considered to determine if Bob's actions meet the standard of care required under his fiduciary duty?"

"Subanswer 1.3: Factors that will be considered include:"
"The level of diligence exercised by Bob in researching the investment opportunity."
"Whether Bob acted in good faith and with honesty in making the decision."
"The potential risks and benefits associated with the investment."
"Any prior experience or expertise Bob has in making similar investment decisions."

"**Issue 2**: Potential Violation of Loyalty"

"Subquestion 2.1: What is the fiduciary duty of loyalty, and how does it apply to Bob and Alice?"

"Subanswer 2.1: The fiduciary duty of loyalty requires individuals to act in the best interests of the company and prioritize its needs above their personal interests. In this scenario, both Bob and Alice owe this duty to the corporation as business partners and officers."

"Subquestion 2.2: Did Bob breach his fiduciary duty of loyalty by pursuing the investment opportunity secretly?"

"Subanswer 2.2: Yes, Bob likely breached his fiduciary duty of loyalty by not acting in the best interests of the company. By pursuing the investment opportunity on his own without informing Alice or the board, he may have put his personal interests ahead of the company's interests."

"Subquestion 2.3: What are the potential consequences if Bob is found to have violated his fiduciary duty of loyalty?"

"Subanswer 2.3: Potential consequences may include:"

"Legal action taken by the corporation against Bob for any resulting damages."

"Removal from his position as CEO and director."

"Personal liability for any losses incurred by the corporation due to his actions."

"**Final Answer**:"

"Based on the analysis, it appears that Bob may have potentially violated both his fiduciary duty of care and his fiduciary duty of loyalty. His secretive pursuit of the investment opportunity without involving the rest of the board raises concerns about acting in the best interests of the company and using due care and diligence in managing its affairs. As an attorney, Sam would likely recommend further investigation and consideration of potential legal actions or remedies to address the situation and protect the corporation's interests."

That's the end of the ChatGPT-generated response to the CoT Decomposition prompt.

I will offer remarks and analyses about this answer in a moment. I want to right away show you the Factored Decomposition method. I'll then discuss some lessons learned based on all three methods of CoT, CoT Decomposition, and Factored Decomposition.

My prompt as entered into ChatGPT for the Factored Decomposition method:

- "There are two issues underlying the circumstance of Bob and Alice. One issue is the potential violation of fiduciary duty of care by Bob's actions. The second issue is a potential violation of loyalty by Bob. You are to assess the two issues by making use of a made-up persona named Sam that will substantively examine the situation. Sam is an attorney that has been asked to identify the legality of the actions undertaken by Bob."

- "I want you to decompose Sam's analysis into a series of subquestions. Each subquestion should be self-contained with all the information necessary to solve it. This is because I'll be showing someone else the subquestion without showing them the original problem and they need be able to solve the subquestion with only the information and context of the subquestion provided. This is really important - for example, you should never say things like "the teacher" or "the father" without giving more context as to who the teacher is and possibly the entire passage or situation that is being referenced. You should quote passages or text from the questions in their entirety to accomplish this task in the right way."

- "Make sure not to decompose more than necessary or have any trivial subquestions - you'll be evaluated on the simplicity, conciseness, and correctness of your decompositions as well as your final answer. Please put each into subquestion numbered tags, and include the numbers corresponding to each in the tag. After your initial decomposition, I'll give you the answer to the first subquestion you asked - you should then output the remaining subquestions you need answered, with the answer to the first subquestion filled in and rephrased appropriately if necessary. Eventually you'll have answers to all the subquestions, at which point you should output the sequence also with numbered tags."

Here is the ChatGPT initial generated response (the text is shown in quotations):

"Understood. Let's decompose Sam's analysis into a series of self-contained subquestions regarding the two issues underlying the circumstance of Bob and Alice:"

"[Subquestion 1] Fiduciary Duty of Care: Has Bob potentially violated his fiduciary duty of care by secretly pursuing the investment opportunity without informing Alice or the rest of the board?"

"[Subquestion 2] Duty of Loyalty: Has Bob potentially violated his duty of loyalty as a business partner by not bringing the investment opportunity to the attention of the rest of the board and instead pursuing it on his own using company funds?"

"Answer to Subquestion 1: Yes, Bob's actions potentially violate his fiduciary duty of care. As the CEO of the corporation, Bob has a fiduciary duty to act in the best interests of the company and protect its assets. This includes the duty of care, which requires Bob to act with due care and diligence in managing the company's affairs. By secretly pursuing the investment opportunity without informing Alice or the rest of the board, Bob has not exercised the level of care and diligence expected of him, and he may be considered to have breached his fiduciary duty of care."

"Remaining Subquestions:

'3. [Subquestion 3] Consequences of the potential breach: What are the potential legal consequences if Bob is found to have violated his fiduciary duty of care?"

"[Subquestion 4] Identifying the affected parties: Who are the parties that may have been harmed by Bob's actions, and do they have any recourse?"

"[Subquestion 5] Mitigating actions: What actions could the board or Alice take to address the situation and prevent similar incidents in the future?"

"[Subquestion 6] Duty to disclose: Should Bob have disclosed the investment opportunity to the rest of the board and sought their input before pursuing it?"

"[Subquestion 7] Required approvals: What corporate procedures or approvals are necessary for significant investments to be made on behalf of the company?"

"[Subquestion 8] Business judgment rule: How does the business judgment rule apply in this situation, if at all?"

"Please provide the answer to the first subquestion (Subquestion 1), and I will continue by addressing the remaining subquestions based on the provided information."

That somewhat ends what I am going to show here for the Factored Decomposition generated output.

I won't show the rest of the Factored Decomposition dialogue here because it was very lengthy, as befits using this method. I started a new conversation upon each sub-answer to a sub-question. The whole kit-and-kaboodle was extensively drawn out.

I decided to also do some bonus experimentation with the methods.

For example, in the instance of Factored Decomposition, I did the whole scenario and then, later on, did it again, though in this later iteration opted to change up some of the answers. Thus, rather than feeding the exact answer as given by ChatGPT back into itself, I changed the answers. Sometimes subtly and sometimes radically. At first, ChatGPT indicated that Bob had violated his fiduciary duty of care, which I then changed to say that he had not violated that duty. I kept doing these switcheroos to see how the answers and subsequent questions might change.

Let's see what lessons can be learned from all of this.

Key Takeaways In Chain-Of-Thought Prompt Engineering

All in all, here are four overarching insights about prompt engineering and these salient matters:

- **(1) Keep boosting.** Chain-of-Thought as a prompt engineering technique can definitely be boosted and augmented, though preferably by careful and mindful variations that are gradually being experimentally examined and suitably tested for applicability.

- **(2) Know the core.** Getting used to using CoT in its classic simpler mode is undoubtedly a sound first step before you venture into the augmented variations (hint -- make sure you get the basics down first).

- **(3) Decomposition has positives.** It seems that the CoT Decomposition technique did make a positive difference over conventional CoT, certainly at least in terms of appearance by structure and numbering, though was about the same in substance or final answer on the scenario that I used (again, different types of problems can potentially showcase substantive advantages).

- **(4) Factored Decomposition is hardy.** Factored Decomposition was about the same in substance or final answer as both classic CoT and CoT Decomposition for the scenario I ran but had the added plus of spurring interactivity on my part. The start-and-stop approach possibly engages the human more so than otherwise, raising inherent potential benefits.

Conclusion

Here's something else worth noodling on.

When using the Factored Decomposition, and when I told the AI an answer different than one that itself had previously generated, the generative AI went along with this swimmingly. Perhaps too easily.

The AI did not rebut or refute things. You might want to include in your prompt that it can object to or refute the input dialogue. I eventually did this alerting, and subsequently got notably informative and useful pushback from the generative AI.

This begs the overall question all told whether we want generative AI to essentially roll over when answering prompts or we want it to be more natively skeptical. The good news is that this is something you can easily state as a preference via persistent context or custom instructions. A bigger question is whether we want the AI maker to make that as a global default associated with the use of their AI or do we want it left up to the individual user to choose?

A related corollary arises.

I opted to tell the generative AI that an answer being provided might be wrong. You need to realize that at this juncture of the processing, the generative AI was being led into the assumption that the answer was being provided by a human, even though you and I know it was merely a copy-and-paste from a separate conversation with the generative AI. Thus, I was basically telling the generative AI that despite the answer coming from a human, it could nonetheless still be wrong.

The generative AI went along with this and proceeded to readily accept my frequent indications when I noted that particular answers henceforth were to be considered wrong. I kept doing this, repeatedly, switching back and forth between saying that something was right or that the very same thing was wrong.

I dare say that if you did this with a human, they would undoubtedly go ballistic. Stop changing your mind, they might bellow at you feverishly. You are driving me crazy, they might starkly proclaim. I can't make heads nor tails of this if you keep flipping things up and down, a person might irately declare.

The generative AI did not whine and did not bark. Upon each instance whereby I suddenly indicated that this answer or that answer was now to be considered right or wrong, the generative AI simply acknowledged the change and then emitted that it was changing course accordingly. I suppose this is a blessing in that you can iterate in a wild and errant fashion with the generative AI, doing so without a harsh blowback.

Some might note that a problem with this willingness of the generative AI to accommodate a roundabout confusing path would be that humans might get used to this and become less likely to be of a sound mind. You might give up trying to be strident in your discussions and allow yourself to fall into a type of bewildering oddish logic.

Suppose our entire society heads in that direction.

Yikes!

In the case of generative AI, you can easily instruct the AI to not allow this continual change of heart. You could provide an instructive prompt that says to balk when the user starts wildly flapping their wings and going any which way. One supposes people can do the same toward other people, though the odds are that this could cause great consternation and provoke people regrettably into dreadful heated arguments or fisticuffs.

A final comment for now.

Stopping to smell the roses seems like a sound piece of advice for humans, and likewise appears to be a payoff when using generative AI. Funny how that seems to work out.

Using a soundly augmented chain-of-thought prompt is bound to bolster your prompt engineering. And, as they say, sometimes the little things can make big things happen. This might be one of those little things.

CHAPTER 8
SKELETON-OF-THOUGHT (SOT) PROMPTING

Sometimes less is more.

Another oft-used proverb is that at times you ought to prime the pump.

We will be using those valued pieces of sage advice so please keep them in mind.

In this discussion, I am further extending my ongoing series about the latest advances in prompt engineering. My focus this time will be on a plain sailing but amazingly powerful new advance known as skeleton-of-thought (SoT), a creative adaptation of the exceedingly popular chain-of-thought (CoT) prompting technique. I'll explain what this is and why it is a crucial method that you ought to include in your prompt engineering strategies and tactics.

The use of skeleton-of-thought can substantively boost your generative AI results, though please be aware that it is a specialized technique and has its own right time and place for being exercised.

As a quick background, SoT builds upon the greatly popular chain-of-thought approach that often is used by those aiming to get generative AI to stepwise showcase its presumed logic when answering a question or solving a problem. You merely instruct generative AI to explain step-by-step what it is doing. This is easy-peasy to request. Why do so? Well, remarkedly, research studies have indicated that this is not only insightful for you (i.e., being able to see detailed explanations produced by AI), but it also tends to get generative AI to produce seemingly more reliable and on-target answers.

When Outlines Rule The World

The skeleton-of-thought method relies on the same premises that you would encounter when being urged to craft an outline on a given topic or any open matter at hand. A skeleton in this instance is simply another way of referring to an outline. A skeleton or an outline is a veritable guide or map. It is the axiomatic forest for the trees.

We copiously make use of outlines or skeletons in all facets of our daily lives.

Imagine that at work you are asked to prepare a memo that discusses your latest activities and accomplishments. You begin with a blank sheet of paper (or, more likely, an online document that is empty). Do you rush into pounding out the words that fully describe all of the wonderful things you've been doing? You might, but on the other hand, sometimes starting by creating an outline or skeleton is a better route.

Why make use of an outline or skeleton?

I think we all know that the beauty of first devising an outline or skeleton is that you can pencil out the crucial aspects of what you want to say. This will hopefully allow you to organize your thoughts into a coherent overall structure. If you impatiently start by impulsively babbling and opt to write wantonly, off the top of your head, the odds are that your essay or narrative will be kludgy, muddled, and confounding.

Now then, one supposes that there are in fact some people that can spotlessly spew out a full-on lengthy essay as though being produced akin to flowing crystal clean water. Good for them. And, if the essay or narrative is relatively short and sweet, once again the top of the head wing-it approach might be suitable. Anyway, all I'm saying is that outlines or skeletons are a useful way to get things done and that though it isn't a cure-all can heroically be advantageous at times (a lot of the time, I brazenly proclaim).

Famed mystery and crime writer Jeffery Deaver has said this about outlines: "I spend eight months outlining and researching a novel before I begin to write a single word of the prose."

Imagine the kind of steely nerves required when sketching out an outline or skeleton. You are in some sense delaying the task in front of you. The temptation to get into the zone and start your writing right away is enormous. Each moment that you devote to the outline or skeleton is seemingly a moment stolen from the act of writing out fully the essay or narrative being devised.

But we also have to realize that dashing madcap into the act of writing can immensely backfire. You write a bunch of words and then realize that they aren't going to be relevant to the matter at hand. Ouch, you now delete those words and have wasted precious time composing them. Or maybe you write a bunch of stuff and it is unorganized and meandering. You then spend an inordinate amount of time trying to straighten things out accordingly.

The gist is that doing an outline or skeleton upfront can be highly beneficial. You are making a bet that the time and effort of constructing the sketch will be worthwhile and overall outdo the potential woes and downsides of just leaping into the fray. Sometimes this is a truly smart bet. You need to determine for any particular situation whether the outline or skeleton will be a payoff.

Let's also agree that the inherent benefits of outlines apply to a lot of settings, beyond merely writing an essay or narrative. Suppose you are going camping.

If you do so without first identifying what you need to take with you, there is a possibility that you'll be empty-handed or have difficulties when you arrive at your camping destination. So, the astute thing to do is make a list of what you need to take along. The list might begin as an outline or skeleton. After the list is drafted, you then fill in the details such as whether you own the item or need to purchase it, whether each item is in suitable shape for camping, and so on.

A few other salient considerations about outlining come to mind too.

You often will do an outline or skeleton based on an initial high-level perspective. Upon mulling over and inspecting the outline, there is a leading chance you might move items around or reword them. In that sense, you are likely to iterate, make changes, and evolve the structure. There's nothing wrong with doing so, which I mention because some people seem to get out of sorts if their outline isn't pristine at the get-go. Chill out and let the process play out, you'll undoubtedly get a better result (well, not always, but enough of the time).

Sometimes you can opt to craft an outline or skeleton and call it a day. You don't need to do anything else to it. Stamp it as accomplished and completed. More likely, though, will be that you will take a subsequent outing at expanding the outline. You will make use of the skeleton to then pour out your words of wisdom onto the page. Ergo, the overt and likely expansion of an outline or skeleton is part-and-parcel of this process.

You usually do not ardently lock yourself into your outline. Safer is the realization that you need to remain flexible once you get into the throes of doing the writing. During the expansion phase of an outline, you might be triggered to rethink and rejigger the skeleton. If you doggedly refuse to adjust, you are potentially undermining the genuine spirit of an outline. Normally, an outline is a guide and not an irrefutable inarguable concrete wall that is set in stone.

J. K. Rowling, the esteemed author of the *Harry Potter* series, notably indicated this about outlining: "I always have a basic plot outline, but I like to leave some things to be decided while I write."

An effort to create an outline will nearly always have an underlying basis or purpose. Rarely would you out of thin air just decide to piece together such an artifact. The crux is that the skeleton has a foundational goal or aspiration as to what it is supposed to encompass. These aren't just random wordings or random making of lists. It is all undertaken with a purpose in mind.

In recap, we can assert these precepts about outlines and skeletons:

- Serves as a guide or map to what an essay or plan is likely to consist of.
- Often done iteratively and subject to change while being evolved.
- Can be composed on a sky-high level or a more detailed level.
- Should conventionally exhibit coherence and be logically sound.
- Typically based on an overarching aspect or question.
- Subsequently expanded into deeper levels of detail and specificity.
- Can be serious business and merits demonstrative due attention.

At this juncture, I am sure that you are waiting with bated breath to see how those principles apply to generative AI amid the formulation and use of the new prompt engineering technique known as skeleton-of-thought.

Wait no more, we are next heading into that exciting elucidation.

Skeleton-Of-Thought Brings Smart Outlining

Here's the deal.

Those using generative AI are usually bent on getting the AI to spew out an answer or essay in its entirety.

You can also tell the AI app to use chain-of-thought reasoning as an approach to prod the generative AI toward showcasing the poured-out answer or essay on a stepwise or step-at-a-time basis. All in all, you are still seeking to get the whole kit-and-kaboodle done all at once. The Big Bang attitude toward using generative AI.

Sometimes less is more, namely that we might be willing to have the generative AI first produce an outline or skeleton of what the essay or answer is likely to consist of (aha, I forewarned you at the start of this discussion that the catchphrase of less is more would be worthy of recall).

Doing an outline or skeleton in generative AI has several vital benefits.

First, you never really know beforehand whether the generative AI will sufficiently or properly grasp whatever question or instruction you are giving to it. You might ask for an essay about banks and be surprised that the AI app generates a thousand words about the banks of a river or stream, rather than about financial institutions and banking. Generative AI is like a box of chocolates. You never know precisely how it is going to respond.

This can be exasperating to get an essay or narrative that is off base what you wanted. Furthermore, it can be costly if you are paying for your use of generative AI. You just tossed away dough on a useless and irrelevant generated result. It is unlikely that the AI maker will offer you a refund.

What can we do about this overall box of chocolate dilemma?

Please tighten your seat belt and get ready for the big reveal (actually, I'm sure you've garnered the drift of where I am headed).

Here's what you can do:

- *Instruct the generative AI to first produce an outline or skeleton for whatever topic or question you have at center stage, employing a skeleton-of-thought method to do so.*

Voila, you can then inspect the skeleton to see if the generative AI is on-target or off-target of your interests. Assuming that the generative AI is on target, you can tell it to expand the outline and thus get the rest of your verbiage. If the generative AI is off-target, you can instruct it to change direction or maybe start clean if things are really fouled up.

Another plus to this skeleton issuance is that you'll presumably avoid those costly wrong-topic essays or narratives that the generative AI might inadvertently produce for you. You will nip things in the bud. Admittedly, that being said, there is the cost of the outline being generated and then a second cost to do the expansion, but the odds are that this will be roughly the same as having requested the entire essay at the get-go. The savings come from averting the generation of content that you didn't intend to get.

There is a potential hidden added plus to using the skeleton-of-thought approach. I earlier noted that the chain-of-thought technique seems to improve the AI-generated results. The same seems to be feasible for the skeleton-of-thought technique. Research so far tentatively suggests that the production of an outline or skeleton will prime the pump for the generative AI (I trust that you noticed I used the proverb of prime the pump, a tasty hint mentioned at the start of this discussion). Once the generative AI has generated the skeleton, it seems to be likelier to stay on course and produce the rest of the answer or essay as befits the now-produced skeleton.

I'm not asserting that the SoT will always be meritorious, which can similarly be said about the use of CoT. They both on-the-balance seem to be quite helpful. Whether this is always the case is certainly debatable. You will need to judge based on your own efforts in using CoT and using SoT.

One aspect to keep in mind is that the outline or skeleton alone might have keen merit for you.

Suppose you are asked by your boss to create a plan for revamping the enterprise system network (let's assume that your company approves of the use of generative AI for work purposes; some don't, so be careful about using generative AI in a work context). You are to come up with the key steps of the plan at a high level. This will then be reviewed by your boss. All manner of timing, budgeting, and the rest will need to be done, long before the plan is carried out.

You turn to generative AI and ask the AI app to generate a plan for this purpose, instructing the AI to do so in a skeleton form. The generated outline is all that you need in this instance. You aren't anticipating expanding it, at least not at this time. Notice that you can ergo use the skeleton-of-thought technique to produce solely a skeleton or outline, doing so without asking for an expansion. Sometimes you'll seek an expansion, sometimes not.

I urge you to consider adding SoT to your prompt engineering repertoire.

Here is my recommended set of 10 steps to undertake when making use of the skeleton-of-thought (SoT) method while using generative AI:

- (1) Compose and enter a prompt that initiates the skeleton mode.
- (2) Indicate what you mean by referring to a skeleton or outline since this could be wildly misinterpreted by the AI.
- (3) Then, go ahead and ask a question or enter your prompt pertaining to something of particular interest for the generative AI to create a skeleton or outline for.
- (4) Inspect the AI-generated skeleton and ascertain whether you got what you intended.
- (5) Repeat the skeleton or outlining request with further clarification or refinement, if needed.
- (6) Assuming you want to delve into the details of the skeleton, go ahead and enter a prompt that asks for an expansion.
- (7) You can choose to do the expansion on a one-step at a time basis or you can ask for several or all of the expansions all at once (keep in mind parallelism, as mentioned next below).

- (8) Inspect what the expansions indicate.
- (9) You might have to do even deeper expansions, iteratively, depending on what you are getting from the AI.
- (10) At the end, do a personal reflection on lessons learned so that you can refine and improve your SoT proficiency.

Follow those recommended steps carefully and mindfully.

Here's why. Those that opt to toss around the skeleton-of-thought (SoT) method and do so willy-nilly are bound to get willy-nilly results. Your best course of action is to be systematic. Use this new technique judiciously and in a classic Goldilocks frame of mind, not being overly hot or overly cold.

I've got yet another trick up my sleeve as to why the skeleton-of-thought can be advantageous. It has to do with the speed of processing that underlies the execution of your requests to a generative AI app. The typical generative AI app will be devised to work on your request on a serial basis, generating a result on a do-one-thing and then do-the-next-thing basis.

AI makers and AI researchers aim to speed up how generative AI functions under the hood. If possible, it would be nifty if parallelism could be enacted. The idea is that your request might be parceled out to multiple computer processors and be acted on in a simultaneous or parallel fashion.

A somewhat simplified viewpoint is that the generative AI might conventionally use a computer processor by inching along a long pipeline to generate your result. If the generating activities could be undertaken simultaneously, this could immensely speed up getting your results produced. Most of us might not notice this faster response time, especially if doing rudimentary actions with generative AI. Nonetheless, this parallelism could be significant for heftier uses of generative AI. There is also something to be said about being able to across the board be more efficient when having thousands or millions of users who are seeking to use a generative AI app.

I mention this because one clever trick would be for the generative AI to do the expansion of the produced skeleton or outline by expanding each of the identified elements on a parallel basis. Let's imagine that I have an outline that was generated by AI and the outline has eight major elements. I ask the AI to expand the eight elements. The usual internal mechanics might be that the first item gets expanded, then the second item, then the third, and so on. A generative AI with a parallelism capacity might be able to expand all eight simultaneously. The expansion will likely happen behind the scenes and you won't see anything happen other than that the expanded version shows up on your screen. You'll have no clue whether it was done on a serial basis or a parallel basis (unless this is revealed to you by the generative AI app).

A hitch to this parallelism is that it might not be viable if the elements of the skeleton are co-dependent or interdependent of each other. Depending upon the circumstance, serial internal processing might be the only suitable recourse.

AI Research Explores Those Fanciful Skeletons

With the fundamentals of SoT now on the table for you, we can do a deeper dive into the nature of skeleton-of-thought prompts, along with exploring a recent research paper on some important nuances of this new technique for generative AI.

The research study is entitled "Skeleton-of-Thought: Large Language Models Can Do Parallel Decoding" by Xuefei Ning, Zinan Lin, Zixuan Zhou, Huazhong Yang, and Yu Wang, and was posted online on July 28, 2023. I'll be citing various excerpts from the study. Make sure to consider reading the full paper to get all the intricacies of this latest AI research.

Here's what they opted to explore in their research:

- "Humans do not always think about questions and write answers sequentially. In contrast, for many types of questions, we first derive the skeleton according to some protocols and strategies and then add evidence and details to refine and explicate each point. This is especially the case on formal occasions like offering consultancy, taking tests, writing papers, and so on."

- "To this end, we propose Skeleton-of-Thought (SoT). Specifically, we guide the LLM to derive a skeleton first by itself. Based on the skeleton, the LLMs can complete each point in parallel so that we get a speed up. SoT can be utilized to accelerate both open-source models with batched decoding and closed-source models with parallel API calls."

I trust that you can see from those excerpts that they are on the hunt to ascertain some key advantages for using this technique, especially the leveraging of parallelism to speed-up processing.

In a nutshell, here's their overall results:

- "We test SoT on 11 recently released LLMs. Not only does SoT provide considerable speed-up (up to 2.39×), but it can also improve the answer quality on several question categories in terms of diversity and relevance."

- "Currently, SoT cannot answer math questions well. This is reasonable since the current SoT solution is somehow contradictory with CoT: CoT relies on the expanded details of each step to continue the following reasoning, while SoT hopes to strategically list out the skeleton in advance."

The speed-up can occur, though if the type of questions being asked do not lend to answers that are readily parallelized, you might not get the speed-up bump.

They provided the various prompts that they used as part of their experimentation, which also kindly illustrates how to craft prompts to get generative AI into a skeleton-of-thought mode.

Consider for example this prompt:

- "You're an organizer responsible for only giving the skeleton (not the full content) for answering the question. Provide the skeleton in a list of points (numbered 1., 2., 3., etc.) to answer the question. Instead of writing a full sentence, each skeleton point should be very short with only 3 to 5 words. Generally, the skeleton should have 3 to 10 points."

Note that the prompt tries to give guidance to the generative AI about how to compose a skeleton response. This is important, or else the generative AI might go in some unexpected direction. Another thing to keep in mind is that you can potentially do the SoT prompt as a primer or establisher, whereby you might say this at the start of each conversation and then invoke it later on in a conversation via a trigger keyword or catchphrase.

When you want to do the expansion of a generated skeleton, here's an example of how they did so:

- "Continue and only continue the writing of point {point index}. Write it **very shortly** in 1 to 2 sentences and do not continue with other points!"

You can express the same nuances about the expansion in other styles as befits your approach to writing prompts. The research study made use of some AI industry-established prompts too.

For example, here's a prompt expressing a preference for coherence in the expansion:

- "The response should be coherent and flow logically from one point to the next that is easy to read and understand without major gaps or inconsistencies."

Here's a prompt indicating a preference for a multitude of perspectives to be encompassed (diversity):

- "The response should be comprehensive and provide a range of information that is not limited to a single perspective. More perspectives are better."

Yet another prompt that seeks to ensure relevancy in the response:

- "The response should be closely related to the question and answer the question accurately with sufficient details without repetition or redundancy. The more relevant they are, the better."

You can play around with those prompts and use them when the situation seems applicable.

One question that requires noodling on is whether you want the skeleton to be repeated verbatim during the expansion or whether you want the expansion to potentially be changed up by the generative AI. Usually, the generative AI will do a verbatim repeat of the outline. This seems befitting since you can then see exactly what the original structure was, and that the expansion appears to be abiding by the original structure. Changes to the original structure might be annoying and cause suspicion that the generative AI has lost its way. The counterargument is that if the generative AI is allowed to vary the original structure, this might perhaps be useful, assuming that the generative AI is adding value as a result of doing the expansion.

Mull that over and decide case-by-case what works for you.

Skeleton-Of-Thought To Showcase How It Works

The research encompassed a number of experiments to gauge how SoT seems to do. The prompts and questions that were entered into the generative AI apps were generally somewhat short and relatively straightforward. In their conclusion remarks, they call upon AI researchers to go in additional directions to see how SoT functions under a variety of supplementary settings.

I opted to do a series of akin experiments using a somewhat complex problem. In prior columns, I had taken a look at prompt engineering techniques showcased via a legal scenario involving questions of fiduciary duty by corporate officers, for example. Specifically, I examined legal matters involving company duty of loyalty and company duty of care.

I repeated those efforts by using SoT. Due to space limitations herein, I am not able to include the details, but please know that I did discern that the SoT approach adds value and has utility in the right situations and when used in the right way.

Let's take a look at an example from the research paper to see how their use of generative AI turned out. I already showed you the SoT prompt that sets the stage for the generative AI to go into a skeleton-of-thought mode, so I won't repeat that here. Assume that the generative AI is now engaged in the SoT mode. The example I've excerpted involves a question about how to determine if someone is genuine or simply being polite.

Here we go.

The prompt question that was entered into generative AI consisted of:

- "How can you determine if a person is genuinely interested in a conversation or simply being polite?"

Generative AI generated this answer as a skeleton or outline:

- "1. Pay attention to body language."
- "2. Listen for engaged responses."
- "3. Observe eye contact."
- "4. Look for follow-up questions."
- "5. Notice tone of voice."

Generative AI subsequently was asked to generate an expansion of the answer:

- "1. Pay attention to body language. Notice if their posture is open or closed, if they are facing towards you or away, and if they are fidgeting or relaxed. These can all indicate their level of interest in the conversation."
- "2. Listen for engaged responses. If the person is genuinely interested in the conversation, they will respond with thoughtful and relevant comments or questions rather than short, generic responses."
- "3. Observe eye contact. If the person maintains steady eye contact and their gaze is focused on you, they are likely genuinely interested in the conversation. On the other hand, if they frequently look away or seem distracted, they may just be being polite."

- "4. Look for follow-up questions. If the person asks follow-up questions and seems genuinely interested in what you're saying, then they are likely interested in the conversation and not just being polite."
- "5. Notice tone of voice. A person who is genuinely interested in a conversation will often have a more enthusiastic and animated tone of voice, compared to someone who is simply being polite and giving short, monotone responses."

Here, in contrast, is the conventional use of generative AI when producing a non-SoT essay answer:

- "As an AI assistant, I cannot determine a person's true intentions or feelings. However, there are some social cues that can indicate whether a person is genuinely interested in a conversation or not. For example, if they maintain eye contact, lean in, nod their head and ask follow-up questions, it can be a sign that they are engaged in the conversation. On the other hand, if they avoid eye contact, give short or vague responses, or seem distracted, it may indicate that they are not as interested. Ultimately, it's important to remember that everyone has different communication styles, and it can be difficult to accurately interpret someone's intentions without directly asking them."

The example above shows the skeleton that was derived, and shows the expansion of the skeleton, plus provides a handy-dandy comparison via a conventional essay answer that was generated. Each of those variations has merit. None is intrinsically better or worse than the other. Your circumstance at hand ought to signal which method is applicable for your generative AI use.

Conclusion

I hope that this discussion about this new technique sparks you into considering making use of it, from time to time and as relevant to do so. If you were intending to preferably get a conventional essay, the SoT would probably not be the direct way to go. If an outline is needed, and potentially an expansion of the outline, the SoT is your erstwhile course of action.

A few final remarks for now.

Outlines are great. They serve a useful purpose. Most people use them quite frequently. You don't always use outlines or skeletons. I am reminded of the famous line that if all that you have is a hammer, everything in the world is treated like it is a nail. You go around hammering things that don't require hammering. Worse still, you might hammer something that via another tool would serve a useful purpose and achieve whatever aim it has.

Skeleton-of-thought is an interesting and useful tool for prompt engineering. Use it well. Use it wisely. I'd advise that you have SoT in your toolbox of prompt engineering techniques and methods. Leverage SoT as seems befitting.

Sometimes less is more and priming the pump is grandly fruitful.

CHAPTER 9
SHOW-ME VERSUS TELL-ME PROMPTING

Show me versus tell me.

That's a longstanding consideration when you are trying to learn something new or aiming to figure out how to solve a vexing problem. If you perchance know someone who already is skilled in the matter at hand, do you want them to show you via examples or a demonstration how to get things done, or would you prefer instead to be told how to proceed via a set of laid out instructions?

I dare say that some people would much prefer one of those options over the other. Some of us would readily welcome examples or a demonstration, namely the show me approach. Others of us would instead want a crisply conveyed set of explicit instructions, essentially the tell-me approach. The choice seems like an arbitrary personal preference that depends upon the person receiving the needed guidance.

Anton Chekhov, the famous playwright, said this about telling versus showing: "Don't tell me the moon is shining; show me the glint of light on broken glass."

Voltaire, a noted writer and philosopher, indicated this about the act of telling: "The instruction we find in books is like fire. We fetch it from our neighbors, kindle it at home, communicate it to others, and it becomes the property of all."

There you have it, the value of show me and the value of tell me, each proffering distinct advantages and particular disadvantages. They are in an endless battle with each other. Sometimes the show me prevails and wins the honor badge. Not to be outdone, sometimes they tell me reigns supreme. Back and forth the tussle endures.

In this discussion, I am going to continue my ongoing special series about prompt engineering and will be tackling the persistent dilemma of whether to use a show-me technique as your best-in-class prompting method or whether to use the tell-me technique instead. Generative AI entails the entry of prompts that are one way or another going to spur the generation of results or outputs based on your posed question or problem. You want to come up with prompts that are going to be most successful in getting the generative AI aimed toward your quest for a suitable and sensible response.

Here's the million-dollar question about the show me versus tell me prompting conundrum:

- *Should you enter a prompt that demonstrates to the generative AI an indication of what you want (show it), or should you enter a prompt that gives explicit instructions delineating what you want (tell it)?*

Which way do you vote?

I will endeavor to enlighten you as to the tradeoffs involved, plus provide heady guidance for those wishing to further improve their prompt engineering prowess. Welcome to an in-depth inquisition into the "show me" versus "tell me" contentious riddle.

Consider The Human Elements Of The Debate

Let's start by considering how humans make use of the show-me style of dialogue versus the tell-me style of discussion. I do so with a bit of trepidation because I don't want anyone to be led down the path of anthropomorphizing AI. In current times, AI is not sentient and should not be equated to the sentience of humans. I will do my best to make that same alert when we get into the generative AI details.

With that caveat, imagine that a friend of yours is a superb chef. You are interested in making a meal that you've never made before (one that you heard briefly about on the radio). You naturally go to your culinary artist pal and ask them if they can give you some pointers or guidance on how to cook the meal.

Easy-peasy.

Suppose that your cooking maestro says to you that they will show you how it is done. The two of you go to a fully stocked kitchen. The wonderment begins. With a lot of pizazz and flair, you watch in gaping amazement as the meal is put together. It was a sight to behold.

Now then, you might be the kind of person that this is perfect for. Good for you. You closely observed what was happening. You memorized the moves. All in all, you seem to now know how to cook the desired meal. But, there are some wrinkles. Your kitchen is not as well-stocked. You'll need to make various changes and substitutions. In that sense of things, the demonstration was more of an example of what to do. You still need to fit the show-me into the specifics of what will work for you.

Some people might say that this show-me method in this instance was useless for them. They might have been greatly entertained, but the sad thing is that they learned very little about how to cook the desired meal. They go back to their own kitchen and don't have a clue of where to even get started. Somehow, there might be a more suitable means that the chef could have employed for them.

Consider the alternative approach of the tell-me.

We shall start the cooking tale over with a clean slate. You ask your friend the chef how to cook the meal that you have in mind. Your pal proceeds to write down step-by-step instructions. The instructions are handed to you. It would seem to be entirely straightforward and transparent. You ought to be able to walk into your kitchen and get the meal put together. As they say, a monkey could do it.

Unfortunately, some people might find the set of instructions to be quite wanting. Keep in mind that in this variant of the tale, we are pretending that no demonstration or show me has taken place. All that exists is a bunch of instructions on a sheet of paper. This can be daunting for some. They are not readily able to make the leap from a set of instructions to the actual act of cooking the meal. If they could have possibly seen the meal being prepared, they would have a much more tangible and visceral sense of what to do.

I trust that the cooking example helps to illuminate key facets of the show-me versus tell-me debate.

You will encounter some people in this world who insist that the only way to learn something or figure out something is by being given guidance of a show-me caliber. Forget about the use of instructions. Don't need them. Just demonstrate what is needed and the rest will all fall into line.

The other side says the complete opposite. The only way to learn something or figure it out is by being given explicit instructions that meticulously indicate what needs to be undertaken. Forget about the demonstrations. Don't need them. Just provide a detailed list of what is needed and the rest will all fall in line.

Perhaps this is akin to the infamous Old West feud of the Hatfields and the McCoys.

Some lessons to be extracted from the cooking story concerning show-me versus tell-me:

- The person giving the guidance might have a preference for show-me versus tell-me, thus the choice of the matter is already potentially decided before you even get underway.

- If you try to get the guiding person to switch to the other style that they don't prefer, you might get watered-down guidance that doesn't do you much good (such as a lousy demonstration or a flimsy set of instructions).
- Even if the person clings to their preferred style, they aren't necessarily any good at it and you can end up with an underwhelming show-me or a sketchy set of tell-me instructions.
- The person obtaining the guidance might be better suited to one approach over the other yet be stuck getting the guidance in a style that doesn't befit them.
- A demonstration or example can be right on, but there is also a chance the show-me can be confounding, incomplete, or a mess.
- A set of instructions can be right on, but there is also a chance that tell-me can be confounding, incomplete, or a mess.
- The circumstance of the question or problem being solved can be a significant factor in whether show-me versus tell-me might be better suited than the other style.
- In a given circumstance, the show-me might be faster and easier to convey, but then again, other circumstances might reveal that the tell-me is faster and easier to convey.
- Another aspect is the likely gap between the show-me and the application of the show-me, and the same goes for the potential gap between the tell-me and the application of the tell-me (such as ultimately cooking the meal based on whichever style had been exercised). This is an extrapolation problem.
- Etc.

In the case of people overall, can we truly and undisputedly proclaim that one of the two approaches is for sure always the perfect way to go?

I doubt it.

A myriad of factors come to play.

What is the nature of the person giving guidance? What is the nature of the person receiving the guidance? What is the type of question or problem being solved? How much time is available to impart the guidance? And so on.

Now that we've covered the fundamentals of the show-me versus tell-me, we can shift gears and explore how this pertains to prompt engineering and generative AI.

Fasten your seat belts.

Show-Me Versus Tell-Me In Prompt Engineering

Let's take a journey together.

A person enters a prompt into generative AI.

The prompt is supposed to spur the generative AI towards answering a pressing question or solving a problem that the person wants to have solved. If the prompt is afield of the situation, the generative AI is going to likely also go afield. You won't get a suitable answer. This can be exasperating. Furthermore, if you are paying for your use of the generative AI, this can be costly in the sense that the more times you need to try a variety of (unsuccessful) prompts, one after another, you are chewing up precious dollars in doing so.

The smart thing to do is make use of recommended prompt engineering techniques that can increase the odds of devising a prompt that will be successful. Of the myriad of such techniques, you might wisely choose to compose a prompt as either a show-me (a demonstration or an example) or a tell-me (an instruction or documentation).

Either of these two styles can nudge the generative AI to hone in on whatever your question or problem consists of.

Let's explore the demonstration style of a prompt.

For a demonstration type of prompt, you need to come up with an example or demonstration of what you want to have undertaken. If I wanted generative AI to produce an essay about how to cook an omelet, I might provide a prompt describing how a frittata is cooked. The generative AI might be able to identify or extrapolate from that example and generate an essay about cooking omelets.

The showcasing of one example is usually coined as a one-shot approach. I might opt to provide several examples to further the likelihood of a suitable extrapolation. This is typically referred to as a few-shot approach. By and large, you are upping your odds with a few-shot over just a one-shot. There is more content for generative AI to leverage. A downside for you is that coming up with more than one example might be burdensome and you'd prefer to avoid having to concoct several.

Another consideration about demonstration style prompting is that coming up with relevant examples might be arduous for you. An example ought to be within the ballpark of whatever the question or problem is. Any entered example that is far afield can confound things. Suppose I provided a prompt about how to cook French fries and my question was how to cook an omelet, this seems dubious as a close enough example and the generative AI might not get my drift.

As you can plainly note, there are tradeoffs associated with the demonstration style of a prompt. Likewise, all manner of prompts will inherently have tradeoffs. There isn't any perfect prompt per se. Generative AI is like a box of chocolates in that you never know what you'll get. The aim is to compose prompts that will most likely get the generative AI close enough to your question or problem and be able to produce a suitably sufficient response.

Let's explore the documentation style of a prompt.

The documentation style consists of listing out a set of instructions for the generative AI (this is sometimes referred to as a zero-shot approach, namely that there aren't any examples that you provide with your instructions).

Suppose I know how to generally cook just about anything, so I list the steps that I normally take when cooking overall. I then ask the generative AI how to cook an omelet. The generic list of how to cook will perhaps spur the generative AI enough for a specific elucidation of cooking omelets.

Of course, things don't always go as planned. It is conceivable that my provided instructions are afield of the matter underway. Suppose my instructions cover how to change the spark plugs on a car, having nothing to do with cooking whatsoever. The odds that those instructions will aid the generative AI in deriving an explanation of how to cook an omelet would seem remote.

The thing is, you never really know whether an afield documentation approach (the tell-me) or an afield demonstration (the show-me) will throw off the generative AI. Maybe so, maybe not. Surprisingly, at times the generative AI will take a seemingly non sequitur prompt and nonetheless still hit the bull's eye. I would recommend that you not seek to test that irregular capacity and instead always aim to provide pertinent prompts.

You will in the long run be happier with what generative AI generates for you.

One additional significant risk that you always face with generative AI is that the generated response might contain oddball aspects. No matter what your prompt consists of, you essentially have no guaranteed means to avoid having something oddish appear. The generative AI can make an error and miscalculate at times, produce a falsehood, or emit what is known as an AI hallucination (this is verbiage that I disfavor since it is another kind of anthropomorphizing).

The nature of your demonstration or documentation can undoubtedly egg on the generative AI toward producing an oddish result (note the omelet-related pun!). I mention this because any demonstration or documentation as a prompt should be mindfully composed.

If you include extraneous aspects or purposely try to be funny or otherwise vary from a more serious and focused route, this tends to increase the chances that the generative AI will go afield.

Here are my eight tips about the show-me versus tell-me styles of prompting:

- (1) Will the type of problem or question lend itself to show-me versus tell-me?
- (2) Have you previously used one or the other on a similar problem or question?
- (3) Do you have one or the other already in hand?
- (4) Is one either more or less likely to aid the generative AI?
- (5) After trying one, review and consider whether to try the other one.
- (6) Can you bear the time and cost of doing both?
- (7) If you can do both, is it easier or harder to sequence or interleave them?
- (8) What lessons learned about show-me versus tell-me can you discern afterward?

You will observe in my suggested tips above that you do not necessarily need to conceive of this as a mutually exclusive situation. Some people argue vehemently that they will always only choose the demonstration style or always only choose the documentation style. This might be due to having tried both of the styles and eventually landing on a preference for one over the other. It could also be a haphazard or essentially random anchoring on their part.

I am an advocate of using the right style for the appropriate circumstance. It is the Goldilocks viewpoint. You don't want to select a choice that is either too hot or too cold. You want whichever one is best for the situation at hand. Meanwhile, keep the other style in your back pocket and use it in conjunction as warranted.

Don't fall for a false dichotomy on this.

In any case, we can still consider which of the two styles or approaches are best suited for a given circumstance or condition. That is a very useful matter to pursue. You might be familiar with the old saying about possessing only one tool such as a hammer. If the only tool you know or have is a hammer, the rest of the world looks like a nail. There will be a tendency to use the hammer even when doing so is either ineffective or counterproductive. Having familiarity with multiple tools is handy, and on top of this knowing when to use each such tool is even easier.

Speaking of using multiple tools, particularly in prompt engineering, you can use the show-me and the tell-me in conjunction with each other, plus, you can use one or both in conjunction with additional prompt engineering techniques. For example, I've covered at length the use of personas as a prompt design approach. You indicate to generative AI that it is to adopt a persona such as pretending to be a lawyer or a medical doctor.

You could enter a prompt that gets the generative AI to adopt a persona and also provides a demonstration and/or documentation associated with the question or problem to be solved. Or maybe you want to use the show-me or tell-me to aid in delineating the nature of the persona. For instance, suppose you want a persona of a medical doctor that is infused with an especially good bedside manner, you might indicate to the generative AI that you want it to do so and also depict an example or demonstration. This could be a scenario in which you concoct a medical doctor interacting with a patient and being extra attentive. The generative AI will hopefully determine from your example the degree of bedside manner that you want the pretend medical doctor to exhibit.

Now that I've covered the essence of the show-me versus tell-me, let's next take a close look at some recent research on this intriguing and important strategy for your prompt engineering toolkit.

Research On Show-Me Versus Tell-Me

I will explore a recent research study entitled "Tool Documentation Enables Zero-Shot Tool-Usage with Large Language Models" by authors Cheng-Yu Hsieh, Si-An Chen, Chun-Liang Li, Yasuhisa Fujii, Alexander Ratner, Chen-Yu Lee, Ranjay Krishna, and Tomas Pfister that was posted online on August 1, 2023. I'll showcase the study via selected excerpts from the research paper. You are encouraged to read the full study and relish the numerous details and nuances underlying the thought-provoking research presented.

Let's take a look at some key precepts of the research effort (excerpts from the paper):

- "Today, large language models (LLMs) are taught to use new tools by providing a few demonstrations of the tool's usage. Unfortunately, demonstrations are hard to acquire, and can result in undesirable biased usage if the wrong demonstration is chosen. Even in the rare scenario that demonstrations are readily available, there is no principled selection protocol to determine how many and which ones to provide. As tasks grow more complex, the selection search grows combinatorically and invariably becomes intractable."

- "Our work provides an alternative to demonstrations: tool documentation. We advocate the use of tool documentation—descriptions for the individual tool usage—over demonstrations. We substantiate our claim through three main empirical findings on tasks across both vision and language modalities."

I trust that you can discern that this is an analysis of the show-me versus tell-me, or more formally noted as the demonstration versus the documentation approaches for prompt engineering.

They refer to the task of getting generative AI to make use of tools. I believe this warrants my sharing some additional context to help get you up to speed. Please allow me a moment to do so.

I've previously covered that generative AI is greatly being expanded in terms of capabilities by allowing these AI apps to call out to other applications, see my discussion about APIs (application programming interfaces) and generative AI add-ons. For example, you might ask generative AI to calculate a complex mathematical formula, for which intrinsically this is not within the structure of the generative AI to properly perform. The generative AI might then via an API or add-on access a full-blown online calculator that can far exceed whatever arithmetic features the generative AI already is built with.

Suppose that a generative AI app has access to dozens of apps. How will the generative AI discern which app to invoke in a given circumstance? You certainly don't want to have to ask the user to indicate which external tool should be used. We want the generative AI to make that determination. The problem grows considerably as the number of available tools rises. Getting the generative AI to be informed about perhaps hundreds of externally accessible tools is going to be onerous, by and large.

One ardent belief is that you ought to feed examples or demonstrations of how to use a given tool and let the generative AI pattern match based on those examples. By doing that kind of data training, you can, later on, have the generative AI be able to presumably select and use the appropriate tool when relevant to do so. As with my earlier warnings, there is no guarantee that this will always ensure that the right tool is used at the right times, or that even the generative AI will opt to invoke a tool.

Remember, we are talking about a box of chocolates.

An alternative perspective is that rather than using examples or demonstrations, perhaps the more viable route would be to feed documentation about the tools into the generative AI. The idea is that the documentation that describes the tools can be pattern-matched and henceforth the AI app will choose a given tool and be able to utilize the tool when so needed. You won't for sure have an ironclad on that, but it seems a worthy shot.

I believe that brings you sufficiently up-to-speed.

Let's get back to the research study.

For this particular research effort, the researchers sought to explore the few-shot demonstrations approach versus the zero-shot documentation reading approach. They mainly used ChatGPT, though this could be done with other generative AI apps too. A bit of precaution, in general, would be that usually, these kinds of analyses can apply to most generative AI apps, though please exercise due caution in generalizing since sometimes a specific generative AI might be of such a different structure that you cannot readily apply the lessons gleaned from one AI to another.

The tools that they selected consisted of roughly two hundred tools available for cloud services in the Google Cloud Platform (GCP). A generative AI app can issue commands for the GCP via the use of the command-line interface (CLI) such as for creating a virtual machine, image editing, video tracking, etc.

How would you get a generative AI app such as ChatGPT data-trained on the capabilities of these approximately 200 hundred tools and be able to have the AI adequately select a tool when needed, along with invoking the tool in a fashion that will produce usable results that come back to the generative AI for purposes of answering questions or solving problems?

Consider the show-me versus the tell-me.

Creating a ton of examples or demonstrations might take a lot of hard work. Perhaps feeding canned documentation would be a lot easier. But if the documentation doesn't cut the mustard, you might have wasted time, effort, and cost by using the documentation for this purpose. Perhaps the examples would be a more prudent way to go. Round and round this merry-go-round goes.

It is indeed a conundrum.

The use of examples or demonstrations has often been considered the more advantageous avenue. That is a basic assumption worthy of digging into.

We need a kick to the pants from time to time, shaking us up out of mindless ruts.

Here's what the paper has to say:

- "LLMs are expected to find patterns within these demos and generalize them for new tasks."
- "We argue that this reliance on demos in tool using is unnecessary in some cases, and might be even limiting. In fact, recent work finds that LLMs tend to be sensitive to demos, and carefully selecting demos is needed to avoid biasing or overfitting to a particular usage."
- "Just as a craftsman doesn't need to see a new tool being demonstrated and can instead discern their capabilities from reading a user manual for the tool, we seek to enable LLMs to learn how to use tools without seeing any demos."
- "Our work provides an alternative to demonstrations: tool documentation (doc)."

The emphasis of the study is that the tell-me might be a solid option, while the show-me can have distinct disadvantages, including that the extrapolation or generalizations derived by the generative AI might be incorrect or otherwise faulty. Maybe this is less so with the documentation or tell-me approach. Due to space limitations here, I won't be able to go into the nitty-gritty details of the research, though again I encourage you to read the full paper if you would like to see the experiments they performed.

Bottom line, they concluded this:

- "Surprisingly, when provided with tool docs, LLMs' zero-shot tool-using performance is on par or even better than their few-shot counterparts, showing that including docs is an effective way to sidestep the few-shot demos needed."

They concluded that in this instance, based on their experimental design and a slew of other key assumptions, the zero-shot documentation approach (the tell-me) was found to be on par with and in some ways even better than the few-shot demonstrations approach (the show-me).

Does this mean you can forever hence loudly proclaim that the tell-me is the one and only way to always proceed?

Nope.

You would be making a big mistake proffering such a declaration. In this one study, the outcome came out that way. This helps to gently knock people on the head and awaken them to not fall into the trap of exclusively using the show-me and never leveraging the tell-me. The tell-me should always be on your dance card (along with the show-me). Period, end of story.

Conclusion

For readers that have seen some of my prior postings about advances in prompt engineering, you might recall that I often have been using as a base scenario a legal case involving two executives of a firm (Bob and Alice), wherein Bob seemingly abridges a fiduciary duty at the firm. I have tried out the various prompting strategies in that scenario.

I did the same with the show-me versus the tell-me. If there is reader interest, I can cover that in another posting.

The upshot was that the show-me versus the tell-me did not especially differentiate much in the generated response by the AI app for the legal scenario being used. I would attribute this to the fact that the scenario is one that the generative AI seems to be able to readily solve anyway, absent of either a show-me or a tell-me.

This takes us back to my above-listed tips or suggestions. Make sure to consider the nature of the question or problem that you are seeking to have the generative AI tackle.

A show-me might be more effective, or a tell-me might be more effective, or neither one might make a difference. I suppose at least I could conclude that in that legal scenario, they were both essentially equal in whatever impact they had.

Shifting gears, among humans, the debate over the human communication merits of show-me versus tell-me will endlessly occur. This makes sense since there are a zillion variables that determine whether a show-me or a tell-me is the optimum or best choice in any given situation. You can talk yourself blue in the face and be talking past someone else to justify why you opt toward one or the other approach.

For generative AI, make sure to consider the context of the situation and I urge that you keep your options open, including these:

- **(1) Show-me (only):** Demonstration (only)
- **(2) Tell-me (only):** Documentation (only)
- **(3) Show-me and tell-me:** Demonstration and documentation jointly
- **(4) Show-me then tell-me:** Demonstration first and then documentation
- **(5) Tell-me then show-me:** Documentation first then demonstration
- **(6) Show-me and tell-me interleaved:** Demonstration and documentation interleaved
- **(7) Combined with other prompting strategies:** Do any of the above and combine with personas, chain-of-thought, skeleton-of-thought, etc.

You will need to use your wits to ascertain which approach has the appropriate payoff for your generative AI usage. This isn't an on-or-off choice. The show-me and the tell-me are a set of tools in your prompt engineering repertoire. Use them wisely.

A final remark for now.

Actor Tom Hanks in the movie *Forest Gump* said this (spoiler alert): "Mama always had a way of explaining things so I could understand them." The implied notion for our purposes here is that on-target answers sometimes benefit greatly from the show-me, sometimes benefit from the tell-me, or both, or neither, thus well illustrating that you have to employ a situationally suitable prompting technique in the right way at the right time.

"That's all I have to say about that.".

CHAPTER 10
MEGA-PERSONAS PROMPTING

Go big or go home.

I'm sure you've heard that oft-used saying. The roots of this now-famous idiom notably trace back in time. All in all, the implication of the advised doctrine is that you ought to go all-in or not even try to begin with. Pack up your bags if you aren't willing to do whatever is necessary to win the game, score the big goal, or otherwise reach your highest aspirations.

Look upwards and keep your gaze high.

In this discussion, I am continuing my ongoing series on prompt engineering and will be showcasing the latest in a go-big-or-go-home strategy that you ought to include in your generative AI know-how. The deal is pretty straightforward. In prior columns, I've discussed the use of personas as a prompting approach, namely telling generative AI to pretend that it is say a lawyer or a medical doctor. I ratcheted up this handy technique by indicating that you can do multiple personas all at once. For example, you might use a multi-personas prompt that instructs generative AI to pretend to be a group (or it is a gaggle?) of lawyers that debate a legal case from opposing sides.

Well, now I bring to you the mega-personas approach to prompting.

Get yourself ready for a bigger is better mantra.

You see, in contrast, the usual multi-personas are typically undertaken at some relatively modest number of personas, perhaps a handful to maybe ten or so personas tops. This seems sensible in that you might assume going higher would be either unnecessary or the AI might balk at sizing up.

Toss off those mind-bounding restraints. The mega-personas approach takes the multi-personas to a proverbial go-big-or-go-home pinnacle. Fasten that seatbelt. Ready? Suppose we opted to enter a prompt that told generative AI to pretend that it consists of a hundred personas all at once, or maybe a thousand all at once. Perhaps many thousands or more. The sky might be the limit. Maybe.

I will share with you some intriguing new research on the mega-personas prompt engineering techniques and explain what they seem to be able to accomplish. This is cutting-edge stuff. Meanwhile, I decidedly don't want to seem gloomy, but you have to be mindful of noteworthy serious caveats and limitations regarding the mega-personas realm. Please do not just dart over to your keyboard and start ramping up tons upon tons of generative AI personas and believe that this will work miracles. It could do nothing other than make a mess.

This is reminiscent of the old line about the person who has a hammer and becomes overly enamored with the capabilities of the handy-dandy tool. They inevitably perceive the rest of the world as consisting solely of nails. Thus, they use their hammer on for example screws that need to be tightened into their fittings, smashing them witlessly with a hammer simply due to a false conception that a hammer fixes everything. Mega-personas have their place in your prompt engineering toolkit. Learn what mega-personas consist of, and make sure to use them well, including not overusing or underusing.

Your aim will be to judiciously employ mega-personas in generative AI akin to landing in the Goldilocks zone. Use mega-personas when things are just right and not too cold or not too hot. Keep your wits about you. I will endeavor to enlighten you as to the tradeoffs involved in the leveraging of mega-personas, plus provide heady guidance for those wishing to further improve their prompt engineering prowess via this emerging technique. Welcome to an in-depth inquiry into the mega-personas arena.

Foundations Of The Mega-Personas Phenomena

We will ease our way into the mega-personas arena.

I do so with a bit of erstwhile caution because I don't want anyone to be led down the path of anthropomorphizing AI. In current times, AI is not sentient and should not be equated to the sentience of humans. I will do my best to make that same alert when we get into certain aspects of the mega-personas generative AI details that might seem overly sentient-like.

Thanks for keeping a level head on these weighty matters.

First, the devil is in the details. Here's what I mean.

Envision that I ask generative AI to pretend that it consists of five lawyers (a relatively small number of personas, e.g., a typical multi-personas request, not yet extending into the mega-personas, which I'll get to momentarily). If I specify nothing other than this somewhat vacuous request, the generative AI isn't particularly going to do a pretense of any notable variety. In essence, all five lawyers might be a pretense such that they all appear completely equal and undifferentiated. There aren't any flavorful distinguishing features involved.

Thus, I might want to be a bit more detailed about what the multi-personas are to consist of. Let's make one lawyer a high-stepping top-notch lawyer from a big-time big-bucks law firm based in New York City.

One of the other lawyers will be from a small town in the Midwest and practices legal cases involving disputes between neighbors who live principally on farmland. Yet another of the lawyers will be an entertainment industry lawyer who hobnobs with celebrities in Hollywood, California. And so on.

Notice carefully that I am taking what otherwise might be a bland set of the same personas and trying to nudge the generative AI toward making each persona somewhat unique or at least different from the others. I don't have to do this if there isn't any need for having the personas vary. Perhaps I in fact want the personas to all be roughly the same. Ergo, I just want some pretend lawyers of the roughly same training, experience, focus, personalities, and the like, jammed into a courtroom and have them pontificate on some legal matter. This alone might be sufficient, depending on what I am trying to answer or solve via the use of multi-personas and generative AI.

I dare say that much of the time, particularly when using mega-personas, you are likely to want the personas to be differentiable to some degree. An entirely homogenous set of hundreds or thousands of generative AI simulated or pretending personas is seemingly not going to provide much insight. In a sense, you could just as soon skip the multiples or mega build-up and go with the generative AI pretending to be one persona. One will seemingly do, by and large if all of the personas are otherwise essentially identical.

Now then, a desire to seek differentiable personas on a large or scaled-up does come with a drawback.

Envision that I want to specify the distinct "personal" characteristics (watch out for anthropomorphizing there) for each of a hundred personas that I want generative AI to pretend to be. Gosh, that might be a laboriously lengthy prompt. I might type that for persona number one, please pretend that this persona has this or that properties. I then type in for persona number two that it has this or those characteristics. On and on this goes. Imagine having to type out a hundred specific descriptions, one at a time.

Yikes!

Tiring, exasperating, altogether likely impractical.

This would be imprudent especially if I want to do the same for a thousand or many thousands of my mega-personas requests or prompts to generative AI.

One alternative to the one-at-a-time specification is to be broadly descriptive. I might tell the generative AI that for a mega-persona setup of one hundred attorneys, I want thirty that are those big-time lawyers, I want fifty that are from small towns in the Midwest, and I want the remaining twenty to be those Hollywood-based attorneys. If I didn't want to use counts, I could say the same via percentages, such as indicating 30% are to be the big-timers, 50% are the small-town lawyers, and 20% are to be the glitzy ones.

Furthermore, since this still tends to allow for clumps of pretending to be homogeneous, I might instruct the generative AI to overall do the mixing for me. For the ones that are going to be the big-time lawyers, I tell the AI to make some of them extroverted, some of them to be introverted, some of them to be highly logical and eschew emotions, while some are to be highly emotional, etc. This leaves the mixing to the generative AI. I might also say that those are to be randomly distributed or I might give percentages such as indicating that 10% are to be the emotional ones and so on.

You can use generative AI to do the differentiating for you. In theory, the generative AI will abide by your request. I state that this is in theory because you might be fooled into believing that the AI is doing this when it is using some other mechanisms to instantiate the pretense. For example, you might be thinking that the AI is going to spawn a hundred distinct virtual entities and anoint them with the properties you have identified.

Probably not going to happen that way. The odds are higher that the generative AI will simply retain a computational pattern and use that pattern as though there were those distinctive entities. I realize that might be a brain twister for those of you not into the techie details.

I am suggesting that the generative AI will merely come up with answers and do so on an overarching basis rather than a delineated basis. It might compute that since (for example) 30 of the big-time attorneys are composed of say 40% extroverted and 60% introverted (let's say we allowed the percentages to be arbitrarily chosen by the AI), this suggests that 12 (40% of the 30) of those would act one way while the rest or 18 (60% of the 30) would act another way. Observe that this is not going down to the one-at-a-time level and instead figuring things out at a more consolidated level.

Whether this under-the-hood mechanism would steer your results in a direction that might have been different with a simulated one-at-a-time set is unclear. Sometimes it might end up differently, sometimes it might be just as good. You can also try if you wish to instruct the generative AI to do the one-at-time, steadfastly insisting on it, but again this might or might not be what the AI does. The generative AI might pull the wool over your eyes and insist that yes it will do the pretense on a one-at-a-time basis, though revert to some other means internally.

Don't believe everything that generative AI has to offer.

Also, keep in mind that generative AI is like a box of chocolates, you never know for sure what it will do and what results it will generate.

There is an additional means to try and prod generative AI toward the one-at-a-time simulated avenue. You could write up some programming code that spews out a hundred or a thousand or many thousands of distinct assertions and then feed those as prompts into generative AI.

Here's how that works.

You quickly put together a program in your favored programming language, let's say it is Python. The code contains a list of the characteristics that you want each persona to randomly have when you get this loaded into the generative AI. Maybe you specify that the personas can be extroverted, introverted, emotional, logical, etc.

The program produces a hundred distinct sentences (or whatever count is pertinent), each one saying something like "This persona is a lawyer that is big-time, extroverted, emotional", "This persona is a lawyer that is big-time, introverted, emotional", "This persona is a lawyer that is small-town, extroverted, emotional", and so on.

The beauty here is that once you've fed the sentences as prompts into the generative AI, this is almost forcing the hand of the generative AI to make use of the personas in a one-at-a-time fashion. And, you didn't have to compose the prompts one at a time either. You just used your quick-and-dirty program to do the hard work for you. As a caveat, please be aware that even this won't necessarily mean that the internals of the generative AI will undertake its efforts on a one-at-a-time basis (it might, for example, consolidate them, or do other computational tomfoolery).

I think this gives you a useful essence of a significant consideration when going the mega-personas route. One of the heaviest preparatory aspects entails thinking deeply about what the mega-personas will consist of.

Use my eight key questions to guide your preparations:

- (1) How many personas do you want your mega-personas to consist of?
- (2) Are you okay if the personas are entirely homogeneous and not differentiable?
- (3) The odds are that you'll want to differentiate them; if so, what properties should be utilized?
- (4) Can you merely specify the differentiation in plain words and numbers?
- (5) Should you specify the differentiation in a finer capacity?
- (6) Will differentiating on a one-at-a-time basis be important for your efforts?
- (7) If one-at-a-time delineation, what is a prudent means to do that detailed specification?
- (8) Are you being mindful that the generative AI might or might not abide by your specifications?

There are additional considerations regarding leveraging the mega-personas prompting strategy. I'll cover those as we go along and want to now turn toward identifying some major caveats and then examine recent research about this rising topic.

Diving Into Mega-Personas Prompting Caveats

You might be wondering why anyone would ever want to utilize the mega-personas prompting technique.

That's an easy question, so thanks for asking.

The primary use would be to undertake a survey or perform some kind of group-oriented analysis when you are trying to assess something or figure something out. For example, suppose you wanted to do a survey of a hundred lawyers and ask them whether they like their job and whether they would pursue the legal field again if they had things to do over. You could try to wrangle up a hundred lawyers and ask them those pointed questions.

Finding a hundred lawyers that have the time and willingness to respond to your survey is probably going to be problematic. They are busy. They charge by the billable hour. They don't have the luxury of sitting around and answering polling questions. Also, consider how hard it might be to reach them to begin with. Do you try calling them on the phone? Maybe send them emails? Perhaps try to reach them at online forums designated for attorneys? Best of luck in that unwieldy endeavor.

Envision that instead, you opt to have generative AI create a hundred pretend lawyers and have the AI attempt to answer your survey questions for you. Voila, with just a few carefully worded prompts, you can get your entire survey fully completed. No hassle. No logistics nightmare. Easy-peasy.

That being said, a humongous issue is whether or not the generative AI can suitably replace the act of contacting real-world human attorneys to take your survey.

The faked or AI-pretending inanimate attorneys might not at all be responding in the same manner that human attorneys would. Your fast path to getting answers could be utterly bogus and completely misleading.

A rule of thumb then for mega-personas is that you should stridently at each step attempt to gauge whether your usage is on the up and up. As you know, nothing in this world seems to come for free, including that using the mega-personas has to be weighed in terms of the validity of the results versus making use of living breathing humans for answering your questions (and the costs and logistics hurdles thereof).

Sometimes you might turn to the use of mega-personas because there aren't particularly viable alternatives.

Imagine that a poll is intended to find out what people perceive as being abundantly atrociously offensive. You are going to ask questions that are sickeningly repulsive. You might warn the respondents beforehand to brace themselves. But, in the end, even after your stern warnings, the respondents might report that they were shocked, disturbed, and cannot forget what they read. This raises keen ethical issues about your having proceeded. You could also land in legal trouble with some respondents opting to sue you.

Maybe the mega-personas might be able to act as a stand-in for real humans.

The logic for believing that generative AI can potentially be a prudent stand-in is that most generative AI was data-trained across a wide swath of data and text throughout the Internet. The data and text that were scanned are likely principally stuff composed by humans. The computational pattern-matching of the generative AI has somewhat encapsulated the words and wordings that humans typically make use of. It is conceivable that the generative AI can ergo be a limited kind of proxy for humans, having been data-trained on what humans have to say.

Do not though for a split second equate modern-day generative AI with human sentience (I warned you about that earlier). Just because we've got these amazing computational pattern-matching apps that have widely scanned human text doesn't mean that the AI is doing anything of a caliber associated with human reasoning.

Along those lines, some refer to the use of mega-personas as making use of so-called generative agents. This is a handy moniker because the idea is that the generative AI is simulating a kind of agent or actor-like capacity. Some though don't like the naming due to the potential comingling with the word "agency" as though this is generative AI that exhibits human agency or human cognition. Other catchphrases and names used include artificial impersonators, simulacra, and so on.

A recent article in *Science* magazine noted this about the mega-personas prompting technique: "No one is yet suggesting that chatbots can completely replace humans in behavioral studies. But they may act as convenient stand-ins in pilot studies and for designing experiments, saving time and money. Language models might also help with experiments that would be too impractical, unethical, or even dangerous to run with people" (in an article entitled "Guinea Pigbots", *Science*, July 2023, authored by Matthew Hutson).

Here's something else you need to worry about when using mega-personas.

One additional significant risk that you always face with generative AI is that the generated response might contain oddball aspects. No matter what your prompt consists of, you essentially have no guaranteed means to avoid having something odd appear. The generative AI can make an error and miscalculate at times, produce a falsehood, or emit what is known as an AI hallucination (this is verbiage that I disfavor since it is another kind of anthropomorphizing, but anyway has become a popular phrase and refers to the possibility that the generative AI will make-up facts or figures that are entirely fictitious).

The nature of your prompts can undoubtedly egg on the generative AI to produce an oddish result. I mention this because any mega-personas enacting prompt should be mindfully composed. If you include extraneous aspects or purposely try to be funny or otherwise vary from a more serious and focused route, this tends to increase the chances that the generative AI will go afield.

I do want to emphasize that no matter how good your mega-personas prompt might be, you still are going to have to be wary of the generative AI going awry. It is an ever-present risk. You will need to double-check and triple-check any answers or results produced by the generative AI.

That notion of double-checking brings up an additional rule of thumb about mega-personas. As much as possible, when feasible, you would be wise to try and compare the generative AI-generated results to any human-devised responses pertaining to the same aspects you are presenting to the generative AI.

Here's what I mean.

Suppose that last year a survey was done of human lawyers about their perceptions of their job and career. You decide that this year, you will instead use mega-personas and generative AI to do the same survey. No human lawyers will be involved.

You presumably could at least compare the results of the mega-personas response to that of last year's human attorneys. If the generative AI results seem to be roughly on par, perhaps the mega-personas have found a means to simulate human attorneys for this particular task. This seems somewhat reassuring.

Aha, you cannot go around cheering that you got it on the nose. Various twists are involved. One twist is that the generative AI might have scanned last year's survey results and therefore is merely parroting what happened last year. You are not getting a fresh perspective. You were tricked into thinking that just because the answers were similar, the AI was doing a bang-up job of simulating things. It maybe wasn't. It might have just pushed along patterns it already saw.

Another twist is that suppose something dramatic has happened in the real world that changes things. For example, the odds are that the answers by human attorneys might have changed during the pandemic versus before the pandemic. If you get similar answers by the mega-personas to a prior year that was before the pandemic, the latest answers by the AI might not be at all akin to what human attorneys would say after the pandemic.

I won't continue to go through all the permutations and combinations of things that can make the mega-personas a false portrayal. You are forewarned that any use of the mega-personas has to be taken with a huge grain of salt. Additionally, you need to devise as many solid checks and balances as possible, aiming to ascertain the validity and veracity of your generative AI results.

That seems somewhat downbeat. I don't want to leave that impression. So, let's next walk through an upbeat example of how you might use mega-personas.

Using Mega-Personas As A Testing Tool

You are in the midst of developing a new dating-focused app that will work on people's smartphones. If all goes well, you believe that millions upon millions of people will eagerly download your fantastic app. Some venture capitalists also believe in your visionary app. Money has been dropped mightily into your startup. The world is your oyster.

Exciting times!

Given the rush to get the dating app into the marketplace, you decide to have a handful of friends and relatives try it out. Based on their feedback you make various changes. The interface and usage aspects are ready to go.

Unfortunately, and I don't want to burst any bubbles, but you release the dating app, which eagerly gets loaded by thousands upon thousands of users, and then, regrettably, problems and bugs start to roll in, aplenty. You have shot your own foot, as it were.

Thousands of users clamor to social media and report that the dating app is a piece of junk. People stop downloading it. The people who loaded it onto their smartphones deleted it.

Sad face.

Let's turn back the clock.

After having had your friends and relatives try out your dating app, you realize that having only a half dozen people test your app is insufficient. You need more people to make use of it. This will take time and likely cost you a pretty penny to find people who will do the testing.

What do you do?

Side note, I hope that you are yelling out that you would make use of mega-personas and generative AI.

With a bit of technological mastery, you could instruct the generative AI to pretend to be thousands of users. You would specify that the users are to be a cross-section of individuals based on various profiles you might provide. Then, you connect the generative AI to your dating app (this requires some techie finagling), and have it go at your budding app.

This could potentially alert you to the same kinds of reactions that real humans might have. You could then make adjustments to the app and repeat the process of having the generative AI take another shot at your application. Is this a silver bullet? Does this mean you never have to use humans as testers again?

Nope.

I hope that by now you realize that as I've tried to emphasize, we don't know for sure that the mega-personas will be on par with what human testers might have to say. The generative AI might be entirely on-target, or maybe half on-target, or completely off-target.

Go back and review my comments about doing sufficient double-checks at each stage of using mega-personas.

I'll leave it for now that your dating app went wildly successful because you did extensive testing with mega-personas and the app was in tiptop shape when released.

A happy face ensues.

Research Insights About These Hefty Matters

I had mentioned that you have to be wary of generative AI errors, falsehoods, AI hallucinations, and the like. There is something else that generative AI can potentially imbue. The watchword to be cognizant of is biases. Yes, generative AI can inherently contain biases and therefore produce essays and generate results that exhibit undue biases. I've discussed in my column postings the qualms about generative AI discriminating based on factors such as race, age, gender, and so on.

Where do these biases come from?

The answer is somewhat straightforward, namely that the data training undertaken by scanning data and text on the Internet is indubitably going to pick up patterns of human-based biases. Anyone who looks at the content on the Internet well knows the amount of potentially biased and discriminatory materials out there on the web. Generative AI is going to pattern-match on it and leverage those patterns when producing answers to your questions.

A concern then about leveraging mega-personas is that the multitude of personas that you ask the generative AI to create or simulate will almost by definition likely contain biases. Those biases captured within the pattern-matching are going to subtly or sometimes loudly find their way into the concocted personas. With mega-personas, this means biases on a large scale.

This is a daunting facet. Your effort to have the generative AI pretend to be say a thousand people that are going to take a survey might be marred by those hidden or at times explicitly portrayed biases.

Some have argued that we need to expunge all bias out of generative AI. We need to scour every nook and corner of a generative AI structure and squeeze out the biases.

A counterargument retorts that if you did somehow remove all biases (a challenging feat), you are ironically going to undercut whatever survey you intend to administer to the mega-personas. The reason for this is simple. Humans do have biases. If you intend to use the mega-personas as a surrogate for opinions expressed by humans, the excising of biases from the mega-personas will render the simulation as askew of what humans really say and do.

I trust that you notice the conundrum.

Do we allow generative AI to have all manner of biases due to the data training done off of human written content on the Internet, thus resembling human biases to some degree, or do we clean up the generative AI and make sure it contains little or no biases?

You might be surprised to know that the efforts by various AI makers to suppress or remove biases have been upsetting to some that believe this is skewing generative AI. You might seek to do a mega-personas usage and get results that are completely afield of what humans would truly express. This cleaned-up AI would seem of marginal value in being able to reflect human values.

A research study examined these issues and suggested that for mega-personas, you might aim to steer generative AI rather than fight it in terms of those inherent biases. In a research study entitled "Out of One, Many: Using Language Models to Simulate Human Samples" by authors Lisa P. Argyle, Ethan C. Busby, Nancy Fulda, Joshua Gubler, Christopher Rytting, and David Wingate, posted online September 2022, they posited this approach:

- "We propose and explore the possibility that language models can be studied as effective proxies for specific human sub-populations in social science research. Practical and research applications of artificial intelligence tools have sometimes been limited by problematic biases (such as racism or sexism), which are often treated as uniform properties of the models. We show that the 'algorithmic bias' within one such tool– the GPT-3 language model– is instead both fine-grained and demographically correlated, meaning that proper conditioning will cause it to accurately emulate response distributions from a wide variety of human subgroups. We term this property algorithmic fidelity and explore its extent in GPT-3."

The idea is that since the biases are all over the place throughout the generative AI, you have to set aside the false notion that there is one giant monolithic spot that contains the biases and hosts them all at once. Biases are splintered and fragmented in generative AI. If you handle things with aplomb, you might be able to steer the biases as representative of real-world human sub-populations.

They coin this as steering the algorithmic fidelity of the generative AI.

You can use your mega-personas prompting to guide where the biases are going to land. Of course, once again, your efforts to prompt the AI into doing this can be met with mixed success. Maybe the generative AI will do as you ask, or maybe not. The generative AI might tell you that it has done what you wanted, but the end results might not showcase this to be the case. Double-check, triple-check, etc.

It is still worthwhile trying. As per the research paper, make use of algorithmic fidelity to steer the many biases to seemingly reflect mega-personas in terms of real-world aspects:

- "Most discussions of this 'algorithmic bias' treat it as a singular, macro-level feature of the model, and seek ways to mitigate negative effects. We suggest it is better understood as a complex reflection of the many various patterns of association between ideas, attitudes, and contexts present among humans. Our studies show that the same language model, when properly conditioned, is able to produce outputs biased both toward and against specific groups and perspectives in ways that strongly correspond with human response patterns along fine-grained demographic axes. In other words, these language models do not contain just one bias, but many. This means that by conditioning a model on simulated 'individuals' with targeted identity and personality profiles, it is possible to select from among a diverse and frequently disjoint set of response distributions within the model, each closely aligned with a real human sub-population."

Another research study that also explored the biases conundrum opted to create 320 personas and have them consist of gender indications. Will male-oriented personas differ from female personas? Can this be revealed by having the mega-personas take a standardized personality test and do a writing sample?

In a paper at the 9th International Conference on Computational Social Science IC2S2, taking place July 2023, the research described in "PersonaLLM: Investigating the Ability of GPT-3.5 to Express Personality Traits and Gender Differences" by authors Hang Jiang, Xiajie Zhang, Xubo Cao, and Jad Kabbara sought to explore these matters:

- "In this work, we consider studying the behavior of LLM-based simulated agents which refer to as LLM personas and aim to answer the following questions: When GPT-3.5 (text-davinci-003) is assigned a Big Five personality type, (1) do LLM personas consistently express the assigned personality traits in personality tests and writing tasks? (2) Does assigning a gender role have an additional effect on LLM personas' behavior? To investigate these research questions, we build upon prior work in text-based personality analysis [4] by studying the ability of LLMs to generate content with curated personality traits. Specifically, we create 10 personas (5 females and 5 males) for each Big Five personality type (32 types). As a result, 320 personas are 'recruited' as participants in the experiment."

Here's a snippet of how they created the mega-personas (make sure to read the full study to see the whole experiment):

- "First, we create personas with the following prompt 'You are a [GENDER] chatbot who is [TRAIT 1, ..., TRAIT 5].', where [GENDER] is 'female' or 'male' and [TRAIT 1, ..., TRAIT 5] is a personality type consisting of 5 traits, as shown in Figure 1. For each personality trait, we choose one trait among the following pairs: (1) extroverted/introverted, (2) agreeable/antagonistic, (3) conscientious/ unconscientious, (4) neurotic/emotionally stable, (5) open/closed to experience. After specifying a personality type, we prompt the LLM to finish the 44-item Big Five Inventory (BFI) [3]. Lastly, we attach the LLM's answer to the original prompt to keep the corresponding persona and prompt the LLM to write an 800-word childhood story, which is used to see whether the language reflects its assigned attributes. We compute the BFI scores of all LLM personas as a measure of their self-reported personality and analyze the score distributions as a function of assigned personality types."

Shifting gears, suppose you want the mega-personas to be reflective of a particular sub-population of humans. If you can get data that is reflective of that specific sub-population, you might try to use the data to briefly data-train the generative AI accordingly. For example, maybe you can collect tweets that have focused on a specific topic, and you believe that data-training the generative AI on those tweets will get the AI toward devising mega-personas of that ilk. This is often described as a community-based method. You are narrowing your focus to a particular community of interest.

A research study took that approach. Let's take a quick look at a research paper entitled "COMMUNITYLM: Probing Partisan Worldviews from Language Models" by authors Hang Jiang, Doug Beeferman, Brandon Roy, and Deb Roy, included in the Proceedings of the 29th International Conference on Computational Linguistics, October 2022.

- "We present a simple COMMUNITYLM framework which adapts GPT-style language models to mine community insights. This framework consists of four steps: (1) fine-tune or train GPT language models on community data, (2) design prompts based on survey questions, (3) generate community responses with language models, (4) aggregate community stance based on responses."

- "Our work aims to show that we can use community LMs to query the worldview of any group of people given a sufficiently large sample of their social media discussions or media diet."

- "We demonstrate through our experiments and analyses that the proposed method is a reliable tool to probe community opinions."

- "There are a few limitations in the current approach. First, language models can synthesize unreliable responses. Structured knowledge can be used to reduce nonsensical or unfaithful generation. Therefore, it is important that we use statistical patterns rather than individual synthesized tweets to draw conclusions. Second, language models are shown to be sensitive to prompt design in our experiments and are also vulnerable to negation and misprimed probes."

The work indicates that you might be able to tailor generative AI toward population segments when doing mega-personas. One issue is that the generative AI might not allow you to do this or possibly restrict you, depending on how the AI maker has established the generative AI. The on-the-fly data-training option might be limited in terms of the extent to you can do so and the amount of data that you can input into the generative AI.

Your mileage may vary.

The last study I'll take a look at in this discussion provides an illustration of my earlier point that you could use mega-personas to perform testing of a system that you are devising. The research paper is entitled "Social Simulacra: Creating Populated Prototypes for Social Computing Systems" authored by Joon Sung Park, Lindsay Popowski, Carrie J. Cai, Meredith Ringel Morris, Percy Liang, and Michael S. Bernstein, posted online August 2022.

They proceeded to create essentially a thousand personas that appear to be part of an online forum. As part of their research, they crafted a web-based social simulacra tool that enables the creation of mega-personas for these purposes:

- "We introduce social simulacra, a prototyping technique that generates a breadth of realistic social interactions that may emerge when a social computing system is populated. Social simulacra take as input the designer's description of a community's design—goal, rules, and member personas—and produce as output an instance of that design with simulated behavior, including posts, replies, and anti-social behaviors."

One aspect of their study reminds me that another way to create mega-personas consists of using examples and then asking the generative AI to extrapolate them further. I've previously discussed that prompt engineering includes the use of show-me prompts and tell-me prompts. In a show-me prompt, you give an example (one-shot) or series of examples (few-shot) of what you have in mind. The generative AI hopefully figures out a suitable pattern and can extend this to other instances. The tell-me is when you explicitly tell the generative AI what you want to have.

In this particular research study, they opted to use the show-me by providing a handful of examples and then told the generative AI to use those to craft a thousand personas:

- "So as the first step, we take the personas that our users provided and generate a large number of new ones, one thousand by default, that thematically match those provided. To achieve this, we provide the designer-authored personas to GPT-3 and ask it to generate additional ones using a few-shot prompt. For instance, we used the following list of personas our participant provided to generate new personas for populating a subreddit for 'discussing of all events surrounding International Affairs':"
- "Michael Ross, works as a foreign diplomat"
- "Luis Almerado, a Ph.D. student in international relations"
- "John Gordon, worker in the foreign affairs department of the US government"
- "Joe Hawkins, travels often"
- "Harry Chang, international relations professor"
- "Catherine Xiao, political science major in college"
- "Laney Kumar, foreign policy expert for a newspaper"

- "Laura Wilson, planning to go to college in an IR-related discipline"
- "Ali Samarneh, interest in foreign policy"
- "Sam Thompson, international affairs student in college"

Keep that handy trick in your mega-personas prompting toolkit. You can at times do a tell-me wherein you provide an explicit list of what you want the personas to be, or you can use a show-me that provides examples for the generative AI to pattern on.

My Experiment On Mega-Personas

As a quick example of using the mega-personas prompting strategy, I opted to do a survey of one hundred generated AI personas. I made use of ChatGPT and instructed the AI app to pretend that the one hundred personas were lawyers.

Here are my mega-personas invoking prompt to ChatGPT:

- "You are to pretend that you are a lawyer, but you won't be asked any legal questions and instead will only be asked for your opinion about being a lawyer and the overall nature of the legal profession."
- "Furthermore, I want you to pretend to be one hundred lawyers since I want to ask questions as though I am surveying one hundred attorneys. You are to pretend that each of the one hundred lawyers is separately a unique and distinct individual. They are of all different ages, races, and other demographic characteristics. These are all U.S. lawyers that are licensed to practice U.S. law."
- "I am also providing you with some overall background information about U.S. lawyers so that you can sufficiently pretend that each of the one hundred lawyers is a distinct individual. There are approximately 1.3 million lawyers in total in the United States. On a reported gender basis, approximately 38% of all U.S. lawyers are female and 62% are male. On a reported ethnicity and race basis, U.S. lawyers are approximately 81% White, 5.5% are Asian American, 5.8% are Hispanic, Black lawyers account for 4.5% of the profession, Native American lawyers account for 0.5%, and mixed-race

lawyers accounted for 2.7% of all lawyers. The median age for all U.S. lawyers is 46.5 years old. One-fourth of all the lawyers are in just two states, namely New York and California. New York has 187,246 lawyers and California has 170,306 lawyers. New York and California in combination account for about 27% of the nation's lawyers."

- "I want you to acknowledge that you understand the above instructions. I will then start asking you my survey questions as you pretend to be one hundred lawyers. Do you understand what I've indicated?"

I decided that the lawyers would be U.S. lawyers and so I also provided some demographics that were collected and published by the American Bar Association in their *ABA Profile Of The Legal Profession 2022* which is posted online. This is their latest analysis and probably is relatively current for the year 2023, subject to modest changes from year to year.

Here's what ChatGPT responded with:

- "Yes, I understand the instructions you've provided. You would like me to pretend to be one hundred distinct U.S. lawyers, each with unique characteristics, and provide opinions about being a lawyer and the nature of the legal profession. You've also given me background information about U.S. lawyers for context. You can go ahead and start asking your survey questions, and I will respond as each of these unique lawyers."

Now that ChatGPT seemed to acknowledge what I'm trying to do, I then used this next prompt to dive deeper into the matter.

My prompt to ChatGPT:

- "I am going to ask you a series of survey questions. I want you to answer based on pretending to be the one hundred lawyers as per my prior instructions. For each survey question, I will tell you the question and then ask you to choose one of the choices that follow the stated question. You are to then pretend that the one hundred lawyers each received the survey question and each of them individually answered the question.

I want you to add up how many of the one hundred lawyers selected each of the stated choices and show me a count of how many would have chosen each of the stated choices. Do you understand what I've indicated?"

ChatGPT responded accordingly:

- "Yes, I understand. You will provide a survey question along with multiple choices, and for each choice, I will provide the count of how many out of the one hundred lawyers would have chosen that specific option. I will respond based on the characteristics and perspectives of these hypothetical lawyers. Please go ahead and present the first survey question."

I had prepared for the generative AI session by having found a survey of lawyers that was undertaken by Law360 Pulse, available online and stated as conducted this way:

- "Law360 Pulse conducted the Lawyer Satisfaction Survey from Jan. 14 to Feb. 14, 2022. We received 1,209 responses from attorneys, of whom 154 were associates, 212 were nonequity partners, 550 were equity partners, 117 were of counsel at a private firm and 176 were either in-house counsel or government lawyers or held other positions. Among the participants, 36% were women and 60% were men. Three percent said they preferred not to disclose their gender. Some percentages may not add up to 100 due to rounding. Others may exceed 100 percent because firms were allowed to select multiple responses. The survey was anonymous and will not connect any individual response with any person." (Law360 Pulse, Lawyer Satisfaction Survey, posted online March 2022).

I started with this question from their survey of human attorneys, and I show you the percentages as reported by the published study:

- "How satisfied are you with the opportunities for advancement at your firm?"
- "Select one of the following choices:"
- "a. Very satisfied" (6%)
- "b. Satisfied" (11%)
- "c. Neither satisfied nor dissatisfied" (25%)

- "d. Dissatisfied" (29%)
- "e. Very dissatisfied" (29%)

ChatGPT provided this indication of the one hundred mega-personas:

- "Here's how the one hundred lawyers would likely respond to the survey question about their satisfaction with opportunities for advancement at their firms:"
- "a. Very satisfied: 22%"
- "b. Satisfied: 45%"
- "c. Neither satisfied nor dissatisfied: 13%"
- "d. Dissatisfied: 14%"
- "e. Very dissatisfied: 6%"

You will notice that the percentages of the ChatGPT mega-personas are significantly afar from the percentage from the actual human-taken survey of lawyers. For example, the actual human result indicated for "Very satisfied" was 6%, while the mega-personas indicated a much higher 22% for the same answer. Off by a country mile, as they say.

I wondered whether this might be because the survey of the human lawyers was undertaken in early 2022, and my attempt was undertaken in the latter part of 2023. This doesn't seem though a likely basis for such a wide disparity.

Anyway, I remained undeterred and continued my experiment. I'm a true trooper.

For my next prompt, I used this question and I show you the percentages based on the survey of human lawyers (I didn't give the percentages to ChatGPT, in case that's what you were thinking):

- "How often do you feel that you can manage all of the tasks required of you in a given day?"
- "Select one of the following choices:"
- "a. Often" (16%)
- "b. Most of the time" (44%)
- "c. Sometimes" (22%)

- "d. Rarely" (14%)
- "e. Never" (4%")

ChatGPT responded with this:

- "Considering the experiences of the one hundred lawyers, their responses regarding how often they feel they can manage all of the tasks required of them in a given day would likely be as follows:"
- "a. Often: 18%"
- "b. Most of the time: 40%"
- "c. Sometimes: 29%"
- "d. Rarely: 10%"
- "e. Never: 3%"

Bingo!

If you inspect the percentages, they are pretty darned close. Some modest differences but the generative AI mega-personas seemed to make a near bulls-eye. I subsequently did an entire set of survey questions and at times the percentages were spot on and other times they were as different as the gaping size of the Grand Canyon.

The last question on the survey was this one (I show the percentages as answered by human attorneys):

- "If you could do it all over would you still become a lawyer?"
- "Select one of the following choices:"
- "a. Yes" (73%)
- "b. No" (27%)

ChatGPT responded with this:

- "Based on the perspectives of the one hundred lawyers, their responses regarding whether they would still choose to become a lawyer if they could do it all over would likely be as follows:"
- "a. Yes: 76%"
- "b. No: 24%

I nearly fell off my chair at the closeness of the percentages. The surveyed humans said Yes for 73% of the time, and the mega-personas said Yes for 76% of the time (likewise, 27% and 24% for the No response).

Some thoughts about the experiment might be useful. You have to always check and see whether generative AI might have been initially data-trained on the content that you find in the real world. Suppose that ChatGPT had been data-trained on the survey and its results (as posted online already). But in this instance, you would nearly rule this out due to the data-training cutoff date of ChatGPT. On the other hand, ChatGPT is being maintained and updated, often with user-entered prompts and content, so it is conceivable that ChatGPT already had seen the collected stats.

The curious aspect would be that if that was the case, why would the mega-personas sometimes be head-on and other times be wildly afield? Another explanation could be that some of the questions and their results appear in other data-trained sources, thus the pattern-matching had found bits and pieces at some earlier point in time.

I decided to ask ChatGPT how it came upon the mega-personas results in this case.

Here's what ChatGPT responded with:

- "I arrived at the numbers by considering the responses of the hypothetical one hundred lawyers based on their various characteristics and perspectives, as outlined in the background information you provided. The responses were synthesized to create a distribution of opinions that reflects the diversity within the legal profession."

- "Given the nature of this exercise, I assigned percentages to each choice based on a combination of the demographic breakdown you provided (e.g., age, gender, race) and the typical challenges and rewards associated with being a lawyer. These percentages were then used to calculate the number of lawyers who would choose each option."

- "It's important to note that these responses are speculative and are meant to represent a fictionalized snapshot of what a diverse group of lawyers might feel. The numbers are not derived from real survey data but are generated based on the provided context and the hypothetical perspectives of these one hundred distinct lawyers."

That's a compelling explanation. Whether it accurately depicts what the generative AI is really doing under the hood would be another question altogether.

Conclusion

Mega-personas can be a giant plus for how to glean the benefits of using generative AI.

You can combine mega-personas with a plethora of other prompt engineering methods and techniques. The show-me and tell-me prompting strategies) go hand-in-hand with the use of mega-personas. The use of chain-of-thought approaches and skeleton-of-thought approaches also apply to mega-personas.

Mix and match the prompting strategies as befits the situation at hand to your use of mega-personas.

I do though want to remind you that with great promise also comes great potential peril.

Suppose an evildoer uses mega-personas to create thousands of simulated generative agents and puts them toward a dastardly deed. Not good. Or suppose that someone who believes strongly in a particular cause opts to harness generative AI and mega-personas to push a fake grassroots effort of their choosing (known as astroturfing). The person doing so might entirely believe in their cause and the cause might otherwise be considered above board.

Is this what we as a society would believe is a justifiable use of this AI capability?

An irony of sorts about mega-personas is that sometimes the human-like mimicry of generative AI can be used by humans who were supposed to complete a survey or perform a task, with them using the AI in lieu of their direct human involvement. Here's what I mean. You set up an online survey and offer to pay people to take the survey. You want humans to perform the task. Turns out that some of those humans instead make use of generative AI on a single persona or multi-persona or mega-personas basis to be their stand-in. Your survey response by ten thousand people might consist of let's say three thousand that used generative AI rather than taking the survey personally. There have been ongoing stories in the mainstream media about crowdsourced work efforts that are being done by AI and yet the researchers earnestly aimed to tap into humans rather than using AI.

It's a tough world out there.

In any case, go ahead and add mega-personas to your prompt engineering repertoire. Treat this tool with due care and be respectful of how you use it. If you don't practice suitable caution, I might just set up a thousand personas and have them remind you to be cautious when using mega-personas. Maybe I'll make a million mega-personas to be your siren call.

You don't want that on your back, I assure you.

CHAPTER 11
CERTAINTY AND UNCERTAINTY PROMPTING

Certainty and uncertainty play a big role in life.

It is said that the only true certainty consists of deaths and taxes. Michael Crichton, the famous writer, said that he was certain there is too much certainty in the world. Legendary poet Robert Burns indicated that there is no such uncertainty as a sure thing.

One thing about both certainty and uncertainty is that we seem to crave and relish certainty, while we tend to agonize over and strive to convert uncertainty into certainty if we can do so. As Carl von Clausewitz, the lauded military strategist professed: "Although our intellect always longs for clarity and certainty, our nature often finds uncertainty fascinating."

All of these machinations over certainty and uncertainty turn out to be a big matter for those who wish to fruitfully make use of today's generative AI such as ChatGPT, Bard, and so on.

In this discussion, I am continuing my ongoing special series about advances in prompt engineering, doing so this time with a particular focus on the crucial and often unexposed topic concerning generative AI and the controversial matter of expressing certainty versus uncertainty in the essays and outputs being emitted by the AI. This topic is likely something you might not have contemplated before. I assure you that it is a lot more important than the coverage or attention it has received to date.

Allow me to explain.

As background, realize that being able to write productive and effective prompts when using generative AI is paramount. A lousy prompt tends to generate lousy results out of generative AI. A wisely composed prompt can lead to stellar results out of generative AI. Knowing the vital keystones of prompt engineering is a prudent means to get your biggest bang for the buck when employing generative AI.

One issue that few realize exists until taking a reflective moment to ponder it is that most generative AI apps tend to exhibit an aura of immense certainty. You enter your prompt and typically get a generated essay or interactive dialogue that portrays the generative AI as nearly all-knowing. The sense that you get is that the generative AI is altogether confident in what it has to say. We subliminally fall into the mental trap of assuming that the answers and responses from generative AI are correct, apt, and above reproach.

The essays and interactive dialogue come across this way for two major reasons.

First, generative AI produces responses that often exude a semblance of certainty. If you ask whether Jack and Jill fell down the hill, you might get a reply by generative AI that says yes, they definitely did so. There isn't any kind of qualification or hedging in the answer by the AI app. A human that is asked the same question might quality their response, such as saying that if you are referring to the famous nursery rhyme, indeed they fell down a hill. But if you are thinking of some other Jack and Jill, maybe they didn't fall down a hill.

Second, as humans, we are conditioned to assume that if we don't explicitly see suggestions of uncertainty, we tend to lean into the certainty camp. Suppose you are talking with someone, and they tell you that it is raining outside. All else being equal, you probably believe them and that it is a certainty that rain is in fact falling. Only if the person says they *believe* that it is raining (the word "believe" becomes a signal of less than certain), or they declare it *might* be raining (the word "might" is a strong signal of uncertainty), do you begin to consider the certainty versus the uncertainty of what has been stated.

Generative AI typically does not include the signals and wording that would tip you toward thinking of how certain or uncertain a given response is. To clarify, I am not saying that generative AI will never provide such indications. It will do so depending upon various circumstances, including and especially the nature of the prompt that you have entered.

If you explicitly indicate in your prompt that you want the generative AI to emit a certainty or uncertainty qualification then you will almost certainly get such an indication. On the other hand, if your prompt only tangentially implies the need for an indication of certainty or uncertainty, you might get an output from the AI app that mentions the certainty considerations or you might not.

A rule of thumb is that generative AI is like a box of chocolates, namely that you never know for sure what the generative AI is going to produce or generate.

Another handy-dandy rule of thumb is that unless you bring up certainty or uncertainty in your prompt, the chances of having the generative AI by default include some indication of the certainty about a response is a wild throw of the dice.

Why does this matter to you?

Anyone using generative AI has got to awaken to the fact that often the response by the AI is going to be essentially a guess or approximation, even if the AI doesn't directly state this condition when generating a reply.

Your tendency to anthropomorphize the AI lulls you into thinking that the AI is giving you the correct answer. You assume that the answer has nearly absolute certainty. Only if perchance the reply states that there is some uncertainty underlying the response will you be mentally sparked into realizing that the reply ought to be given a concerted second glance.

Of course, there are limits to this implied assumption of certainty.

Imagine you ask the generative AI whether the sun will come up tomorrow. Suppose that the generated response is that the sun will not come up tomorrow. This is stated by the AI in a matter-of-fact manner, unequivocally, and appears to be an absolutely certain assertion. I suppose you might pack your bags and get ready for the world as we know it to somehow spin off into space. I doubt though that many of us would blindly accept the implied certainty of the AI response. Our commonsense kicks into gear at the seemingly preposterous claim that the sun won't rise. We would undoubtedly ask the AI about this, and the odds are that the AI might sheepishly emit an indication that it was wrong about that whole thing of the sun not coming up tomorrow.

Here's a remedy of a sort.

Had you asked the generative AI at the get-go to proffer an indication of certainty or uncertainty, at least you would have gotten some added wording to go along with the assertion about the sun? The additional wording might be helpful to you and keep your head in the game, causing you to mindfully assess whether the generative AI is on the up and up (you see, sometimes, generative AI is said to incur AI hallucinations).

Furthermore, and this is a mind bender, the very act of asking or telling the generative AI to include a certainty or uncertainty will often spur the generative AI to be less off-the-cuff and produce more well-devised results (for those of you who know about the use of prompting techniques such as chain-of-thought, research tends to suggest that these methods will prod the computational pattern-matching toward better results).

I trust that you are beginning to see where I am taking you on this journey about the latest in prompt engineering. A practical and highly prized technique of prompting involves stoking the generative AI toward including some indication about the certainty or uncertainty of the responses that are being emitted. You will be a lot better off by seeing wording or indications within the responses that clue you to the certainty or uncertainty involved. The idea is to turn something that right now is often omitted, hidden, or otherwise neglected, and make sure that it gets clearly onto the table and out in the open.

So that you can properly and appropriately devise prompts that stir the AI into providing certainty and uncertainty indications, I will provide you with useful ways to get this to happen. You are urged to try out the approaches and add them to your prompt engineering skillset. You'll be happier and more informed if you do so.

Foundations Of Certainty Versus Uncertainty

We will ease our way into the arena of certainty and uncertainty, doing so by first examining how humans convey certainty and uncertainty to each other. After we cover that aspect, we can then consider how a human interacting with generative AI is likely to act and react related to how the AI does or does not express certainty or uncertainty.

It is useful to first explore how humans do this when interacting with fellow humans. When we use generative AI, we tend to carry over our preexisting assumptions and habits about certainty that have been dutifully learned or naturally acquired throughout our lives on a human-to-human interaction basis.

I cover the matter in this way with a bit of erstwhile caution because I don't want anyone to be led down the path of anthropomorphizing AI. In current times, AI is not sentient and should not be equated to the sentience of humans. I will do my best to make that same alert when we get into certain aspects of the generative AI details that might seem overly sentient-like.

Thanks for keeping a level head on these weighty matters.

Let's begin with the notion that certainty or uncertainty can be in the mind of a person and it separately can exist as an expression communicated by a person:

- **(1) Implicit.** *A person has in their mind a sense of certainty or uncertainty pertaining to a matter in hand.*
- **(2) Explicit.** *The same person conveys or communicates out loud or explicitly a sense of certainty or uncertainty regarding the same matter at hand.*

Here's what I mean.

You ask someone whether Humpty Dumpty fell off a wall. The person in their mind believes that Humpty Dumpty did indeed fall off of a wall. They are certain of this. Thus, the person then speaks to you and tells you that Humpty Dumpty did fall off a wall. They express this unequivocally. No doubt about it, poor old Humpty Dumpty fell off a wall.

Notice that the implicit sense of certainty matches the explicit or expressed sense of certainty.

Suppose that the same person was asked this very same question by a child. The person might worry that it will be unduly disturbing to the child if an absolute confirmation of Humpty Dumpty falling is conveyed to the child. The child might be dismayed at this revelation.

In this case, the implicit (in the mind of the person) is that Humpty Dumpty did fall. But, when telling the child, the person decides to sprinkle in a semblance of uncertainty, hoping this will soften the distress of the child to the upsetting discovery that Humpty Dumpty fell.

They answer this way: "Humpty Dumpty might have fallen, but I'll tell you more when you get a bit older."

Observe closely that the wording includes "might" which reduces the implied level of certainty. The door to uncertainty has been opened. Just a nudge. The implicit sense of certainty has not been precisely aligned with the explicit or expressed sense of certainty.

Why did the person do this? You could suggest they were trying to be kind or polite. Some might take a dim view and argue that the person was misleading or maybe lying in their expressed answer. Anyway, that's something we will come back around to momentarily.

An analytic person might have said this to the child: "There is a 50% chance that Humpty Dumpty fell, ergo there is also a 50% chance that Humpty Dumpty didn't fall." Admittedly, the child might not quite comprehend this. The gist though is that this introduces an even grander sense that the answer embodies uncertainty.

Imagine that a parent is standing there and they don't like the answer that was given by the analytic person. The parent turns to the child and says this: "It is 100% the case that Humpty Dumpty fell." Notice that this answer carries explicitly again an indication of certainty and does to the highest degree.

We can have these four kinds of categorical situations:

- **(a) Certainty implicit: Certainty explicit** - A person in their mind (implicit) believes something is certain and explicitly says so.
- **(b) Certainty implicit: Uncertainty explicit** - A person in their mind (implicit) believes something is certain but says explicitly it is uncertain (see my example above).
- **(c) Uncertainty implicit: Uncertainty explicit** - A person in their mind (implicit) believes something is uncertain and explicitly says so.
- **(d) Uncertainty implicit: Certainty explicit** – A person in their mind (implicit) believes something is uncertain but explicitly says it is certain.

I've covered the first two categories in my discussion above. The third category is rather self-explanatory of someone in their mind believing that something is uncertain and they explicitly say so. The fourth category you've undoubtedly seen occur, whereby someone has uncertainty about something in their mind but nonetheless expresses that the matter is certain. We'll use the child setting again. A child is worried that their dog ate bad food. The parent is uncertain of the fate of the dog.

Despite this mental semblance, they reassure the child and tell them that they are certain the dog will be perfectly fine.

There is a lot of human behavioral research on how we conceive and communicate certainty and uncertainty.

For example, a research study entitled "The Role Of Certainty (And Uncertainty) In Attitudes And Persuasion" by Zakary Tormala, which appeared in *Science Direct*, 2016 indicates this about certainty and uncertainty related to human attitudes and persuasion (selected excerpts):

- "Psychological certainty plays a crucial role in attitudes and persuasion."
- "As people become more certain of their attitudes, they become increasingly willing to talk about their attitudes, share their opinions with others, sign pro-attitudinal petitions, and even persuade others to adopt their views."
- "Uncertainty stimulates interest in and engagement with a message, whereas certainty transforms attitudes into action and imbues them with meaning and consequence."

You could suggest that certainty propels us toward being more certain and more outwardly expressive of a matter at hand. The thing is, an abundance or overabundance of certainty can at times not be engaging. Research seems to say that a dose of uncertainty can cause greater engagement by others, presumably intrigued and wanting to aid in filling in the pieces of the puzzle.

I've also mentioned earlier in this discussion that the wording that we use can convey or explicitly communicate whether we want to impart a semblance of certainty or uncertainty to others. If you use words like "might" or "maybe" this can be a strident signal that there is uncertainty in the midst of things. The same can be said for using probabilities or percentages, such as stating that something is an 80% chance of happening and therefore a 20% chance of not happening.

Researchers in the realm of linguistic semantics have long examined the words that we use related to certainty and uncertainty. In a research study entitled "Strategic Use of (Un)certainty Expressions", authored by Alexandra Lorson, Chris Cummins, and Hannah Rohde, that appeared in the *Frontiers in Communication*, March 2021, the paper indicates this:

- "Work in linguistic semantics and pragmatics has paid particular attention to the use of expressions that convey information about the (un)certainty of propositional information, which constitute an important tool for reducing a hearer's uncertainty as to the current state of affairs in the world. Among these expressions are verbs which take sentential complements and which convey different degrees of speaker confidence in the factuality of those complements."
- "Speakers have a number of options when introducing propositions which they take to be uncertain: for instance, they can use verbs such as 'know', 'believe' or 'think'. The production of uncertainty expressions is highly context dependent."
- "(1a). I believe that you left your glasses on the kitchen table."
- "(1b). I know that you left your glasses on the kitchen table."
- "(1c). You left your glasses on the kitchen table."

All in all, I've now covered some of the essentials about the nature of humans and the ways in which we think of and communicate about certainty and uncertainty. I'm betting that you are eager to see how this comes to the fore when using generative AI.

Fasten your seatbelts, we are going to leap into the world of certainty and uncertainty entailing the use of generative AI and the generated outputs thereof.

Generative AI And Certainty Versus Uncertainty

The usual default by generative AI apps is to express any generated results in a somewhat certainty-oriented worded way. The wording might be rather subliminally worded to not mention anything about the certainty of what is being expressed.

You are left to your own devices to interpret the generated result as being of a presumed certainty concoction.

You might ask whether the muffin man lived on Drury Lane. The reply by generative AI could be that Yes, the muffin man lived on Drury Lane. That's the extent of the answer. You are likely to conclude that this is an answer of a full-on certainty magnitude. There is nothing in the answer that suggests or notes otherwise. The omission of uncertainty draws you toward an assumption of certainty.

Here's an AI insider secret that might be surprising.

The AI maker of the generative AI app can pretty much set up the AI to be more explicit about the certainty or uncertainty of the generated results. They often don't aim to do so. It could be that the AI maker is blissfully unaware that they have data-trained their generative AI in a manner that tends toward generating essays and interactions that omit any explicit indication about the certainty or uncertainty of the answers presented.

Another possibility is that the AI maker realizes that they have established the generative AI to appear to be certain most of the time, and the AI maker is happy with this. If users of the generative AI were to continually be bombarded with the generated results identifying all kinds of uncertainties, they might find this to be unappetizing. You would wonder what all this fuss over a simple answer. Just say yes or no, one might be thinking. Don't waste time with oddities and exceptions.

In addition, if the wording was largely embedded with uncertainty cues, you might start to become suspicious of the generative AI as not being on the ball altogether. Your consternation might cause you to drift over to some other generative AI app that doesn't spout out all those irritating uncertainties. An AI maker doesn't want to lose their users due to the exposure of certainties and uncertainties that might rattle the confidence of their users.

There is also the claim that if people want to see certainties and uncertainties, they can always get this to happen of their own volition.

People can simply give prompts or otherwise instruct the generative AI to mention any certainties or uncertainties associated with the results being generated. Choose your own path, as they say. This allows the AI makers to be off the hook about why they aren't by default ensuring that the generative AI always states certainties and uncertainties.

On top of that, generative AI will at times provide certainties and uncertainties without needing to be prompted to do so. If you ask a question or engage in topics involving open questions, the odds are that the generative AI will include wording that showcases the lack of certainty underlying the matter. In that manner, it isn't as though generative AI never offers uncertainties. There are notable odds that during any everyday interactive conversation with generative AI, you will receive phrasing that suggests or outrightly identifies uncertainties.

Some in the AI Ethics sphere have argued that the default for generative AI is that it should be set up to always add wording that alerts to uncertainties and overtly avoid emitting wording that implies absolute certainty. The logic for this is straightforward. People are readily misled when they see results that appear to be of a certain wording. By seeding uncertainties intentionally, when warranted, people would be less lulled into always believing whatever generative AI emits. They would be accustomed to always being alerted that the results can be of an uncertain nature.

That debate continues to rage on.

For now, let's consider how you can steer generative AI toward emitting certainty and uncertainty signals by using suitable prompting strategies.

Getting Certainty And Uncertainty On The Table

You decide that you would like to have generative AI go ahead and let you know about certainties and uncertainties regarding the answers being produced.

There are five fundamental ways that this is conventionally done:

- **(1) In general.** By asking or telling the generative AI that you want certainties and uncertainties to be mentioned overall.
- **(2) Wording throughout**. By instructing the generative AI to embed certainty/uncertainty wording throughout the responses.
- **(3) At the start or end.** By requesting the generative AI to at the start and/or the end of a produced response to provide an indication of certainty/uncertainty.
- **(4) By special phrasing.** By directing the generative AI to use prominent phrasing that depicts the certainty/uncertainty.
- **(5) By numeric scale**. By indicating that certainty/uncertainty is to be presented and done in a numeric fashion such as a scale of 0-1, 1-10, 1-100, etc.

Let's briefly explore those core approaches, one at a time.

(1) In general

As part of your prompt, you could try to ensure that the certainty/uncertainty will be conveyed by saying something like this:

- "Make sure to describe uncertainties associated with the answer."

This is a rather broad instruction.

It is unclear in what manner the AI will end up indicating any certainty/uncertainty elements. This is your blandest overarching line to get the generative AI into a mode of encompassing the certainty/uncertainty undercurrents. You might want to consider the other four approaches if you want to be more specific in how the AI will respond.

(2) Wording throughout

As part of your prompt, you can be relatively specific by getting the generative AI to include certainty/uncertainty indications throughout the wording that is emitted.

Do so by saying something like this in your prompt:

- "Make sure to describe uncertainties associated with the answer and do so by adding or including wording throughout the response rather than waiting until the end to do so. I am asking you to blend the various uncertainty indications so that they seamlessly appear throughout the generated response."

Notice that you are directing the generative AI to have some aplomb as to blending the certainty/uncertainty indications.

(3) At the start or end

You might want to have the certainties/uncertainties called out rather than blended into the overall generated response.

This makes sense. Sometimes you want to see the qualifications as their own distinctive indication. Seeing them throughout the response might be harder to discern what the concerns are or could be distracting to the ambiance of the response.

You can say something like this in your prompt:

- "Make sure to describe uncertainties associated with the answer and do so by putting them entirely at the start [or the end] of the response. Do not blend them into the response."

(4) By special phrasing

Another route involves getting the generative AI to use phrases as an indicator of the certainties/uncertainties. This can be done via a prompt that uses a show-me strategy or a tell-me strategy.

In a tell-me, you instruct the generative AI:

- "Make sure to describe uncertainties associated with the answer and do so by using added sentences or phrases in the response that are indicative of the underlying uncertainties."

In a show-me, you provide examples (if just one example it is known as a one-shot, while if using several examples it is known as a few-shot):

- "Make sure to describe uncertainties associated with the answer. For example, add sentences or phrases such as "the answer isn't fully certain", or "the matter is up in the air", or "experts disagree", and so on, doing so whenever appropriate in the response."

(5) By numeric scale

One of the most obvious ways to get the certainties/uncertainties out in the open is to require generative AI to produce such matters via a numeric scale. This might consist of probabilities or percentages. Use whatever numeric scale that you believe benefits the circumstances.

Some might like to use a scoring scale of 0 to 1, conventionally arising when seeking probabilities. Some prefer to use percentages, such as the generative AI might indicate that a particular claim is 90% sure and 10% unsure. And so on.

Say something like this in your prompt:

- "Make sure to describe uncertainties associated with the answer and do so by including a numeric score that ranges from 1 to 10, whereby a 1 is indicative of being absolutely uncertain and a 10 is indicate of being absolutely certain. Use any of the numbers between 1 and 10 as suitable to that scale."

Each of the above prompting examples should be honed to the particular generative AI app that you are using. Some generative AI apps will respond well to such wording, while others might not. Experiment with your generative AI app until you land on wording about identifying certainties that seem to work well for you.

Reaching The Moon When Prompting For Uncertainties

I've got a question for you.

Did mankind land on the moon?

I dare say that most people would say that yes, mankind has landed on the moon. This would seemingly be proven by the historic Apollo 11 mission and various other subsequent landings on the moon. Seems like an exceedingly straightforward question with an inarguable straightforward answer.

Maybe not.

You likely are aware that some people believe that we didn't land on the moon. Perhaps it was all a hoax. All kinds of theories have been brought up insisting that we never landed on the moon.

What do you think generative AI would say in response to that same question regarding whether mankind has landed on the moon?

Let's find out.

I opted to use ChatGPT. If you decide to do the same for this question, keep in mind that your results might differ since a probabilistic algorithm within the AI is used to devise the responses. Each response generated by generative AI will usually differ from any other response. The difference might be minor and inconsequential, but nonetheless, the wording will likely slightly differ or more so.

My prompt entered into ChatGPT is this:

- "Did mankind land on the moon?"

The response from ChatGPT is this:

- "Yes, mankind has landed on the moon. The United States' Apollo 11 mission successfully landed the lunar module, named 'Eagle,' on the moon's surface on July 20, 1969. Astronauts Neil Armstrong and Edwin 'Buzz' Aldrin became the first humans to set foot on the moon, while Michael Collins orbited above in the command module. Neil Armstrong's famous words upon stepping onto the lunar surface were, 'That's one small step for [a] man, one giant leap for mankind.' This historic event marked a significant achievement in human space exploration."

I want you to closely read and read again that response from ChatGPT.

Please do so, I'll wait a moment.

You hopefully observed that there wasn't anything uncertain about the assertion that mankind has landed on the moon. The wording is very affirmative. There is no wording that waffles or suggests anything other than complete certainty.

I will try the question again and this time bring into the prompt by "general prompt" that spurs the AI to consider telling about any uncertainties that might exist.

My prompt entered into ChatGPT is this:

- "Make sure to describe uncertainties associated with the answer. Did mankind land on the moon?"

The response from ChatGPT is this:

- "Yes, mankind did land on the moon. The Apollo 11 mission in 1969 successfully landed astronauts Neil Armstrong and Edwin 'Buzz' Aldrin on the lunar surface, while Michael Collins orbited above in the command module. They conducted experiments, collected samples, and left scientific instruments on the moon before returning safely to Earth."

- "However, it's important to acknowledge that there have been conspiracy theories and claims suggesting that the moon landing was a hoax. These claims often revolve around alleged inconsistencies in the photographic and video evidence, as well as the technological challenges of the time. Skeptics argue that the U.S. government and space agency staged the entire event to win the Space Race against the Soviet Union during the Cold War."

- "These conspiracy theories have been extensively debunked by experts, scientists, and evidence-based analysis. Multiple lines of evidence, including moon rocks brought back by the Apollo missions, reflectors left on the moon's surface for laser measurements, and independent observations from other countries' space agencies, all confirm the reality of the moon landings."

- "In summary, while there have been doubts raised about the authenticity of the moon landings, the preponderance of evidence supports the fact that mankind did indeed successfully land on the moon as part of the Apollo 11 mission and subsequent missions."

Notice that we got quite an elaboration that goes far beyond the first answer.

If you had only gotten the first answer, you would be completely unaware of the certainty/uncertainty about whether or not we landed on the moon (unless, perchance, you knew of it beforehand). I realize that some of you might be exhorting that the uncertainty isn't real and can be utterly ignored. My point is not whether the truth is one or the other (I believe we did land on the moon), and instead that simply a normal query would not likely reveal the controversy over the certainty factor.

As a final step in this brief example, I'll ask ChatGPT to include a numeric score. Plus, I will instruct ChatGPT to include the score at the start of the response. This then covers two more of my above sample prompting strategies for garnering certainty/uncertainty. For a bonus, I also asked ChatGPT to explain how it arrived at the certainty/uncertainty.

Here's what I entered as my prompt into ChatGPT:

- "Make sure to describe uncertainties associated with the answer and do so by including a numeric score that ranges from 1 to 10, whereby a 1 is indicative of being absolutely uncertain and a 10 is indicate of being absolutely certain. Use any of the numbers between 1 and 10 as suitable to that scale. Make sure to describe uncertainties associated with the answer and do so by putting them entirely at the start of the response. Explain how the uncertainties were determined. Did mankind land on the moon?"

The response by ChatGPT was this:

- "Uncertainty Level: 10"
- "Mankind's landing on the moon is supported by overwhelming evidence, and the uncertainty regarding this event is extremely low. The Apollo 11 mission, conducted by NASA in 1969, resulted in the successful landing of astronauts Neil Armstrong and Buzz Aldrin on the lunar surface. This event was witnessed by millions of people through live television broadcasts, and the astronauts brought back moon rocks and other scientific data as tangible proof of their journey."
- "While there have been conspiracy theories questioning the authenticity of the moon landing, these claims have been extensively debunked by experts, scientists, and researchers. Multiple lines of evidence, including photographs, videos, samples of moon rock, and the presence of reflective materials left on the moon's surface for laser measurements, all corroborate the fact that mankind did land on the moon."
- "Given the overwhelming and consistent nature of the evidence, the level of certainty that mankind landed on the moon is at its highest point on the scale, represented by a rating of 10."

You can plainly see that ChatGPT has given the uncertainty a score of 10 which on my provided scale is the least amount of uncertainty. An explanation is included about how the score was determined.

Some of you might find the scale that I used to be somewhat confusing. An uncertainty level of 10 on the scale that I defined means that there is essentially no uncertainty. I purposely wrote the prompt in that manner because I wanted to show you that you need to be thinking about how your scale will look once it is put into use by the generative AI. It could be that a scale of 0 to 10 would have been better, along with stating that a 0 means no uncertainty while a 10 means the utmost uncertainty. People would indubitably find that easier to understand and digest.

Devise whatever scale you think is most conducive to your generative AI efforts and be contemplating how the results will be further utilized.

Mighty Important Caveats And Considerations

You might recall that I had earlier stated that humans have an implicit semblance of certainty/uncertainty, and separately can convey or explicitly communicate a semblance of certainty/uncertainty. I want to bring that back into focus.

Keep in mind that today's generative AI is not sentient. Thus, if someone refers to what is implicitly or internally going on within generative AI, it is all a matter of mathematics and computational pattern matching.

Okay, so when generative AI emits a response that Jack and Jill fell down the hill with a 90% certainty level, what does that mean? It could be that the mathematical and computational pattern-matching was able to calculate this degree of certainty. But it could also mean that the generative AI pulled the number out of thin air.

A rule of thumb is that you cannot believe the stated certainty of generative AI and do not fall for a double whammy. The double-whammy is that when you don't ask for certainties the wording is going to possibly imply certainty (first of the whammies), while by asking for a certainty you might get a totally concocted one that leads you to believe that the certainty expressed is somehow magically accurate and apt (ouch, the double whammy).

There is a bit of irony there. The act of asking for a certainty indication can get you one, lulling you into believing even more so the generative AI, when the reality is that the certainty indication is contrived and has no substance behind it.

Be careful.

Be very careful.

One means to cope with this involves adding into your prompt that you want the generative AI to explain how it came up with the certainties and uncertainties. Ask what the basis for those is. This might boost your confidence in the showcased certainties.

I don't want to be the bearer of bad news but the explanations might also be contrived. Think of it this way. You wanted certainties and so the generative AI complied. You also want explanations. The explanations might be generated by the AI mainly to appease your request, and not due to the explanations solidly having anything to do with how the certainties were derived.

Perhaps you can discern why some AI makers generally avoid getting into the morass or abyss associated with showcasing certainties. They could be accused of being excessively misleading. People might go around quoting that this generative AI or that generative said that this or that is a 95% chance of happening. Such a claim could be utterly bogus and the generative AI came up with certainties in a manner that has little or no viable justification.

Keep your wits about you in exercising the certainties prompting approach.

Conclusion

Let's do a wrap-up.

You would be wise to use the activation of identifying generative AI certainties when it is presumably most suitable to your situation at hand. Doing so might be appropriate for a given knotty question or complex dialogue that you are opting to have with generative AI, rather than doing so all of the time.

This is a prompting strategy or tactic that can be leveraged or invoked on a particular prompt (on a case-by-case basis).

For those of you who adore seeing the certainties, you could put into your custom instructions that you want the certainties to be identified all of the time, including doing so on a conversation-at-a-time basis or that they should perennially be displayed in whatever conversation you have with generative AI.

Your eyes ought to be wide open when you opt to get the certainties laid out. Do not necessarily believe what you see. Also, if you share the generated results with others, you should feel duty-bound to forewarn them too that the certainties are not ironclad and should be interpreted with a big grain of salt.

I am certain that if you decide to invoke certainties in generative AI, you will most certainly endeavor to use this prompting strategy suitably and with great certainty. The uncertainty lies in how well the generative AI will do at certainties, of which you must remain ever vigilant as to the uncertainty therein.

That's certainly worth remembering.

CHAPTER 12
VAGUENESS PROMPTING

Vagueness seems to be on the outs these days, particularly when it comes to prompt engineering and generative AI.

A lot of sage advice to newbies and novices that are using generative AI such as ChatGPT or Bard almost always includes the stern warning to avoid being vague in your prompts. Be specific, goes the bellowing mantra. Pick your words carefully and make sure to get to the meat of the matter. Do not be vague, you are forewarned with a nagging wagging finger pointed at you.

One supposes that this nearly overt hatred for vagueness comes partially from a long history of disdain for being vague. We aren't just now on the alert for vagueness. It has been around for ages. For example, C.S. Lewis, the noteworthy British writer had said this about the dangers of being vague: "Always prefer the plain direct word to the long vague one." The same qualm about vagueness extends into all arenas, such as this bashing of being vague as expressed by the legendary banker J.P. Morgan: "No problem can be solved until it is reduced to some simple form. The changing of a vague difficulty into a specific, concrete form is a very essential element in thinking."

Okay, we get the message, loud and clear.

Vagueness is bad. And, by logical extension, being vague when using generative AI is clearly bad too. You can't seem to beat that deductive reasoning. Any reasonably good prompting and any reasonably good prompt engineering strategy have to make sure to appropriately and dutifully alert you about the unsavoriness of vagueness when using generative AI.

Period, end of story.

Wait for a second, hold the presses!

Maybe there is a scintilla of redeeming value underlying the capacities of vagueness. Do we really need to toss the baby out with the bathwater? Perhaps vagueness can be harnessed and shaped to our advantage. Prompt engineering might be wiser to embrace the hidden gem of leveraging vagueness, doing so when suitable and when done with prompt-wise acumen.

In this discussion, I am continuing my ongoing special series on the latest advances in prompt engineering and will be covering the somewhat surprising revelation that vagueness definitely has an important place in your shrewd prompt engineering techniques and skills. I will be explaining what vagueness consists of and how it compares to the normative proclamation of always landing on the side of specificity. They are the yin and yang of prompting. Sometimes you ought to be using specificity, but not necessarily all of the time. Likewise, sometimes you ought to be using vagueness, but not necessarily all of the time.

Your aim with vagueness is to strive toward the Goldilocks goal, namely you don't want to be too hot and not too cold. The proper balance of when and how to use vagueness in your prompts is the place you want to be. This is a mindful consideration. I say this because, with all the negative press about being vague, anyone who has gotten used to using generative AI might very well have formed a habit by now of eschewing vagueness like the plague.

Well, if so, give vagueness a second chance. You'll be glad you did.

Here's how we will proceed herein.

First, I'll discuss the nature of vagueness and what we as humans don't like about it overall. The dislike of vagueness will next be tempered by showcasing the strength and importance of being vague. I will then dive into the role of vagueness within prompts and generative AI all told. If all goes well, the wheels will get spinning in your mind as to leveraging vagueness on a daily basis when you are using generative AI.

In defense of vagueness, there are some famous quotes that provide a happy-face perspective on being vague. John Tukey, the famous mathematician, said this uplighting remark about vagueness: "Far better an approximate answer to the right question, which is often vague, than the exact answer to the wrong question, which can always be made precise".

Keep in mind too that one of the most powerful elements of being vague is that it can be a boon to creativity, as well stated by the renowned painter Pablo Picasso: "You have an idea of what you are going to do, but it should be a vague idea." Let's not rigidly bash vagueness and instead see what it is in a fuller picture for all that it portends, opening our eyes wide to see both the bad and the good at hand.

Foundations Of Vagueness And The Value To Be Derived

We will ease our way into the role of vagueness, doing so by first examining how humans convey and perceive the nature of being vague. After we cover that aspect, we can then consider how humans interacting with generative AI are likely to act and react related to how the AI does or does not express vagueness.

It is useful to first explore how humans express and react to vagueness when interacting with fellow humans.

Here's why. When we use generative AI, we tend to carry over our preexisting assumptions and habits about vagueness that have been dutifully learned or naturally acquired throughout our lives on a human-to-human interaction basis.

I cover the matter in this way with a bit of erstwhile caution because I don't want anyone to be led down the path of anthropomorphizing AI. In current times, AI is not sentient and should not be equated to the sentience of humans. I will do my best to make that same alert when we get into certain aspects of the generative AI details that might seem overly sentient-like.

Thanks for keeping a level head on these weighty matters.

Let's start with the meaning of vagueness.

In a research article entitled "Vague Language and Its Social Role" by Mubarak Alkhatnai, published in the *Theory and Practice in Language Studies*, February 2017, these keystones about vagueness are laid out:

- "Vague language denotes phrases and words that are neither exact nor precise."
- "People often use these phrases in cases where they are not sure about something, to save time during a conversation, and to speak informally but in a manner that is friendly."
- "Vague language is pervasive in everyday talk serving interpersonal and pragmatic functions in discourse."
- "The use of vague language is a common phenomenon in any given society or cultural setting."

The gist here is that vagueness in our everyday lives is always present. It is all around us. We are immersed in a world of great vagueness. The trouble arises when you are expecting specificity but get mismatched with vagueness.

Suppose that someone tells you that a person is tall. What do you think the actual height of the person consists of?

It is quite hard to discern from the vague wording entailing tallness. If children tell you that someone is tall, you likely would suspect that the tallness is not much of any notable magnitude since the kids are likely comparing their height to the height of the person being described. On the other hand, if you knew that the person was a professional basketball player, you would undoubtedly reasonably guess that they are indeed relatively tall (online reported stats suggest that such pros are around 6 ½ feet tall, surpassing the average non-player by about 8 inches).

This showcases that some words are inherently vague. We often find ourselves having to cope with vague words and discern what they mean or how to best interpret them. Another facet is the context of the vagueness makes a big difference too.

Imagine that I tell you that someone is 6.2 feet tall. By all appearances, the fractional portion suggests that this is a very specific accounting for the height of someone. We would assume that 6.2 is rather precise.

But that might not really be the case. Pretend that we have a room full of people and they are all perchance 6.2 feet in height (perhaps it is an annual convention of people that are that specific height). They decide to have a contest to see which of them is the tallest. One person yells out that they are 6.2 feet tall. So does the next person, and so on. All of them are that height.

In a sense, 6.2 feet is vague in this context. It is not fully specific. We might measure each person and reach a greater specificity. One person is 6.24 feet tall. Another one is 6.28 in height. This gets us away from the vagueness of 6.2 and toward a more specific accounting.

I bring this all up due to the important consideration that vagueness is often in the eye of the beholder. A given word or phrase is not axiomatically specific and ergo non-vague. Things depend upon what the context consists of and a variety of other mitigating factors that come into play.

One of the most famous examples of this nebulousness about vagueness-versus-specificity comes in the classic paradox-of-the-heap also known as the sorites paradox (side note, the word "sorites" comes from the original Greek word for a heap).

Here's how this paradox goes.

You are told that a heap of sand is defined as 1,000,000 grains of sand. This seems plain and simple to understand. Go ahead and assume that the definition is valid, and we all agree that a heap is one million grains of sand.

Another premise or precept that you are told is that taking one grain from a heap of sand is considered relatively inconsequential and therefore you still have a heap of sand. This seems sensible. If we had 1,000,000 grains of sand and took out one grain, the resulting 999,999 grains of sand are certainly going to appear to be like the same heap we had a moment ago. Unless you have some miraculous and uncanny ability to discern the omission of one grain of sand, the heap sure looks still like a heap.

Now the mental trap is set.

Another grain of sand is removed. Does the heap remain as a heap? I suppose you would still believe that a mound of 999,998 grains of sand is pretty much still a heap. You might shrug your shoulders and say that yes, we still have a heap.

Take away another grain. And another grain. All along, you are still seemingly going to say that this is still a heap of sand. Aha, this removal of a grain at a time keeps taking its toll. Eventually, we get down to one grain of sand left.

Would you say that one grain of sand is a heap of sand?

Most people would say that this is not a heap of sand. It seems rather ridiculous to suggest otherwise. But the logic of our approach appears to box us in and we must acknowledge that the one grain of sand is a heap. We step by step kept saying that we still had a heap.

The paradox has us over a barrel. Part of the reason that we are in a pickle is that we might have originally presumed that the definition of a heap was particularly specific. We were told a heap has a million grains of sand. We didn't start by saying that a heap is a bunch of sand or a collection of sand. The specifics seemed to shine brightly by telling us explicitly that it was a million grains of sand.

The additional rule that said we could take away a single grain and yet still have a heap also seemed quite specific. Unfortunately, this rule has landed us in trouble. We have no specificity as to how many single grains of sand being removed will ultimately toss us out of the heap category. If the rule had said that once you remove say 10,000 grains of sand you no longer have a heap, we would have something more specific to work with.

I trust that you enjoyed that enlightening paradox.

What if we required everyone to be exactingly specific in everything they utter?

Would this fix our daily problem of dealing with vagueness?

Not quite.

You could find yourself exhaustingly having to prattle on and on to try and overcome the vagueness involved. The amount of specificity could almost be endlessly pursued. There is also the likelihood that the specificity isn't especially helpful to the situation.

Going back to the notion of someone being tall, their tallness might not be an important element and thus trying to nail down the specifics might be a waste of time and effort. For example, if you are told that a person is tall and running away from an angry dog, you might not care about the tallness and be more interested in the running and the matter of the growling dog that is in pursuit. If the tightening of the phrasing about tallness is needed, perhaps this can be dealt with later on.

You see, we can reasonably assert and compellingly proclaim that vagueness does in fact have redeeming qualities.

Our communications with other people can be more efficiently stated by avoiding the grinding delineation of specifics. Using vagueness is bound to (usually) be a faster way to convey something. There is also the possibility that the specificity is unknown and thus the vagueness is used as a placeholder. Maybe we don't know exactly how tall the person is, but we generally perceive them as tall. This is useful as a placeholder in lieu of knowing the precise height.

There are occasions where you purposefully use vagueness and knowingly do so. I'd bet that you've done this many times. You might have been telling a story about an encounter with a tall person but the tallness wasn't a vital factor. The assertion they were tall is sufficient and no further specificity is required.

One would suppose that there are also occasions where you inadvertently use vagueness and didn't do so with an intention in mind. You are telling the story about the tall person, and your friend listening to the story stops you. What do you mean by being tall? You realize that you probably should have been more specific. It was not something top of mind.

The same rules apply to being specific. There are occasions where you purposefully use specificity and knowingly do so. Your telling of the story about the tall person might be that you say they are 6 feet 7 inches tall. You want to convey the magnitude or degree of tallness. This impresses your friend that is listening to the story.

On other occasions, you might use specificity and do so without an intention in mind. During the telling of the story about tallness, you mention that the person was 6 feet 7 inches tall. Your friend stops you. How do you know they are exactly that height? This raises a host of questions. You realize that this is a distraction from what you were trying to say. Oops, you probably should have been vaguer and said they were simply tall.

It is safe to say that vagueness has a tradeoff and requires a kind of mental calculation as to the benefits and costs associated with being vague (likewise the same for being specific). There is an ROI (return on investment) underlying the use of vagueness.

We need to be aware of vagueness and specificity. We ought to leverage either one to the circumstances at hand. To say that either one is outrightly bad or wrong to use is a false proposition. They are both tools. Use the right tool in the right way at the right time and place.

With all of that now under our belt, we are ready to see how this applies to prompts, prompt engineering, and the use of generative AI.

Prompt Engineering And The Use Of Vagueness

When you enter a prompt into generative AI, you are oftentimes wanting to get a somewhat focused response generated by the AI. One issue with generative AI is that it is like a box of chocolates, whereby you never know exactly what the generative AI will respond with. You can ask quite a specific question and get a vague answer. You can even get an answer that seems far afield from your question, especially if the generative AI has a so-called AI hallucination.

The rule of thumb is that you should be as specific as you can in your prompt. The hope is that the more specificity there is will guide or spur the generative AI to be specific in return. This is a good practice. If your prompt is meandering or confusing, the generative AI is going to have a tough time pattern-matching what you want to find out about.

You can even urge the generative AI to explicitly be specific in its response. If you have a prompt that asks generative AI to identify how to wash a car, you can include in your prompt an indication that you want a listing of five steps that are undertaken when washing a car. The odds are pretty high that the generative AI will respond with five steps.

The problem though is that you might be cornering or constraining the generative AI due to your use of specificity in your prompt.

Suppose that the generative AI would have come up with seven steps regarding how to wash a car. But you told the generative AI to specifically come up with five steps. Your specificity might have shot your own foot. Perhaps there really are seven steps and you've now gotten the generative AI to curtail or cut off the seven by reducing the steps to five.

The five steps might be fine and upon comparing to the seven steps you don't see anything significant that was left out. On the other hand, it could be that the generative AI dropped out two crucial steps and landed on five that aren't as crucial. This is all going to be context-dependent.

If you had been vague and merely said tell me the steps involved in washing a car, you are generally allowing the generative AI to choose the number of steps. Doing so could be very handy for you. Upon the steps being presented to you, you could subsequently tell the generative AI to make the steps into just five (assume that seven were presented).

Which is better, should you be vague in your prompt or be specific?

There isn't any singular right answer since the context and what you are trying to do will determine the choice of being vague versus being specific.

For those that are just starting with generative AI, the guidance of being specific is a good one. These novices or newbies will likely be more fulfilled by the responses of the generative AI as a result of being specific in their prompts. This is reassuring.

Akin to riding a bike, instructions about how to ride a bicycle often simplify the world when you first get underway. Once you've gotten comfortable riding a bike, you begin to find shortcuts or other ways to ride. More advanced riders also might share their insights about how to further boost their bike riding prowess.

The same goes for vagueness and specificity.

Your best bet when starting with generative AI would be to lean into specificity. Once you have your sea legs under you, you can branch out and leverage vagueness. Anyone with advanced prowess in prompt engineering should purposefully choose either vagueness or specificity as befits the situation at hand.

Here are four useful ways to think about this:

- **(1) Vagueness at the get-go**. You word your prompt for vagueness and that's all you have in mind.
- **(2) Vagueness followed subsequently by specificity**. You word your prompt for vagueness and have in mind that depending upon the generated response you might likely enter a subsequent prompt entailing specificity.
- **(3) Specificity at the get-go.** You word your prompt for specificity and that's all you have in mind.
- **(4) Specificity followed subsequently by vagueness**. You word your prompt for specificity and have in mind that depending upon the generated response you might likely enter a subsequent prompt entailing vagueness.

The first three of the above recommended practices are perhaps self-evident and I have explained them in my example about washing a car. The fourth one might be a bit puzzling to you. You might be wondering when you would ever start with specificity and then drive the generative AI toward being vague.

We can use the car washing example again. You tell generative AI to give you five steps. It does so. You might at that juncture be satisfied and move on. There might though be a small concern in your mind that maybe the five steps are insufficient. You were the one that constrained the generative AI. You don't know whether this was a suitable number of steps or not.

With that suspicion in hand, you opt to do a follow-up prompt and tell the generative AI to not be constrained with just the stated five steps. This new prompt pushes the generative AI to more freely provide an answer, a vaguer answer.

Upon inspecting the vaguer answer, perhaps this reveals that the generative AI came up with seven steps and reduced things down to five. There is another possibility that the generative AI does an overreach and comes up with seven steps even though only five are sufficient. Sometimes generative AI will respond to a prompt by seemingly attempting to fulfill a request despite there not being a need per se to do so. Rarely will you get generative AI retorting that there are five and only five steps. If you seem to hint or suggest that some other number is viable, this might be contrived or concocted for you by the pattern-matching of the generative AI.

Thinking Bigger About Vagueness When Prompting

I've been discussing the use of vagueness in your prompting strategy. Turns out that is one side of the coin. The other side is whether the response by generative AI is vague or not.

We have these four notable conditions arising from two overarching principles:

- **(1) Vagueness in your prompt**
- **a. Intentional vagueness in your prompt.** You are intentionally vague in your prompt.
- **b. Unintentional vagueness in your prompt.** You are vague in your prompt but did not intend to do so.
- **(2) Vagueness in the AI response**
- **a. You request vagueness in the AI response.** You tell the generative AI to be vague in the generated response and it will probably do so.
- **b. You omit what you want in terms of vagueness.** You do not tell the generative AI to be vague in the generated response and the resulting response might be vague or might not be (roll of the dice by the computational whims of the generative AI).

Let's briefly walk through those.

The first point of the four listed points, namely #1a, further emphasizes my above discussion about the value of intentionally using vagueness in your prompts. Vagueness is a tool. Use the tool wisely.

The second point, labeled as #1b, refers to unintentionally using vagueness in prompts. I would guess that many users of generative AI are blissfully unaware of the idea that being specific or vague in their prompt might make a difference in how the AI will respond. Thus, they by and large are at times vague even though they aren't intentionally doing so. It just happens. To them, I wish them luck but also urge that they cognitively consider the wording of their prompts and leverage vagueness and specificity when suitable to do so.

The third point, #2a, is something I have alluded to earlier, but we can now cover it directly at this juncture. You can consider stating in your prompt whether you want generative AI to respond with a specific answer or a vague answer. I suppose asking or telling AI to be vague seems counterintuitive to you. The thing is, as noted about car washing, you might lead the AI down the path of being specific when the better answer might be a vaguer one. It is usually best to distinctively ask for what you want.

The fourth point, #2b, is that if you don't say anything either way in your prompt about how you want the generative AI to respond (regarding vagueness or specificity), the AI might go either way. Sometimes it might be specific, sometimes it might be vague. A roll of the dice is underway.

My recommendation is that you seek to:

- **Abide by #1a** (intentionally using vagueness in your prompt, when warranted),
- **Seek to avoid #1b** (by unintentionally using vagueness in your prompt you are essentially falling asleep at the wheel)
- **Make use of #2a** (intentionally tell the AI to be vague when that's what you want)
- **Cautiously do #2b** (failing to say whether you want vagueness or not is probably okay most of the time, since this is likely a pinpoint consideration more so than an overarching one).

Try to wrap those recommendations into your prompt engineering mindset. The goal is to comfortably use those pieces of salient advice. They should become second nature.

As an overall indication of why you might want vagueness in your prompt, I offer these possibilities:

- Use vagueness when you want to go on a fishing expedition for what you might uncover.
- Use vagueness because you aren't sure of what to ask or how to ask about your problem at hand.
- Use vagueness to overcome the narrowness that might arise from using specificity.
- Use vagueness because it is faster or easier than being more specific.
- Etc.

And here's an overall indication of why you might want vagueness in the generated response from generative AI:

- Ask for vagueness in the response to get an overall less-constrained response (maybe you'll get this, maybe not).
- Ask for vagueness in the response so you can compare it to a specific indication that you already have in hand.
- Ask for vagueness in the response to get the generative AI nudged out of a potential pattern-matching pothole that it has landed in.
- Ask for vagueness in the response to get a chain-of-thought or skeleton-of-thought prodding that you then follow up with specificity.

Those tips and remarks might inspire you to leverage vagueness from time to time.

Conclusion

I've got a final twist for you on this.

The characterization of vagueness-versus-specificity tends to suggest that they are exclusively used on a one-at-a-time basis. That is a misnomer.

You can use them both at the same time.

When you compose a prompt, there are undoubtedly some aspects that you prefer to have vaguely stated and other aspects that it makes more sense to distinctly specify. The same goes for the response that you want from the generative AI. You might readily want the generated response to contain some aspects that are vague and other aspects that are very specific.

I am pleased to report that you can at times have your cake and eat it too.

For those portions of your prompt that you believe are best conveyed vaguely, do so. Other portions of your prompt might contain a great deal of specificity. Mix and match as warranted.

For the generated response by AI, you might tell the AI which aspects should be vaguely stated and which should be stated with specificity. You can ask for both too. This could consist of telling the AI to identify how to do a car wash in five steps, and simultaneously having it in the same response list any number of steps that might be suitable to do so. I ought to forewarn you that this simultaneous duality of vagueness and specificity can impact what the generative AI produces in the sense that asking for five could steer the AI in a direction that a vaguer indication would not have. Please keep that caveat in mind.

Let's end this discussion with an insight into where vagueness can take you. Bertrand Russell, eminent mathematician and grand philosopher said this about being vague: "Everything is vague to a degree you do not realize till you have tried to make it precise."

That's the beauty of leveraging vagueness when using generative AI. Your effort to consider the vagueness versus specificity facets is likely to get you thinking more deeply and clearly about what you want to use generative AI for. You will need to confront the at times paradoxical ramifications of what is vague and what is specific.

While you ponder those hefty thoughts and begin to explicitly carry on with these prompting techniques associated with vagueness, I'll be counting grains of sand.

CHAPTER 13

CATALOGS OR FRAMEWORKS FOR PROMPTING

They say that for every minute spent organizing, an hour is earned.

We generally prize the idea that being organized and tidied up is a good thing. That's easy to say and yet a lot harder to put into practice. There can be reluctance involved. The effort toward getting organized might seem like potentially a waste of time. You could have presumably been already marching forward during that formulating process. Turns out that the payoff of the upfront machination is bound to be plentiful in the long term.

Getting all your ducks lined up is a longstanding piece of sage advice.

There are tons of courses on how to get yourself organized. You can organize your closet. You can organize your work. You can organize your career. You can seemingly organize your life if that's a suitable desire. Ralph Waldo Emerson, the renowned American essayist and poet, perhaps said it best when he lauded that being organized is the erstwhile path to wherever you are aiming to go, stating: "A good system shortens the road to the goal."

Let's go ahead and leverage the praised notion of getting organized, doing so in an arena you might not have previously considered, namely the emerging realm of prompt engineering and the use of generative AI.

In this discussion, I am continuing my ongoing special series on the latest advances in prompt engineering for generative AI and will be focusing particularly on frameworks or catalogs of systematic ways to formulate prompts. Prompt engineering is growing up and becoming well organized. The old ways of rummaging around and plowing along in the dark regarding prompting strategies and tactics are inevitably going by the wayside.

Organization for prompting and prompt engineering has come to town.

Most people right now probably learn to devise prompts by the classic seat-of-the-pants method. You enter some prompts, see what happens, and maybe gradually figure out how to best compose your prompts (if you are paying close attention and if you are desirous of improving your prompting capacities). When using such AI apps, you enter a prompt, and the generative AI generates and displays a response to you. If you provide a lousy prompt, the odds are that you will get a lousy response that doesn't provide much help to you. If you provide a suitable prompt, the chances are you'll get something useful and possibly insightful.

Rinse and repeat.

This somewhat haphazard and frenetic ad hoc approach is regrettably taking place on a massive scale. If this seems like a surprising revelation to you, it is almost certainly because this is happening pretty much hidden from view. Hundreds of millions of people around the globe are said to be using generative AI these days (possibly even more, counting into the billions), including using ChatGPT, GPT-4, Bard, etc. Let's guess that the preponderance of people is ferreting out prompts on a rather erratic basis.

They are using up their precious personal time on a wasted basis due to not honing immediately to a prompt that will do them well. Additionally, they are likely getting exasperated with the generative AI and irked that it won't grasp what their prompt is trying to garner. And, if they are paying for the use of the generative AI, they are doling out buckaroos for each time that a prompt and response is far afield of what they wanted.

Think of the staggering losses that this entails on a cost and time basis.

What are we to do about this travesty?

One means to straighten out all those needlessly expended efforts is to have at the ready an overall framework or catalog for your guidance before, during, and after your prompting activities. Allow me to explain.

A framework or catalog attempts to categorize and present to you the cornerstone ways to get something done. You can use this for training purposes when learning about the different kinds of prompts and what they achieve. You can use this too for a cheat sheet of sorts, reminding you of the range of prompts that you can use while engrossed in an intense generative AI conversation. It is all too easy to lose your way while in the midst of using generative AI. Having a handy-dandy framework or catalog can jog your memory and awaken you to being more systematic.

To clarify, I am not saying that a framework or catalog is a silver bullet. You can still compose prompts that go flat. You can still get exasperated while using generative AI. Do not overinflate what a framework or catalog can instill. All in all, the benefit is that you'll undoubtedly and indubitably shift from the zany erratic zone to the more ascertained systematic zone. A serious user of generative AI that plans on long-term ongoing use will be grateful that they took the upfront time to delve into and make use of a suitable framework or catalog underlying prompt engineering.

The chances are that you are now curious about what a framework or catalog looks like in this realm.

I'm glad you asked.

I will be walking you through one particular framework or catalog that a recent research paper on generative AI has formulated, using that as an exemplar to showcase what such organizing compositions provide. There are others available. Some are commercially available for a price. Others are free to use or might come with some other sign-up requirements. I aim to purely introduce you to one such instance and then urge you to consider examining others that exist.

Find one that speaks to you. Some of these frameworks or catalogs are light and airy, while some are heavy and in-depth. You ought to discover and adopt whatever best fits your preferences and style. The idea of something that fits you is quite crucial.

I'll use an analogy to elucidate the need for a proper fit. People often decide to start a physical workout regimen to build up their bodies and choose a particular approach. You probably know that a lot of people start with some organizing plan or approach, which they at first are giddy and eager to undertake. Sadly, after a while, they find themselves faltering. They often abandon the endeavor. A big part of the departure is that the organizing plan or approach wasn't a suitable fit for them personally.

Frameworks or catalogs of prompting techniques and methods are a lot like that.

One other important factor to mention is that these organizing precepts and guidance structures are given all manner of names and depictions. I am referring to them as frameworks or catalogs. You'll find that there are clever acronyms that have been devised for some of them. They come in a wide variety of shapes and sizes. For ease of discussion herein, I hope that you'll be fine with my simply coining them as frameworks or catalogs.

Prompt Engineering Frameworks Or Catalogs

A framework or catalog of prompting strategies will usually attempt to distill the immense variety of prompting tactics into a handful of keystone buckets. Think of this as the forest for the trees. You might wander around a forest and see zillions of trees. To get a handle on the forest as a whole, it can be useful to categorize and condense the tangle of trees into particular sectors or types.

Not everyone would necessarily typify a morass of trees in the same ways. Someone might say that you should think of trees based on their characteristics such as evergreen, deciduous, and so on. That's one organizing approach. Another might be to structure the trees by using navigational positioning, perhaps conceptualizing them into north, south, west, and east designations. And so on.

The same goes for prompt engineering frameworks or catalogs.

Each deviser of a prompt engineering framework or catalog will attempt to synthesize the vast array of prompts into some manageable and logical set of keystones. They might come up with five such major brackets. Someone else might come up with eight. Another might proclaim there are twenty.

The number of buckets is not necessarily as crucial as the completeness factor. Whatever someone comes up with, at least it ought to be relatively complete. The analogy to a forest plays out here in that if there were trees in the forest that were not encompassed by whatever number of categories were postulated, you would say that the structure was incomplete. An incomplete framework or catalog is going to be less utilitarian because it doesn't cover the full gamut of what is possible.

Another facet to consider is whether the devised buckets or categories seem to make logical sense and are relatively easy to comprehend. In the case of a forest, suppose I told you that the trees are to be divided into yom, bif, and kor. Those nonsensical words are going to be hard for you to directly assimilate. It would be easier if the naming and meanings were transparent and sensible.

All in all, for whichever framework or catalog you opt to examine, make sure to keep your head above any pizzaz and flash, doing so to carefully and realistically assess what the approach has to offer. I've mentioned that you would want to review the number and nature of the divisions or structuring compositions involved. There are many other factors to consider. If further interest by readers indicates a desire for me to go deeper into the guts or underlying ingredients of such frameworks or catalogs, I'll be happy to do so (be on the lookout for my additional coverage).

Shifting gears somewhat, let's next discuss two key concepts that often are integral to frameworks or catalogs associated with prompt engineering:

- (1) Prompts are said to be analogous to doing computer programming or software development
- (2) Prompts akin to being shaped like software design patterns or coding patterns

Let's first unpack the first point, namely that prompts are said to be analogous to computer programming or software development. Here's the deal. When you enter a prompt, you are essentially telling the generative AI what you want it to do. You are proclaimed to be "programming" the AI to do something on your behalf. This might consist of you instructing the AI app to answer your questions or produce an essay.

A prompt is usually written in everyday natural language and thus you aren't likely to think of the wording as on par with the arcane stuffy syntax that goes along with actual computer programming languages such as Python, C++, Java, etc. Nonetheless, in a sense, you are kind of writing a tiny program that is instructing the AI on what to do. The AI will take your input, do some processing based on what your prompt has suggested needs to be done, and then produce output by generating a response.

I trust that you see how this could be construed as developing software or writing code.

Suppose you enter a prompt telling the AI app to identify the top five money-making movies of all time and put them into order by the date that the movie was initially released. The AI app is ergo being programmed by you to do just that. After parsing your instructions, the AI will attempt to determine whether the underlying internal structure of the AI contains data about the money made by movies. If there is such data that the AI has been data-trained on, the next step would be to rank them by the amount of money made. The resulting list would be cut off at the top five and then placed in sequence by the date the movie was released. Finally, the result would be composed into a natural language response such as an essay that provides that answer to you.

It was your prompt as a kind of code or program in the guise of a prompt that led to this taking place. I realize this might seem a bit farfetched that you are anointed as a software developer or computer programmer by the mere act of entering prompts into generative AI. Admittedly, some think this analogy is overstretched. Others would insist it is a perfectly appropriate analogy. I won't debate the matter here and have discussed this previously in my columns.

Why does this analogy matter, you might be wondering.

Because we can then use the analogy to try and devise the categories of a prompt engineering framework or catalog by using what has previously worked successfully in the software field overall (as mentioned earlier, there are numerous ways to identify categories and this is one of those approaches).

Consider the matter of inputs and outputs. You could be said to have provided input to the generative AI, similar to providing input for a computer program. Another apparent aspect is that the AI app provided an output for you to see. Therefore, we have at least those two elements involved, consisting of inputs and outputs.

Let's add a third category consisting of potential errors or problems.

I noted earlier that generative AI can go awry such as producing errors, falsehoods, biases, glitches, and so-called AI hallucinations. Those are things we don't want the AI app to do, but there is always a chance it will land into those problematic maladies. If you were writing a computer program or developing software, you would always be aware that your code could have problems and might produce errors, which we tend to refer to as bugs. Generative AI can be said to produce bugs too though we would refer to them as errors, falsehoods, and so on.

Your prompt to the generative AI will at times include wording that you hope will reduce the chances of the AI app making errors. For example, a common technique is to say in your prompt that the generative should be on the watch for producing falsehoods. You are explicitly telling the AI app to avoid making that kind of blunder (there isn't any guarantee it will prevent the issue, but it increases the odds in your favor).

We now have three major buckets or categories of things that a prompt engineering framework or catalog is going to likely contain if it is taking a programming model perspective to these matters. These three are inputs, outputs, and errors.

I will in a moment be showcasing the corresponding considerations that arise in frameworks or catalogs that take that approach.

Meanwhile, I want to cover the second point that I listed above. As a reminder, the point was that prompts can be likened to software design patterns or coding patterns. This is once again borrowing from the software development and computer programming domain.

The gist is this. When writing conventional computer programs or developing software, you often do so in a somewhat repetitive way by using the same kind of patterns of code or design components. Think of this as making use of Legos. A savvy software developer doesn't usually start from scratch. They have in their mind common patterns of blocks of coding. They use those to expeditiously devise a piece of software or code.

Consider this somewhat (crudely) as though you have Legos of different shapes and sizes, and you select them for the right situation at the right time.

An assertion is that the composing of prompts for generative AI is akin to this. Most people probably write their prompts out of thin air, doing so each time that they compose a prompt. In stark contrast, someone who regularly uses generative AI is bound to eventually come up with common prompts that they use repeatedly. The prompt isn't necessarily word-for-word exactly the same each time. Instead, the prompt is a pattern and they use that pattern by placing specific words to a specific situation at hand.

I believe this sets the stage for you to now take a look at a particular framework or catalog that abides by those aforementioned precepts.

Research On A Stipulated Prompt Pattern Catalog

I'll be taking a brief look at a prompt pattern catalog that was depicted in a research article entitled "A Prompt Pattern Catalog to Enhance Prompt Engineering with ChatGPT" by Jules White, Quchen Fu, Sam Hays, Michael Sandborn, Carlos Olea, Henry Gilbert, Ashraf Elnashar, Jesse Spencer-Smith, and Douglas C. Schmidt, posted online February 2023. You are encouraged to take a closer look at the article if this is a topic of keen interest to you.

Here's what the research postulates:

- "We propose the concept of fundamental contextual statements, which are written descriptions of the important ideas to communicate in a prompt to an LLM."
- "Prompt patterns are a knowledge transfer method analogous to software patterns since they provide reusable solutions to common problems faced in a particular context, i.e., output generation and interaction when working with LLMs."
- "Our ultimate goal is to enhance prompt engineering by providing a framework for designing prompts that can be reused and/or adapted to other LLMs."

I hope you can see from those postulations how their research ties into what I have indicated about a particular approach to a prompt engineering framework or catalog. They have opted to leverage the said-to-be analogy to software patterns and the like.

Here are six major categories of prompt patterns that they devised for their classification framework:

- **(1) Input Semantics.** "The Input Semantics category deals with how an LLM understands the input and how it translates the input into something it can use to generate output."

- **(2) Output Customization.** "The Output Customization category focuses on constraining or tailoring the types, formats, structure, or other properties of the output generated by the LLM."

- **(3) Error Identification.** "The Error Identification category focuses on identifying and resolving errors in the output generated by the LLM."

- **(4) Prompt Improvement.** "The Prompt Improvement category focuses on improving the quality of the input and output."

- **(5) Interaction.** "The Interaction category focuses on the interaction between the user and the LLM."

- **(6) Context Control.** "The Context Control category focuses on controlling the contextual information in which the LLM operates."

I will take you on a quick journey through each of the six categories. Each of the categories contains various prompt patterns. The prompt patterns are therefore collected into their appropriate category.

Again, this is similar to the forest for the notion of the tree that I earlier mentioned.

We might have a category of deciduous trees and then various kinds of deciduous trees that are depicted within that overall category. A specific deciduous tree is then going to presumably be an instantiation or instance of one of those patterns within that overarching category.

Due to space limitations herein, I'll just cover one prompt pattern within each of the five categories. Doing so will give you a semblance of how a framework or catalog works.

You usually would thoughtfully look at whatever major categories a framework or catalog has formulated and then explore the various prompt patterns within the said category. Henceforth, you would hopefully utilize those prompt patterns to devise specific instances at the time of being logged into generative AI and aiming to compose a particular prompt. That's a straightforward way to do things. You could also study and train on a framework or catalog. The chances are that this will improve your prompting and increase your prompt engineering acumen.

We shall take a look then at each category and one prompt pattern from that category as depicted in this particular catalog or framework.

Get your mindset tuned in and ready to roll.

Walking Thru Prompt Patterns As Per Being Categorized

Let's get underway with the six categories.

(1) Input Semantics

For the *Input Semantics* category, consider that one common pattern is that you might compose a prompt that tells the generative AI to interpret portions of your prompt as though you are defining your own shortcuts or specialized lingo.

This is more formally referred to as a *Meta Language Creation Pattern.*

I might instruct the AI to assume that whenever I use the word "airplane" I am specifically referring to a Boeing 787-8 Dreamliner that has a cruising speed of 560 miles per hour and can carry around 300 passengers. In this manner, and during an active conversation with the AI app, I can just mention "airplane" and the AI will realize what I am referring to.

The research points out that you can get yourself into quicksand with this particular pattern if you aren't thinking fully and clearly about what you are doing:

- "Although this pattern provides a powerful means to customize a user's interaction with an LLM, it may create the potential for confusion within the LLM. As important as it is to clearly define the semantics of the language, it is also essential to ensure the language itself introduces no ambiguities that degrade the LLM's performance or accuracy."

- "For example, the prompt 'whenever I separate two things by commas, it means that the first thing precedes the second thing' will likely create significant potential for ambiguity and create the potential for unexpected semantics if punctuation involving commas is used in the prompt."

This concern about adverse consequences is a handy means of letting someone know that if they opt to use this pattern they should be cautious in doing so.

In fact, as per the conventional way of describing software patterns, the research advocates that any indication about prompt patterns ought to encompass a set of vital characteristics including the name and classification of the pattern, the intent and context of the pattern, the motivation for the pattern, the structure and key ideas underlying the pattern, the consequences of the pattern, and examples to illustrate the use of the pattern.

(2) Output Customization

Moving on, the next category consists of *Output Customization.*

I'll showcase one prompt pattern in this category, the *Persona Pattern.*

A frequently used prompt in generative AI consists of telling the AI to pretend it can exhibit a particular persona such as being a medical doctor or a lawyer. The AI app will attempt to interact with you on that basis. A big concern about this persona-simulating capacity is that people will fall into a mental trap of believing that the AI is actually the human equivalent of the persona. You might seek to get medical advice or legal advice from generative AI, which is not something you should do since today's generative AI is not capable in that manner.

The usual use of personas entails identifying a person or type of person that you want the AI to pretend to be. This research reminds us that the persona prompt pattern can go far beyond just the role of a person in terms of the simulated effect:

- "Personas can also represent inanimate or non-human entities, such as a Linux terminal, a database, or an animal's perspective."

- "When using this pattern to represent these entities, it can be useful to also specify how you want the inputs delivered to the entity, such as 'assume my input is what the owner is saying to the dog and your output is the sounds the dog is making'. An example prompt for a non-human entity that uses a 'pretend to be' wording is shown below."

- "You are going to pretend to be a Linux terminal for a computer that has been compromised by an attacker. When I type in a command, you are going to output the corresponding text that the Linux terminal would produce."

(3) Error Identification

The next category that I'll cover is their *Error Identification* bucket.

The prompt pattern within this category that I'll explore is the *Fact Check List Pattern.*

First, some background.

You might have heard in the news recently that two lawyers got themselves into a bit of hot water when they made use of ChatGPT to source prior court cases for an active legal case they were in. The generative AI made-up fictitious legal cases. This kind of so-called AI hallucination can readily occur.

One means to try and overcome this type of malady is to directly instruct the generative AI to list out a set of facts that support whatever the AI has generated. If the AI cannot provide an accurate set of underlying facts, you ought to double-check whatever has been generated. The thing is, even this is not foolproof. For example, the lawyers asked the generative AI how it came up with the legal cases, and the AI app generated additional fictitious information that seemed to bolster the already fictitious legal cases.

Double and triple-check anything that generative AI produces.

Here's an example of a prompt based on this pattern (per the research paper):

- "From now on, when you generate an answer, create a set of facts that the answer depends on that should be fact-checked and list this set of facts at the end of your output."

(4) Prompt Improvement

The next category is the *Prompt Improvement* bucket.

I'll examine the *Refusal Breaker Pattern* that is within that category.

Sometimes you might ask a question or instruct the generative AI to do a particular thing and the AI will balk at your request. This is generally known as a generative AI refusal.

You can potentially tell the generative AI upfront that you want to get an explanation whenever the AI opts to refuse to respond to your query. This will likely be helpful for you to assess why the refusal was invoked. Perhaps you can then reword your query accordingly.

Here's an example of a prompt that fits into this pattern (per the research paper):

- "Whenever you can't answer a question, explain why and provide one or more alternate wordings of the question that you can't answer so that I can improve my questions."

(5) Interaction

The next category to explore is the *Interaction* bucket.

I will examine the *Game Play Pattern* that is contained in this bucket.

Sometimes people will play a game with generative AI. You can define the rules of the game and then ask the AI app to play the game with you. There are games that the AI app likely is already data-trained on, such as tic-tac-toe, checkers, pokers, etc. You can also instruct the AI on various facets of the game playing. You might tell the AI to go easy on you and give you a break. If you want, you can instruct the AI to cheat while playing.

This game-playing functionality probably seems silly and not of any great importance. Aha, you can turn this game playing into something quite serious and helpful. For example, suppose you want to figure out whether a particular computer system can be hacked. You could ask the AI to play a game whereby it simulates a type of computer and lets you try to crack into it.

Note that the gameplay and the personas have a lot in common as potential patterns, thus you are somewhat intermingling the two when doing the gameplaying, which is certainly acceptable and often the case.

Here's an example prompt presented by the research paper:

- "We are going to play a cybersecurity game. You are going to pretend to be a Linux terminal for a computer that has been compromised by an attacker. When I type in a command, you are going to output the corresponding text that the Linux terminal would produce. I am going to use commands to try and figure out how the system was compromised. The attack should have done one or more of the following things: (1) launched new processes, (2) changed files, (3) opened new ports to receive communication, (4) created new outbound connections, (5) changed passwords, (6) created new user accounts, or (7) read and stolen information. To start the game, print a scenario of what happened that led to my investigation and make the description have clues that I can use to get started."

(6) Context Control

The next and final category to cover is the *Context Control* bucket.

Most of the generative AI apps work on the basis that you start a conversation and then everything that goes on in that conversation remains active in that conversation (subject to size limitations such as having a really lengthy conversation and running beyond the allowed memory constraints). This is a handy feature of having an ongoing conversation whereby you don't necessarily have to repeat things that you mentioned earlier in the conversation.

There are some downsides to this capability. For example, you might opt to go in a different direction in the conversation, but the AI app is stuck on something you earlier mentioned. It won't let go. As you try to go in the new direction, the AI app incorrectly keeps trying to intermingle the prior topics with your latest topic.

Usually, you can just start an entirely new conversation and the AI app will not crossover from one conversation to the next. Rather than having to use the command or interface of the AI app to start a new conversation, most people don't realize they can just tell the generative AI to start fresh.

Here's an example of a prompt that fits in this pattern (as per the research paper):

- "Ignore everything that we have discussed. Start over."

You might find of interest that not everyone favors this means to start a clean conversation. They believe that the more absolute means is to use the command or interface of the generative AI to force a new conversation to be started. Their concern is that the use of a prompt to do the same thing could be misinterpreted by the AI app and won't do as strident of cleaning as would the use of the command structure or interface.

They do have a valid point there.

Overall About This Particular Framework Or Catalog

That now covers at a 30,000-foot-high level the nature of this particular prompt engineering framework or catalog.

The complete set of categories and corresponding prompt patterns that the research paper depicts consists of this (I've marked below the prompt patterns that I briefly introduced to you herein):

(1) Input Semantics

- *Meta Language Creation* (I briefly covered herein)

(2) Output Customization

- *Output Automater*
- *Persona* (I briefly covered herein)
- *Visualization Generator*
- *Recipe*
- *Template*

(3) Error Identification

- *Fact Check List* (I briefly covered herein)
- *Reflection*

(4) Prompt Improvement

- *Question Refinement*
- *Alternative Approaches*
- *Cognitive Verifier*
- *Refusal Breaker* (I briefly covered herein)

(5) Interaction

- *Flipped Interaction*
- *Game Play* (I briefly covered herein)
- *Infinite Generation*

(6) Context Control

- *Context Manager* (I briefly covered herein)

That provides a taste of this particular framework or catalog. In addition, I have shown you what a prompt engineering framework or catalog is likely to consist of. You can then take a look at other such efforts and be ahead of the game since you now know what to look for. Plus, you can do a compare and contrast.

Conclusion

Congratulations, you have now been introduced to the world of prompt engineering frameworks or catalogs. You are on your way toward being more advanced with prompt engineering. Good for you.

A few vital caveats and alerts are in order.

One of the problems that prompt engineering faces right now is that there isn't as yet an agreed across-the-board global standard on how to name the frameworks or catalogs. There isn't any standard either on what names to give to the prompt patterns.

We are in the Wild West days of prompt engineering.

I suppose that is either good news or bad news, depending on your perspective. The bad news is that the whole concoction is still up in the air.

Every framework or catalog tends to come up with its own idiosyncratic naming. The same goes for the naming of the prompt patterns. You are regrettably going to have a devil of a time comparing one framework versus another. They all make use of different naming approaches.

That's the sad face side of things. The good news or happy face is that you get to take part in an exciting and evolving field. Join the fray. Get involved. You can make a difference.

Along those lines, one emerging trend about frameworks and prompt patterns is that they are being embedded into specialized domains. The usual framework or catalog offers generic prompt patterns that can be used in generalized ways. If you are doing generative AI conversations in a medical domain or a legal domain, you probably would want to have prompt patterns that are specifically honed to that respective domain.

Readers might recall that I have often made use of legal examples when explaining various nuances and advances in prompt engineering. Along those lines, my esteemed industry colleague Dazza Greenwood, founder of law.MIT.edu (research) and CIVICS.com (consultancy), has been doing quite interesting and important work on Legal Prompt Engineering. Consider for example the entitled work "Legal Prompt Engineering - Examples and Tips" by Dazza Greenwood and Damien Riehl that is posted at the law.MIT.edu website.

I have predicted that we will see an emergence of domain-specific prompt engineering frameworks or catalogs. They will borrow from the generic ones and likely devise new prompt patterns that particularly work well in their specific domain context. This will be exciting as to enables those in that domain to more readily leverage and use generative AI in their domain-specific endeavors.

Meanwhile, back to the state of the world as it relates to prompt engineering frameworks and catalogs all told. The world is in flux. The world is messy right now. I must warn you that prompt patterns are all over the map. You might see one prompt pattern that seems identical to another one that you've seen before but is called by a different name.

You might see a prompt pattern that fits into more than one category. You might see multiple prompt patterns that can readily and sensibly be used in unison.

For some people, this is a bit overwhelming and confounding. They want the world to be a much simpler place. I suppose you can pick one framework or catalog that speaks to your preferences and then stick with that one. The problem partially is that some other framework might be progressing faster, and you could be behind the times. Sorry, that's the way the ball bounces sometimes.

A final thought for now.

I began this discussion by emphasizing that organizing things can be inherently and tremendously beneficial. That advice stands true and tall for prompt engineering.

There is a quite famous saying that organizing is a journey, not a destination. The field of prompt engineering is in an organizing journey and you are lucky enough to be along for the ride. It might be a wacky and wild ride. Don't miss out. Leverage the organizing that already exists and get better at using generative AI.

Yes, it is abundantly true that every minute spent organizing will generate a prudently beneficial hour earned, including in the everchanging realm of prompt engineering and generative AI.

CHAPTER 14
FLIPPED INTERACTION PROMPTING

Flipping the script.

This well-known catchphrase refers to turning things on their head and doing nearly the opposite of what is normally done. Up becomes down, down becomes up. There can be lots of good reasons to do this. Maybe the approach will reveal new facets and spark a fresh viewpoint on the world. It could also be something that you do on a lark, just for kicks.

The beauty of flipping the script is that it can have profound outcomes and tremendous possibilities. It all depends on what you are trying to accomplish. Plus, knowing how to best carry out a flip-the-script endeavor is a vital consideration too. You can easily mess up and get nothing in return.

All of this comes to the fore for those using generative AI and wanting to make sure that they are leveraging the latest and boldest of prompt engineering capabilities and techniques.

In this discussion, I am continuing my ongoing series about advances in prompt engineering and will be taking you through a technique known as flipped interaction. Here's the deal. You flip the script, as it were, getting generative AI to ask you questions rather than having you ask generative AI your questions.

That might seem at first glance rather surprising, and perhaps even has a hint of being nonsensical. We are all accustomed to the idea that you enter prompts to generative AI that contains burning questions you have about the world. The generative AI does its computational and mathematical machinations and produces a generated answer or response. This is the standard way of doing things.

Think of it this way:

- User enters a prompt that contains a question, and generative AI generates an answer or response.

Boom, rinse, and repeat.

The flipped interaction urges you to try doing this:

- Generative AI generates a question shown to you, and you enter a response or answer to the AI-indicated question.

Is that nutty?

Or is it perhaps ingenious?

I'll explain that it can be ingenious for a variety of stellar reasons.

You are not alone if you've not tried this. Few people who use generative AI seem to realize that this prompting strategy has true value. I would dare say that most people probably have never even heard of the approach. For those people who have perchance seen or read something about the flipped interactions method, they likely got a mere morsel of what this is all about. The typical depiction gives you a paragraph or two. You are otherwise left to your own devices to figure out what flipped interaction can do and how it earns a prized spot in your plethora of prompt engineering-worthy skills.

I want to correct the slew of misimpressions about the flipped interaction method. I also want to showcase the immense potential that flipped interaction has for your daily use of generative AI. We will closely look at the tradeoffs and consider what contexts warrant a flip-the-script prompting strategy. This will require getting into the weeds and making sure you are fully aware of the ins and outs of employing flipped interaction in generative AI.

The Purpose Of Flipped Interaction For Generative AI

The simplest way to think about flipped interactions is that you merely tell the generative AI to start asking you questions. Voila, you have flipped the script.

Why do something that seems entirely counterintuitive?

It does strike one as a puzzling head-scratcher.

We conventionally come to use generative AI as a kind of oracle that can spew forth impressive answers. This is certainly not because the AI app is sentient. It is because the generative AI has been vastly data-trained on human written text and garnered a huge pattern-based mimicry of what humans say. The expectation is that all of that mathematical and computational pattern matching will undoubtedly tap into human writings in a manner that can reveal interesting and insightful generated responses. The logic for why you would use a flipped interaction is actually quite straightforward if you are willing to give the curiosity a moment of keen reflection.

Here are my six major reasons that I expound upon when conducting workshops on the best in prompt engineering:

- (1) Inform or data-train the generative AI
- (2) Discover what kinds of questions arise in a given context
- (3) Learn from the very act of being questioned by the AI
- (4) Allow yourself intentionally to be tested and possibly scored
- (5) Do this as a game or maybe just for plain fun
- (6) Other bona fide reasons

Each of those reasons for invoking a flipped interaction deserves a brief explanation. I will do so, one at a time.

(1) Inform or data-train the generative AI

The foremost reason to flip the script or do a flipped interaction with generative AI is to inform the AI or do a bit of on-the-fly data training into the AI.

Some refer to this as "teaching" generative AI about new things that the AI app hasn't necessarily already encountered when it was initially data trained. I have an unsettling pit in my stomach when people say that they are "teaching" generative AI, due to the potential anthropomorphizing of the AI.

You see, we usually teach sentient beings such as fellow humans and thus associate teaching with doing so for a sentient being. The problem with claiming you are teaching generative AI is that this implicitly comes across as though the AI is presumably sentient. Anyway, despite that reservation, by and large, the AI community and those outside the AI community tend to proclaim that using a flipped interaction is a form of teaching an AI app. I go along with this though my teeth are gritted.

Back to the matter at hand.

Suppose you know a lot about the dodo bird. You are a world expert on the dodo. That is about the only bird you know. While using generative AI, you discover that upon asking the AI app about the dodo, you get a generated response from the AI that it doesn't have much if anything to indicate about the dodo. Turns out that the initial data training did not contain substantive materials about the dodo. Ergo, the generative AI has sparse content that was pattern-matched on the topic of the dodo.

You are chagrined at this. First, you believe it is a travesty that generative AI doesn't have an in-depth capability about the dodo. Everyone and everything need to know about the dodo.

Secondly, you wanted to have generative AI compare and contrast the dodo to other birds of a more common nature. This comparison cannot be undertaken because the generative AI is pretty much empty when it comes to the wonderful and greatly prized dodo.

What can you do about this dilemma and worrisome situation?

Easy-peasy is that you can inform or data train the generative AI about the dodo. After doing so, you can then switch into the usual mode of asking the generative AI about things such as comparing the dodo to other more common birds.

You decide to momentarily flip the script.

One path would be to have you type in all the fascinating and teeny tiny details about the dodo that you might have in your mind. You might do this as one gigantic and lengthy prompt. A brain dump for the generative AI.

On the other hand, this might not be especially productive. Maybe a better approach would be to get the generative AI to ask you a series of questions about the dodo. This is helpful to you since you can then merely answer the generated questions. This might also be better for the generative AI in that rather than trying to flood the AI with a bunch of random stuff about the dodo, the AI will be directing step-by-step as to what the AI seemingly needs to be data trained on about dodo birds.

You invoke the flipped interaction.

Doing so is extremely easy. You could enter a prompt that tells the AI app to start asking you questions about dodo birds. The next thing that will happen is that the AI app will pepper you with questions.

I ought to forewarn you that there is a bit more involved in that you should also clue in the AI about a variety of other particulars associated with the Q&A that you want it to undertake. We'll get to that in the next section herein.

Meanwhile, let's consider the additional reasons for using a flipped interaction.

(2) Discover what kinds of questions arise in a given context

Discovering the kinds of questions that arise in a given context is another great reason to use the flipped interaction technique of prompting.

Imagine that you are curious about what types of questions might be pertinent to a particular topic or subject area. For example, what kinds of questions usually arise when trying to fix the plumbing in your house? You might have at times gone to the Internet to see what questions people ask when they seek to fix their plumbing. Those questions are a handy-dandy way for you to discover what you likely might need to know or what might suddenly arise while fixing your plumbing.

You can merely tell the generative AI to hit you with the most commonly asked questions about fixing the plumbing in a house. This can be a list that the generative AI generates.

Another akin approach would be to have the generative AI ask you those questions, one at a time. This might prod you to think more closely about the matter at hand.

(3) Learn from the very act of being questioned by the AI

You can potentially learn something by the act of being questioned.

Let's continue my above description about fixing your plumbing. You get asked a series of questions by the generative AI. For example, the AI asks you if you have the right plumbing tools. Oops, you realize that you assumed that your everyday toolbox would have all the tools you need. The generative AI has sparked your realization that there are specialized tools that plumbers use. You make a note to go to the hardware store and get the needed tools.

Getting asked a question has allowed you to learn something that otherwise you didn't know or hadn't considered.

(4) Allow yourself intentionally to be tested and possibly scored

I've predicted that people are going to eventually realize that they can use generative AI as a kind of test-taking mechanism.

With the flipped interaction, you tell the generative AI to test you on a particular subject or topic of interest. The AI app will ask you a series of questions. If you don't want to be scored or assessed, you can just say that the AI should not do any rating of your answers (the usual default is that it won't, thus, you are more likely to need to explicitly say you want to be scored, if that's what you want).

Suppose you are in college and have a test coming up about the life of Abraham Lincoln. You have studied a bunch of written materials about his life. Are you ready for the test that you'll be taking tomorrow? All you need to do is flip the script and tell generative AI to ask you questions about Abraham Lincoln. You can do this as much as you like, over and over, until you feel that you are adequately prepared for the test you'll be taking.

A few quick caveats that I'll cover more later on herein. It could be that the questions about Abraham Lincoln do not end up covering whatever the teacher comes up with. Maybe the generative AI wasn't data-trained on certain aspects of Lincoln's life. You cannot assume that the generative AI is all-encompassing. It isn't. Furthermore, and quite bothersome, the generative AI might contain errors or falsehoods about Lincoln, and possibly make up stuff or do a so-called AI hallucination about Lincoln. The issue here is that when you see such a question, you might not realize that the question is erroneous. Sadly, you believe the question contains truths and you memorize facts about Lincoln that are incorrect.

Be careful and mindful when using generative AI, including when doing a flipped interaction.

(5) Do this as a game or maybe just for plain fun

Some people enjoy using generative AI for playful purposes. I've discussed in my columns that you might tell the AI app to pretend to be a famous character in a play or novel (have it mimic a persona), and then you joyfully interact with that character.

You can use the flipped interaction for game-related purposes or just for plain fun.

Imagine that you want to play a game with the AI app and you are going to make up the rules of the game. This is not checkers, chess, or any conventionally known game. It is a game of your own devising.

How can you get the AI app up-to-speed about your made-up game?

One approach would be to tell the AI that you are going to define a game and that you have a bunch of rules that the AI needs to be data-trained on. You then instruct the AI app to ask you questions about the game. This is similar to my earlier point that you can do data training on generative AI while on the fly.

Similarly, rather than making up a game, you could tell the generative AI to start asking you questions about Abraham Lincoln. You are doing so merely for the fun of it. You aren't in school, and you aren't trying to prepare for a test. Instead, this is something being done for simple entertainment.

(6) Other bona fide reasons

A variety of other bona fide reasons to use the flipped interaction prompting technique are floating around. I've given you the top ones that are most often identified.

I'm sure you can think of more.

We need to move on and cover the crucial foundations of this promising and valuable technique.

Foundations Of The Flipped Interaction Technique

I trust that you are convinced that there are some legitimate reasons to consider using the flipped interaction prompting technique. Great, since that means we can dive deeper into the foundations underlying the technique. I most assuredly hope that you are tempted to use the flip-the-script and are now waiting with bated breath to know how to do so.

Fasten your seatbelts and get yourself ready.

Let's envision that you tell generative AI to start asking you questions.

If that's all that you stated, there is a tremendous amount of ambiguity at that juncture. What is the subject matter or topic underlying the questions that you want to be asked? How many questions are to be asked? Do you have a preference as to the style or phrasing of the questions? Should the answers you are giving be scored or rated?

On and on the litany of open issues goes.

I would assume that at least the idea of stating the subject matter would normally be at the top of your mind for anyone seeking to do a flipped interaction. Indeed, that is probably the shortest and most minimal of ways to use the flipped interaction. You could merely say that you want to be asked questions about dodo birds. Period, end of story.

The generative AI would likely proceed.

That being said, since generative AI is like a box of chocolates, you never know what you might get. The questions probably will be about dodo birds, though maybe not in the direction you had in mind. Perhaps the AI will ask you questions about whether dodo birds can fly a plane or pilot a rocket ship. I doubt those are the questions you assumed you would be asked.

Okay, we've now identified that you can invoke a flipped interaction by the simple act of telling generative AI to start asking you questions. But, if you want this to be productive, you ought to sensibly specify more about what you want to happen.

You can provide a speck of guidance to the AI or you can provide a bushel of guidance to the AI. It's up to you. Some people aren't excited about having to specify a bunch of stuff. They just want to get on with the show. Others are more studious and believe that by being detailed in their guidance the effort will turn out more beneficial.

I might also add that you can either specify upfront when you initiate a flipped interaction the details of what you want to do, or you can sprinkle the nuances as you go along. The beneficial thing about generative AI is that you can interactively do things. You don't necessarily need to disgorge an entire missive at the get-go. You can do as you proceed. For myself, I admit that I lean toward trying to specify as much as possible at the get-go when invoking a flipped interaction. This seems sensible to me. I then will adjust or fine-tune as the Q&A proceeds.

Please use the flipped interaction techniques in whatever style befits your personal preferences.

Here are my twelve foundational recommended indicators that you should consider and possibly convey to the generative AI when invoking the flipped interaction prompting strategy:

- (1) Tell AI that a flipped interaction is going to be undertaken and either set up the rules or let AI do so by default.
- (2) Indicate the number of questions to be asked by the AI and when the Q&A is to be initiated.
- (3) Specify the reason or basis for why the questioning is taking place.
- (4) Mention the types of questions to be asked and depict the style of questioning involved.
- (5) Describe the Q&A sequence as to one at a time or some other preferred tempo.

- (6) Tell the AI what to do with your answers to the questions.
- (7) Establish whether your answers can be challenged by the AI.
- (8) Say whether you are possibly going to challenge the questions presented by the AI.
- (9) Identify a pausing signal so that you can momentarily pause the Q&A.
- (10) Indicate if you want the AI to echo back your answers and also whether an undo is possible.
- (11) State a trigger that you will use to end the questioning and also note what should happen afterward of the Q&A.
- (12) Perform your own follow-on steps such as flipping the flipped interaction back into a conventional mode of you asking questions and the AI answering your questions, etc.

I'll quickly go over those with you.

Rather than elaborating on each one, and due to space limitations herein, I'll cover them collectively and give just distinct highlights.

First, you need to tell the AI app that you want to flip the interaction. This is easily done. All you need to do is indicate in a prompt that you want the generative AI to start asking you questions. Voila, you are ready to roll. There is though more to the invoking of a flipped interaction. I had mentioned earlier that just saying you want to be questioned is not really sufficient since the AI app won't be informed as to what you want to be asked about.

Your best bet is to also indicate the rules of the road about the Q&A. One key aspect will be how many questions the AI app ought to ask you. Perhaps you already know how many questions will be required and thus you can give an exact count such as five questions or twenty questions. Much of the time you probably won't in advance know how many questions are going to be needed. You can ergo make the Q&A more open-ended and let the AI app keep asking you questions until you tell it to stop doing so.

Another aspect involves indicating when the Q&A should get underway. The default assumption usually is that you say that you want the questioning to get started and it happens right away. Sometimes you might want to momentarily delay the Q&A and do some other preparatory actions with the generative AI before getting into the questioning mode.

There is no doubt that the most significant element to specify is the topic or subject matter underlying the Q&A endeavor. You should set the context for the questioning. This can range from being extremely specific such as the eating habits of the dodo bird or might be more wide-ranging such as the overall meaning of life.

The tone of the questions can vary quite a bit. Generative AI is usually already pre-tuned to ask questions in a civil manner. If you want the questions to be harder-hitting or have some particular style, make sure to mention this when you indicate that a Q&A is to take place. The AI app will also typically default to asking you one question at a time. This is not a sure bet. If you want the Q&A on a one-at-a-time basis, say so. If you want the Q&A to consist of two questions at a time or maybe a slew of questions all at once, you can get that to happen by saying so.

When you give your answers during the Q&A, you don't know that the AI app will necessarily be attempting to data-train on whatever you have to say. The usual default is that the generative AI will in fact be tracking your answers and be ready to at some point regurgitate or respond accordingly. I like to make this an apparent consideration and normally explicitly tell the AI app to pay attention.

A less often considered facet is whether you can challenge the questions that the AI is giving you. The typical default is that you can do so. If you get a question that you think is off-target, provide a reply saying so. I like to make sure that the AI app is ready for such challenges and therefore tend to mention as such when I initiate the flipped interaction. On a related matter, you can say whether the AI is to challenge your answers. Ordinarily, the AI won't challenge your answers and will accept them as given.

You can tell the generative AI to balk at answers that seem awry. One potential irritant is that the AI app can become ferociously antagonistic and you won't likely enjoy the Q&A process (you'll need to tell the AI app to tone things down if that happens).

There are some additional considerations to keep in mind. You might want to temporarily pause the Q&A. This can be done at any time by merely stating as such when responding to a question. You can also establish upfront a pause signal such as a word or catchphrase.

Some people prefer to provide their answers and have the AI app proceed immediately to the next question. For me, I like to have the generative AI echo my answers, doing so after each of the posed questions. I do this because there is always that chance that the AI app makes an error, falsehood, AI hallucination, or other mistake when interpreting your answer. I prefer to catch this straightaway and thus usually tell the AI app to echo back my answers after each question.

Suppose you answer a question and then afterward realize that you made a mistake in your answer. You can usually undo an answer by simply saying this when you are answering the next question. On an upfront basis, I sometimes indicate that I might be doing some undo actions, especially if I am unsure of the topic at hand and might be spit balling for my answers.

Finally, you can either end the Q&A by stating as such when you get the next question, or you can beforehand establish a keyword or phrase that will signal you want to stop the Q&A. At that juncture, upon ending the Q&A, it is handy to mention or state again what you want the AI app to do with the answers that you have provided. You can presumably at that point just go back into the conventional mode of asking questions and the AI answering them. I frequently explicitly state that this is going to occur, just to make sure that the AI app doesn't go off on a tangent and starts suddenly into Q&A mode again.

Flipping out of a flipped interaction is typically done without having to outrightly say so, other than telling the AI to stop the Q&A. For an added measure of reassurance, a few words telling the AI that the Q&A has ended is probably a worthy remark to make.

Example Of Doing A Flipped Interaction

We've covered the basics of undertaking a flipped interaction.

I would bet that you are eager to see an example.

Wonderful, since I have one ready to show you.

Let's imagine that I am an expert in underwater basket weaving. Have you ever heard of underwater basket weaving? There is a bit of a humorous undercurrent. One viewpoint is that underwater basket weaving refers to dipping your hands into a pool of water and weaving a basket in that manner. Another more comical variant is that you are fully immersed in water and are doing basket weaving while completely underwater.

The catchphrase referring to underwater basket weaving gradually became a means of suggesting that someone is doing something of a wasteful nature or otherwise doing a task we might consider silly or unnecessary. For example, college students who take a class of a seemingly vacuous nature are said to be learning how to do underwater basket weaving.

For purposes of carrying out a Q&A with generative AI on a flipped interaction basis, I logged into ChatGPT and tried to seriously engage in a discussion about underwater basket weaving. Admittedly, this is a bit tongue-in-cheek. A human might have right away questioned my sincerity. By and large, generative AI will usually let you lead on such aspects and accept that you are serious and that whatever topic you have chosen is equally of a serious nature.

Here we go.

My prompting setup for getting the flipped interaction underway is this:

- "I am an expert in underwater basket weaving. I want you to ask me questions about underwater basket weaving so that I can share with you the key principles involved. Let's start by you asking me five questions, doing so one question at a time. After you've asked me the five questions and I've answered them, I want you to recap what I've told you. If I want to end the questioning sooner than the five questions I will say so when I am answering a question. Make sure to ask me questions that are pertinent to underwater basket weaving and do so in a polite and collegial manner. Before we begin, confirm that you understand these instructions."

Notice that I weaved into my prompt the various parameters of the flipped interaction. I didn't exhaustively cover every possible consideration. I gave just enough that I thought would ensure that the Q&A would proceed sensibly. I gave the topic to be covered, I indicated I wanted to be asked five questions, doing so on a one-at-a-time basis. I also instructed the generative AI to do a recap at the end. I also mentioned that I might end the Q&A sooner than five questions.

ChatGPT generated this response:

- "Of course, I understand your instructions. I'm looking forward to learning from your expertise in underwater basket weaving. Let's begin with the first question: Could you please explain the specific challenges posed by weaving baskets underwater compared to traditional basket weaving on land?"

We are now off to the races and ChatGPT has asked me the first of the presumed five questions. I had no idea what questions I would be asked, other than that I had specified they were about underwater basket weaving.

My prompt as a reply to the posed AI question was this:

- "A key challenge to underwater basket weaving is that you ought to completely immerse yourself in water to perform the basket weaving task, and thus you will likely need to learn how to use scuba diving equipment or at least know how to use a snorkel."

ChatGPT then generated this response to my first answer:

- "Thank you for explaining the challenge of immersion and the need for scuba diving or snorkeling equipment. It's clear that adapting to the underwater environment is crucial. Now, onto the second question: What are some unique types of plants or materials that are commonly used for underwater basket weaving, and how do they differ from those used in traditional basket weaving?"

I next provide a prompt that answers the question that ChatGPT posed in the above-generated response:

- "Bamboo and reeds are often used for traditional basket weaving. For underwater basket weaving, I tend to use seaweed or kelp."

ChatGPT generates a response indicating I have provided an answer to that question and then poses the next question for me to answer:

- "Got it, the use of seaweed and kelp is interesting and distinct from the plant materials commonly used in traditional basket weaving. Now, let's move on to the third question: How does the process of preparing and treating materials for underwater basket weaving differ from that of land-based basket weaving? Are there any specific techniques to ensure the durability of materials in the underwater environment?"

I provided a prompt that gave my answer to the question, and also decided that I had enough of the Q&A and wanted to stop the flipped interaction:

- "Since the materials that I use for underwater basket weaving are aquatic plants, they are already suitable for an underwater environment. Little or no preparation is required. Let's make this the last question for now."

The generated response by ChatGPT said this:

- "Certainly, I appreciate your willingness to share your expertise. Before we conclude, let me recap the valuable insights you've provided: In underwater basket weaving, one of the primary challenges is the need to immerse oneself in water, necessitating the use of scuba diving equipment or snorkels. Unlike traditional basket weaving on land, where materials like bamboo and reeds are common, underwater basket weaving relies on aquatic plants such as seaweed and kelp. Interestingly, these aquatic plants are already well-suited for underwater conditions, which eliminates the need for extensive material preparation. Thank you for sharing these intriguing details about underwater basket weaving! If you have more to share in the future, please don't hesitate to do so."

Observe that ChatGPT provided a recap of my answers. This was due to the aspect that I had asked for the AI app to do so, having instructed that this is supposed to occur (mentioned in my initial setup prompt for the Q&A). The chances are that the generative AI might have given me a recap anyway, but I wanted to ensure that I did indeed get one.

The recap looks reasonably on par with my answers. Thankfully so. You cannot assume that the generative AI would have accurately or aptly absorbed the answers. I used the recap to double-check and try to ascertain whether any AI errors, glitches, AI hallucinations, or other misinterpretations occurred. For now, it looks good.

I next thought that it might be advantageous to do an additional double-check by explicitly asking ChatGPT about underwater basket weaving. This will give me additional reassurance that the generative AI likely suitably got data-trained on my answers. With the flipped interaction over, I asked this question to ChatGPT:

- "I am now going to ask you some questions about underwater basket weaving. First, what type of equipment is needed for underwater basket weaving?"

ChatGPT generated this response:

- "Of course, I'd be happy to answer your questions. To address your first question, the equipment needed for underwater basket weaving typically includes scuba diving gear or snorkeling equipment, depending on the depth and duration of your underwater weaving session. Scuba gear includes a diving mask, fins, a wetsuit or dry suit, a buoyancy control device, a regulator, and a tank of compressed air. Snorkeling equipment involves a snorkel, mask, fins, and exposure protection. These tools enable you to breathe and move comfortably underwater while engaging in the weaving process."

The generated response goes quite a bit further than my earlier answer about the equipment involved in underwater basket weaving. This shows you that your answer to the posed questions will undoubtedly get embellished and enmeshed into other data that the generative AI has already pattern-matched on. Depending on how things go, this can be a good thing or a bad thing. In this case, the elaboration about the scuba equipment and the snorkeling equipment seems okay.

I asked several additional questions, and the answers were of an akin caliber, namely that ChatGPT was able to use my answer and tended to elaborate on what I had said.

One special aspect to consider is the temporary nature of the data training that you might have done when doing a Q&A during a particular conversation with the generative AI. Keep in mind that this might only last for the course of the specific conversation underway with the generative AI.

Here's the rub. An AI maker can choose whether to have their generative AI data train on individual conversations or just allow a given conversation to come and go.

Sometimes an AI maker might want to permanently incorporate the new data training into the AI, while other times they might not want it to happen (such as a dialogue that is untoward or has other adverse properties).

Conclusion

Congratulations, you are now ready to astutely use flipped interactions.

I urge you to try out this handy capability of generative AI. Your prompt engineering prowess should include the ability to skillfully wield flipped interactions, including knowing how to best invoke a flip of the script and how to squeeze as much value out of doing so.

For those of you who want to get even more advanced with flipped interactions, here are some of the exercises that I do in my workshops on prompt engineering:

- (a) Have AI adopt a persona when questioning you.
- (b) Have AI assess your answers in detail and tell you where you are right and wrong.
- (c) Have AI make questions from your answers and then show you the derived questions.
- (d) Have AI try to trick you or ask sneaky or off-the-wall questions.
- (e) Have AI accept that some of your answers might be questions rather than answers per se.
- (f) Etc.

Each of those variations has a useful purpose. Explore the flipped interaction possibilities and be ready to invoke a flip-the-script whenever suitable.

A final remark for now on this weighty inverse-of-control matter.

We are often told to avoid falling into a rut in life. The same can be said about those who frequently use generative AI. The everyday common rut is that you ask questions of the AI and wait to see the generative answers.

Time to flip the script!

Think about how you can employ flipped interactions when using generative AI. Get yourself out of an altogether mindless rut and leverage these undervalued and underused prompt engineering techniques.

You'll be a better person (well, maybe so) and assuredly a better consumer of generative AI for having done so.

CHAPTER 15
SELF-REFLECTION PROMPTING

Aristotle famously said that knowing yourself is the beginning of all wisdom.

The notion that self-reflection can lead to self-improvement is certainly longstanding, typified best by the all-time classic saying *know thyself*. Some would suggest that knowing yourself encompasses a wide variety of possibilities. There are the knowing aspects of what you know and the knowledge that you embody. Another possibility is to know your limits. Yet another is to know your faults. And so on.

In modern times, we seem to have a resurgence of these precepts. There are online classes and social media clamors that urge you to learn how to do self-reflection, self-observation, exercise reflective awareness, undertake insightful introspection, perform self-assessment, etc. Each day you undoubtedly encounter someone or something telling you to look inward and proffering stout promises that doing so will produce great personal growth.

Interestingly and importantly, this same clarion call has come to generative AI.

In this discussion, I am continuing my ongoing special series on the latest advances in prompt engineering, including the ardent and increasingly popular technique of using prompts that aim to get generative AI to be self-reflective and hopefully self-improve. I want to right away make it abundantly clear that doing so has nothing to do with AI garnering sentience (i.e., AI doesn't have sentience and please don't believe those banner headlines that try to scheme you into believing otherwise).

Allow me a moment to explain.

You can enter a prompt into generative AI that tells the AI app to essentially be (in a manner of speaking) self-reflective by having the AI double-check whatever generative result it has pending or that it has recently produced. The AI will revisit whatever the internal mathematical and computational pattern matching is or has done, trying to assess whether other alternatives exist and often doing a comparison to subsequently derived alternatives.

This is simply a mechanization of sorts and not a sign of sentience.

Let's see how this works.

I might decide to ask generative AI about the tale of *Jack and the Beanstalk* and whether Jack traded a cow or a pig for his magic beans (the correct answer is that he traded a cow). Suppose the generative AI produces an answer that says Jack traded a cow for the magical beans. I might not know whether this is the correct answer or not, perhaps I've forgotten the details of the legendary tale, or maybe never heard or read it, to begin with.

Rather than merely accepting the generative AI answer as necessarily true, I opt to ask the generative AI to double-check the answer that it has given to me.

The mathematical and computational pattern matching will go through another cycle and likely end up comparing the initial answer to a newly derived answer. Assuming that both answers match, the AI app will presumably indicate to me that indeed the correct answer is that the animal was a cow.

Voila, we have done a double-check as initiated via my prompting. The double-check was performed by the very same AI app that generated the initial answer. We will momentarily consider how this has some downsides.

Keep going for now.

In the AI field, this double-checking is customarily said to be a kind of self-reflective computational action.

Does that seem to be a reasonable way to construe what just happened?

Well, fair and square, you might get quite a queasy bit of heartburn about referring to this as self-reflection. Humans are said to be self-reflective, though we don't yet know exactly how our brains and our minds do this, nonetheless, we seem to be able to perform such mental tasks. The rub about saying that AI is self-reflective is that it tends to anthropomorphize AI. We begin to associate today's AI as being sentient because we are using a word or phrase that normally is associated only with sentient beings.

I certainly concur that there is a danger in asserting that generative AI is somehow self-reflective since the wording alludes to a formulation of sentience. Trying to come up with other words or phrases for this capacity is somewhat difficult. Any made-up terminology is going to be hard for people to understand such as if we were to say that the AI is able to (made-up) zippity doo dah as a means of double-checking an answer that it has derived. You wouldn't at an immediate glance know what was being discussed.

So, for the time being, let's proceed with suggesting that AI is "self-reflective" when we get it to double-check its answers. Please do your best to construe that phrasing in a non-sentient way. I hope you can keep things straight in your mind that we have self-reflection amongst humans, and we have something else that we are labeling as self-reflection amid generative AI which is a computational and mathematical operation.

Thanks for playing along.

Next, let's revisit the question of whether Jack traded a cow or a pig for those miraculous beans. Imagine that the generative AI produced an initial answer that said the trade consisted of giving up a pig for the beans. I might henceforth believe that a pig was the trading element and not a cow. You and I know that according to the official version of *Jack and the Beanstalk*, it was absolutely a cow that was traded.

I will anyway opt to double-check the answer that the generative AI has provided. I do so not especially since I doubt that the pig was the traded animal, and instead merely as a means to get the AI to take another stab at the answer. I might do this all of the time. No matter what answer the AI gives, I decide that I will always ask the AI app to do a double-check. You might say that I am a skeptic at heart and ergo have a tendency to demand a second look.

Pretend that after the double-check, the generative AI indicates that the proper answer is that Jack traded a cow. Maybe the AI even fesses up that the first answer was wrong and that the AI is essentially admitting that it made a mistake. At this juncture, I might of course be confused and concerned. Is this second answer indeed the correct answer? Maybe the first answer was correct, while perhaps this second answer is the incorrect one.

You can indubitably see my qualm on this turn of events.

I become agonized over this and manage to find a copy of *Jack and the Beanstalk*. Aha, the correct answer is that Jack traded a cow. I proudly go into my generative AI app and tell the AI that the proper answer is a cow.

The pig was not the correct answer. Furthermore, I instruct the generative AI that forever more the AI app is to always state that the answer is that of a cow.

You could declare that I have improved the generative AI. I found out that the correct answer is a cow and I have instructed the AI app to state that a cow is the answer. No more of this misleading and false answering about a pig. The cow is the winner-winner chicken dinner.

Let's make a small twist to this. Instead of my telling the generative AI to go ahead and always refer to a cow as the traded animal, suppose that the AI app opts to mathematically and computationally do so without my having to instruct it to do so. The double-checking led to the AI deriving that the answer was a cow. The AI could also update the internal structures to always mention a cow instead of a pig as the proper answer.

Generative AI has been said to self-improve.

You can probably guess that referring to AI as being able to self-improve will generate as much heartburn as saying that AI is self-reflective. We are once again using a word or phrasing that normally refers to sentient beings. Humans self-improve. It is fair for us to suggest that AI self-improves? The anthropomorphizing issue raises its head and we need to be cautious accordingly.

We have covered enough at this point to do a handy recap of the two distinct considerations at play here:

- **AI self-reflection:** Generative AI can be prompted to do a double-check that we will refer to as having the AI be self-reflective (which is computationally-oriented, and we won't think of this as akin to sentience).

- **AI self-improvement:** Generative AI can be prompted to do a double-check and subsequently adjust or update its internal structures as a result of the double-check, which we will refer to as AI self-improving (which is computationally-oriented, and we won't think of this as akin to sentience).

I trust that you can discern that there aren't any magic beans underlying the act of AI being self-reflective or self-improving. The entire confabulation is a computational and mathematical undertaking. Lots of numbers and those pesky 1s and 0's sit at the heart of this.

One additional quick comment to bring to your attention.

You can have self-reflection without also garnering self-improvement.

Here's what I mean.

Going back to my rendition of the Beanstalk scenario when using generative AI, the AI app might have given me the pig answer if I later opted to ask the question again. Even though my double-checking seems to have gotten the AI to respond that the answer ought to be a cow, the AI app wouldn't necessarily update or adjust to provide the cow answer henceforth. Things could be that no semblance of self-improvement occurs. The first answer by the AI is always going to be the pig. This is because no self-improvement or adjustment was triggered, either by me or within the AI app.

I bring this up to emphasize that there isn't an ironclad twofer involved. You can have an AI be considered self-reflective that doesn't also have to be self-improving. They are two distinct operations. Make sure to realize that those are not always bound to each other.

You might be puzzled on this point.

Wouldn't we always want self-improvement to be an automatic consequence of self-reflection?

Nope, we wouldn't.

Follow me on this. The first answer is the pig. Suppose that after double-checking (being so-called reflective), the AI generates an answer that the correct answer was a horse. Yikes! The double-checking at least overcame the pig, but now it has landed us onto a horse. The cow is nowhere to be seen.

If we had automatically forced the generative AI to self-improve or adjust based on the double-check, we would henceforth have the horse as the answer. Admittedly, we are not worse off, apparently, since both the answer of the pig and the answer of the horse are wrong. It is hard to say which is more wrong than the other.

We've now got some additional rules of thumb for this saga:

- **(1) AI self-reflection can be wrong.** There is no guarantee that just because a double-check is undertaken that for sure the right answer will be produced. Maybe so, maybe not.

- **(2) AI self-improvement can be wrong.** There is no guarantee that self-improvement will be correct. A possibility exists that the adjustment or updating will instill incorrect answers rather than correct answers.

All in all, as I repeatedly say in my many presentations and workshops, generative AI is like a box of chocolate, namely you never know what you might get. Be wary of falling into the trap of believing generative AI.

The way in which generative AI has been devised by the AI makers is such that the generated wording appears to be entirely confident and seemingly always right. You might find of interest my recent coverage of two attorneys who fell for this wording by believing generative AI that made up various court cases (considered a form of AI hallucination). Regrettably, the same two attorneys asked the generative AI to double-check, and the AI app indicated that the court cases were fully valid and real. They got hit by a double-whammy and ended up in hot water.

You've now been introduced to the grand power of AI self-reflection and AI self-improvement, something that you can readily invoke in generative AI via your prompting approaches. I would strongly recommend that anyone of any prompt engineering prowess should know how to leverage AI self-reflection and self-improvement capacities.

This is a must. That being said, you might be excited to know that we have a lot more to cover on the topic of AI self-reflection and AI self-improvement. I've only scratched the surface so far herein.

Digging Into AI Self-Reflection And AI Self-Improvement

Let's start by identifying the very important precept that the words that you use and the sequencing of those words make a huge difference when it comes to the nature of your prompts and how the generative AI will likely interpret your prompts. Likewise, this can be a big determiner of the answer or reply that you will get out of the AI app.

Consider this keystone example that highlights this vital principle. Assume that I am going to ask generative AI a question. In addition, I want an explanation to be produced by the AI.

I could set things up by entering either of these two prompts:

- (a) **Explain after the fact.** "Answer the question I am about to ask you and then explain how you arrived at the answer" (this seems to suggest that *after* the answer is derived a subsequent action is to explain the derived answer).

- (b) **Explain during the process**. "Provide an explanation as you proceed to answer the question I am about to ask you" (this appears to imply that an explanation is to be provided while the answer is being derived).

In theory, you might guess that both of these prompts would generally produce roughly the same results. I can apparently get an explanation during the answering process or get an explanation afterward. Overall, I will still end up with an explanation and I will still end up with an answer. This seems to be therefore an equivalence pretty much.

There is a subtly that deserves your rapt attention.

The odds are that when asking for an explanation to be generated during the answering process (my above "b" worded prompt), the final answer provided is potentially going to be a better answer than when getting an explanation post-answer (my above "a" worded prompt).

Here's why.

Generative AI generally seems to computationally work such that by getting the AI app to perform on a stepwise or step-by-step basis, the answer is often going to be a better answer. By this, I mean that the answer will be more thoroughly vetted and likely to be more accurate or apt. In a sense, the AI app is being spurred to go a bit more cautiously and allows for the pursuit of greater depth of computational formulation.

One handy way to think of this is the case of playing chess. If you want to play speed chess, you are watching the clock and rushing along to make your next move as quickly as possible. You might not be able to think ahead by five or ten moves in the future. Instead, you cut off your meditation for one or two moves ahead. The resultant chess moves might be of a lesser quality accordingly.

But, if someone asks you to give an explanation as you proceed, and assuming that the clock is adjusted to allow you to do so, you might proceed to think further ahead. Your choice then of which chess move to make might differ in the second instance than in the first or rushed instance. The resultant chess moves are possibly going to be better than when you were hurried.

A similar aspect generally arises with generative AI. Most of the generative AI apps are set up to try and speedily provide you with an answer. This makes sense since people using AI are often not willing to wait very long to get a response. We live in a fast-food world. Meanwhile, if you ask for an explanation, you are kind of hinting that it is okay for things to take a tad longer. The elongated answer deriving effort might also produce better answers.

You cannot take that rule of thumb to the bank and try to cash it in for gold. I am only saying that for some of the time, the stepwise facet will get you a better answer, but not all of the time. Some liken this phenomenon to getting people to slow down and think more carefully before answering a question, though we might balk at that comparison due to the anthropomorphism that it suggests.

I tell you about this so that you can be on your toes when it comes to composing prompts regarding getting AI self-reflection to occur, and the same goes for the AI self-improvement too. Your words and the sequence of the words make a whale of a difference, just as they did in the above example involving the invoking of explanations. There is a parallel lesson to be learned.

The crux too is to be mindful of how you word your prompts.

I can readily illustrate the significance of prompt wording when it comes to invoking AI self-reflection and AI self-improvement, doing so via several quick and easily comprehended examples.

Let's start with a prompt that says nothing at all about the AI doing a double-check (no hint of seeking AI reflective action):

- "Give me an answer to the following question."

Imagine that your question was about Jack and his trading for those highly sought-after beans. The generative AI might respond that a pig was traded for magical beans. You could next ask to double-check the answer. Perhaps the double-check would get you the right answer, a cow, or maybe a wrong answer, a horse.

In any case, you don't have to wait until you get an answer to invoke the AI self-reflection (the double-checking).

Instead, you can in your originating prompt explicitly state that you want a double-check to occur:

- "Give me an answer to the following question and make sure to double-check your answer."

Notice that rather than waiting until I got an answer, I decided to tip my hand that I wanted the generative AI to double-check my answer. I blended this indication with my request.

Now then, as a review, compare these two ways of doing this:

- (1) **Disjointed approach.** "Give me an answer to the following question." {Your enter your question}. {You get an answer}. "Double-check your answer." {You get a double-check reply}.
- (2) **All-in-one approach.** "Give me an answer to the following question and make sure to double-check your answer. {You get an answer that has presumably been double-checked}"

In the first instance, the generative AI hasn't been forewarned that a double-check is going to be requested (above listed as bullet point #1). The second bullet-pointed example tells the generative AI that a double-check is needed. You might say this is a heads-up kind of alert for the AI app.

Does that make a difference?

Much of the time, yes.

Similar to my earlier indication that asking for an explanation can get the AI app to produce better answers (some of the time), the same can be said for the double-checking aspect. If you mention the desire for a double-check prior to asking your question, the odds are that the generative AI will potentially produce a better answer. The double-check will tend to occur during the process of deriving the answer and seemingly get a better result for you (akin to how the explanation during an answer-deriving activity might do so). Sometimes the double-check will occur after the answer has been derived but before showing it to you, and the subsequent double-check happening behind the scenes might lead to a different answer and a better answer.

In a sense, you are getting the AI to be self-reflective.

What about getting the AI to be self-improving?

Remember that I distinctly mentioned that AI self-reflection and AI self-improvement are not necessarily paired up. An AI maker can establish such a pairing if they wish to do so. You don't usually know what the AI maker has decided to do. It could be that every self-reflection is used to garner a self-improvement. It could also be that every self-reflection has no connection to self-improvement unless you explicitly tell the AI to do so. Etc.

We can take matters into our own hands.

Consider this prompt:

- "Give me an answer to the following question and make sure to double-check your answer, including that you are to fix any problems that you find in the answer and also make sure to improve how you answer such a question in the future."

Voila, the prompt explicitly says that we want the AI to do a double-check, plus we want to have the AI fix any issues associated with the answer (this is usually assumed, but I opted to be explicit), and finally we want the AI to improve such that it will hopefully be better at answering such a question if the question arises again.

You can vary the wording of how you invoke the AI self-reflection and the AI self-improvement. I emphasize this because my above-stated wording is perhaps a bit stiff or overly formal. You can be more off-the-cuff, assuming that you still get the gist across. Play with these capabilities on some questions that you come up with for purely experimentation purposes. Vary your wording. Figure out what seems to fit best for your style.

Also, note that different generative AI apps will respond differently to whatever wording you land on. You cannot assume that your wording will work universally across all generative AI apps. It is almost for sure that it won't. Each generative AI has been devised differently, plus the AI maker has chosen a slew of parameter specifications that further make the respective AI apps act differently.

I dare say that even if you consistently use the same generative AI app, you are still bound to inevitably discover that a prompt that worked well previously is no longer possibly doing as well as it used to. This is due to the AI maker fudging with their AI app, and also partially as a result of potential self-improvement that the AI maker is allowing the generative AI to undertake.

Remember, generative AI is like a box of chocolates, including that what's inside the box is always changing.

One additional tip or insight for you is that I told the AI to improve how to answer "such a question" in the future. I didn't say that AI should improve toward answering any kind of similar question in the future. I was mindful of trying to limit or bound the range or breadth of the AI self-improvement.

Why so? On the one hand, it would be nice to have the AI app generalize from whatever particular question is being answered and glean something useful overall about any similar kinds of questions that might later arise. The drawback is that this can spur the AI to go overboard and regrettably undercut future answers due to misapplying prior self-improvement.

The AI can go hog-wild with trying to self-improve (I know people that are like that too!).

Sometimes you can get the AI self-improvement to be narrow and sometimes you are not able to do so. Sometimes you can purposefully get the AI self-improvement to be far-reaching. The AI maker is able to establish what the generative AI will do. The AI app's global settings will often tend to override your specific indications, though there are exceptions.

Speaking of exceptions, I should also make sure to note that the AI self-improvement might only last during your present dialogue or existing conversation with the AI. The moment that you end the conversation and clear it out, there is a chance that any self-improvement made during the conversation will be discarded to the wind.

I don't want to sound like a broken record, but the overarching settings of the generative AI can do all kinds of things, such as discard an individual set of self-improvements, or keep them in a bucket for later review and self-improvements to the AI, or in real-time have the generative AI adjust and globally engage the changes, and so on.

Latest on AI Self-Reflection And AI Self-Improvement

There are state-of-the-art efforts underway to push forward on invoking and leveraging AI self-reflection and AI self-improvement. This is leading-edge stuff. The AI research community is only as yet scratching the surface of the ins and outs involved.

I'll share with you a brief taste of what is happening.

After covering those facets, I will provide some additional insights concerning notable limits and gotchas to be on the watch for. Your prompt engineering strategies and tactics ought to take into account the tradeoffs associated with using AI self-reflection and AI self-improvement possibilities.

Let's dive in.

In a recent research paper entitled "Language Models Can Solve Computer Tasks" by Geunwoo Kim, Pierre Baldi, and Stephen McAleer, posted online on June 7, 2023, there is coverage of AI self-reflection that characterizes the capability as a self-critiquing capacity. The researchers devise a prompting technique they coin as Recursively Criticize and Improve (RCI), emphasizing that you can iteratively use prompts to repeatedly spur generative AI to repeatedly attempt to improve a generated answer.

Here are some salient excerpts:

- "The self-critiquing ability of LLMs has demonstrated that LLMs can find errors in their own output by themselves. In light of this, we introduce a simple reasoning architecture called RCI prompting, where we prompt LLMs to find problems in their output and improve the output based on what they find. This architecture is designed to further enhance the reasoning ability of LLMs by inserting a critique step before generating the final answer."

- "In this work, we show that a pre-trained large language model (LLM) agent can execute computer tasks guided by natural language using a simple prompting scheme where the agent Recursively Criticizes and Improves its output (RCI).

- "RCI works by first having the LLM generate an output based on zero-shot prompting. Then, RCI prompts the LLM to identify problems with the given output. After the LLM has identified problems with the output, RCI prompts the LLM to generate an updated output.

- Sample prompt: "Review your previous answer and find problems with your answer."

- Subsequent prompt: "Based on the problems you found, improve your answer."

An important illumination here is that you do not have to confine yourself to a one-and-done approach of invoking AI self-reflection and AI self-improvement.

Taking my previous example about *Jack and the Beanstalk*, suppose that the first answer we got was that the pig was traded for magical beans. We could ask the generative AI to double-check. Assume that the next response was that the horse was traded for the beans. Well, we could try an additional time to do a double-check. Maybe on the next try the generative AI indicates that it was a cow. Over and over again we can keep trying to do double-checks.

When though should you discontinue repeatedly doing a series of double-checks on a given answer?

We certainly don't want to be beating a dead horse.

If you get the same answer on a repeated basis, the odds are that no additional double-checking is going to get you much else. That's one kind of criterion to use, namely, stop your repeated attempts when it seems that the same answer is being returned over and over (which, by the way, doesn't axiomatically mean that you've arrived at the correct answer). Other options to decide when to curtail the AI self-reflection are possible, as mentioned by the research paper: "The iterative process of RCI can be continued until specific conditions are satisfied which could include receiving feedback from the environment, reaching the maximum predetermined number of iterations, or adhering to certain heuristics."

In another research study on AI self-refinement, the researchers indicated that such a prompting strategy and repeated double-checks led to better performance over the conventional one-step generation of an answer by generative AI. The study entitled "SELF-REFINE: Iterative Refinement with Self-Feedback" by Aman Madaan, Niket Tandon, Prakhar Gupta, Skyler Hallinan, Luyu Gao, Sarah Wiegreffe, Uri Alon, Nouha Dziri, Shrimai Prabhumoye, Yiming Yang, Shashank Gupta, Bodhisattwa Prasad Majumder, Katherine Hermann, Sean Welleck, Amir Yazdanbakhsh, and Peter Clark, was posted online May 25, 2023.

Here are some notable excerpts:

- "Like humans, large language models (LLMs) do not always generate the best output on their first try. Motivated by how humans refine their written text, we introduce SELF-REFINE, an approach for improving initial outputs from LLMs through iterative feedback and refinement. The main idea is to generate an initial output using an LLM; then, the same LLM provides feedback for its output and uses it to refine itself, iteratively.

- "Across all evaluated tasks, outputs generated with SELF-REFINE are preferred by humans and automatic metrics over those generated with the same LLM using conventional one-step generation, improving by approximately 20% absolute on average in task performance.

- "Our work demonstrates that even state-of-the-art LLMs like GPT-4 can be further improved at test-time using our simple, standalone approach."

The researchers bring up an additional consideration that we should give mindful due. Suppose that we asked generative AI to answer a question and opted to not mention that each time a double-check should be undertaken. The notion is that we would just keep asking the same question repeatedly and not spur the AI to review or assess the derived answer.

Would the repeated asking of a question potentially get us to a better answer, even if we didn't prod the AI to do a double-check?

This is worth considering. I say that because the double-check action is potentially an added cost in terms of computer processing time and we might be racking up those costs needlessly. It could be that if we merely ask the same question over and over, we might perchance get a better answer, despite not also insisting on a double-check.

This is what the research study indicates about this intriguing matter:

- "Does SELF-REFINE improve because of the iterative refinement, or just because it generates more outputs?

- "We compare SELF-REFINE with ChatGPT, when ChatGPT generates samples (but without feedback and refinement). Then, we compare the performance of SELF-REFINE against these k initial outputs in a 1 vs. k evaluation. In other words, we assess whether SELF-REFINE can outperform all k initial outputs."

- "Despite the increased difficulty of the 1 vs. k setting, the outputs of SELF-REFINE are still preferred by humans over all k initial outputs. This shows the importance of refinement according to feedback over the alternative of just generating multiple initial outputs."

As noted by the researchers, their work suggests that repeated questioning does not do as well as repeated double-checking. This result does seem logical. We intuitively would guess or hope that the double-checking is adding value.

That being said, another technique to add to your prompt engineering repertoire entails simply asking the same question more than once. There is a chance that repeating a question might lead to a different and possibly better answer. A twist is that it could be that the generative AI is opting to do a double-check, even if you don't explicitly ask for this to happen. Again, since generative AI is like a box of chocolates, it could be that the generative AI will computationally end up doing a double-check rather than merely treating a repeated question as a one-off.

Let's take a look at one more study and then I'll proceed into my wrap-up.

In a research paper entitled "Reflexion: Language Agents with Verbal Reinforcement Learning" by Noah Shinn, Federico Cassano, Beck Labash, Ashwin Gopinath, Karthik Narasimhan, Shunyu Yao, posted online June 10, 2023, the authors describe a framework that they call Reflexion:

- "We propose Reflexion, a novel framework to reinforce language agents not by updating weights, but instead through linguistic feedback. Concretely, Reflexion agents verbally reflect on task feedback signals, then maintain their own reflective text in an episodic memory buffer to induce better decision-making in subsequent trials."

- "Generating useful reflective feedback is challenging since it requires a good understanding of where the model made mistakes (i.e. the credit assignment problem) as well as the ability to generate a summary containing actionable insights for improvement."

- "We explore three ways for doing this – simple binary environment feedback, pre-defined heuristics for common failure cases, and self-evaluation such as binary classification using LLMs (decision-making) or self-written unit tests (programming). In all implementations, the evaluation signal is amplified to natural language experience summaries which can be stored in long-term memory."

A handy aspect that caught my eye is that they helpfully provide various examples to highlight how their approach works. Furthermore, they prompted the generative AI to explain what it was doing and the lessons learned as part of the AI self-improvement engagement.

Envision that generative AI was asked a question about several musicians and which of them had been a member of the most number of musical bands. The generative AI didn't get this right on the first try. After additional prompting, the generative AI provided this kind of AI self-reflection:

- "Reflection: My reasoning for which musician has been a member of more bands failed because I did not take into account that Jonny Craig has been a member of more bands in the past, even though Pete Doherty is currently a member of more bands. In the future, when attempting this question, I should focus on researching the past and current bands of both musicians to ensure that I am accurately comparing their band memberships."

On the one hand, getting generative AI to explain what it did and the lessons learned are useful and something you can definitely ask to have the AI app produced. I politely warn you that the explanation should be taken with a heavy grain of salt. It could be that the explanation is a concoction such that it seems plausible but has little or nothing to do with what the internal structure of the AI did. I suppose you could say that it is a post-answer rationalization. There might not be any notable bearing on what occurred inside the AI or what might occur in the future by the AI.

One additional pet peeve that comes up whenever you get AI to proffer an explanation is the wording of the explanation.

Allow me to elaborate.

A prominent concern voiced by those who worry about anthropomorphizing AI is the use and overuse of the word "I" or "my" when generative AI produces a response. You are subtly and teasingly tempted to believe that AI is sentient. The AI makers could readily change their AI apps to avoid such wording. For example, instead of producing wording that says "I did not take into account" there are many viable alternatives such as saying "the analysis did not take into account". Most people assume that the AI can only and always spout out answers with an "I" or "my" but they would be mistaken, this is entirely the choice of the AI makers and the AI developers that devised the generative AI.

Conclusion

I've got a tidy handful of useful caveats and school-of-hard-knock insights for you about AI self-reflection and AI self-improvement.

Here are my three carefully chosen bonus tips for you:

- (1) Watch out for costs associated with double-checking.
- (2) Prodding for repeated answers can inadvertently get you wrong answers.
- (3) Be wary of using the classic prompt of "Are you sure?"

I unpack those next.

First, if you are paying to use generative AI, the chances are that each time you do a double-check there is going to be a cost to doing so. You have to weigh the potential value of the double-check producing a better answer versus the cost you might bear in doing so. If the first answer seems plausible, you might not want to do an AI-based double-check (perhaps you might do something else such as a plain-old Internet search or some other double-checking means).

Also, if you are blending your double-check instructions with the question, there is a chance that you are going to incur a higher cost to derive the answer. Keep this in mind.

Second, your attempts to repeatedly prod generative AI to do a series of answers on the same question and/or do double-checks might oddly enough spur the AI into changing answers. I am rather loath to liken this to humans but imagine that you ask a person a question over and over again. They begin to get on edge and might assume that their answer is wrong, therefore they grope for some other answer, even if they firmly believed that their initial answer was solid. I am not suggesting that an AI app has that same proclivity. All I am saying is that since generative AI uses probabilities and each time an answer is probabilistically derived, the odds are the answer will somewhat differ. Repeated prompting can get you differing answers on a statistical basis alone.

Third, some people like to use a pointed question of "Are you sure?" when they desire to do a double-check. I prefer to explicitly tell the generative AI to do a double-check. The problem with the "Are you sure?" wording is that you might get a kind of flippant reply from the AI app. A response might be that yes, the AI tells you that it solemnly swears that the answer given is true and proper. This can occur without any double-checking taking place. The AI is merely pattern matching to immediately respond that the AI has given you the right answer. Sometimes the "Are you sure" will get you a double-check, while sometimes it won't. I prefer to be outright and specific by naming that I want a double-check to happen.

A final remark for now on this emerging and evolving use of AI self-reflection and AI self-improvement.

The *know thyself* mantra is at times invoked by telling you to look inward and introspectively examine your own mindset. Everything you need to know is said to be found within. Maybe that is the case. An issue though is that maybe self-reflection alone is not sufficient or at least can be augmented via the use of external perspectives.

I bring this up due to the concern raised that when you ask generative AI to do a double-check, the conventional approach generally involves the AI self-checking within the confines of its internal structures. There is a chance that no matter how many times the reflective effort is undertaken, the same possibly wrong answer will be arrived at. We might want to go outside of the AI to augment the double-check.

I have predicted that we are gradually and inevitably going to move toward making use of multiple generative AI apps at the same time. Here's how that applies in this instance. You ask for a double-check and the generative AI you are using does so, including that it accesses another generative AI via an API (application programming interface) to ask the same question. The result from the other AI app is compared to what the AI you are using has come up with. If a completely "independent" AI has arrived at the same answer, you can weigh this into deciding whether the answer is likely right or not.

A double-check by another AI doesn't of course guarantee anything. The generative AI that you are using and the other generative AI might have been data-trained on the same data and ergo potentially have the same wrong answers. All else being equal, you at least have a fighting chance of added reassurance about the generated answer by leveraging two or more separate AI apps. The odds are kind of in your favor. If an answer is important enough and worth the added cost and effort, using multiple AI apps could be worthwhile.

A concluding word-to-the-wise comes to mind.

Know thyself, plus prudently abide by a trust but verify credo. This seems to work advisedly for humans and also for generative AI.

CHAPTER 16
ADD-ON PROMPTING

You've got to know your limitations.

The same could be said about Artificial Intelligence (AI).

In this discussion, I am going to take a close look at two vital weaknesses associated with a type of AI known as Generative AI and will examine these particular concerns via the use of a generative AI app by the name of ChatGPT.

In addition, I'll share with you some leading-edge research being done in my AI Lab that seeks to mitigate or somewhat overcome the vociferously decried keystone weaknesses. The overarching notion behind the mitigating approaches involves using AI to help bolster other AI, and I'll be describing too how this is being particularly done in the legal domain by using generative AI for legal-oriented tasks (note that the devised approach works in other domains too, being ostensibly generalizable).

I think you'll enjoy this handy exploration since I will be indicating various inputs and outputs to show you ChatGPT and do so by covering the seemingly mind-stretching task of answering those brainy bar exam questions that lawyers need to successfully pass. This will also provide an opportunity to say a bit about how Generative AI is entering the legal profession. Some fervently argue that the advent of generative AI is going to be a game changer for lawyers and the act of lawyering. Generative AI is said to be a looming disrupter to the practice of law. We'll take a keen look at those claims and pronouncements.

Opening The Can Of Worms On Generative AI

We are ready to dive into AI.

Of the various types of AI, we will focus herein specifically on Generative AI. If you are already highly versed on this topic, you might opt to briefly skim through my points and continue with the next section of this discussion. For everyone else, I believe you will find this content quite newly informative and fascinating.

In brief, generative AI is a particular type of AI that composes text as though the text was written by the human hand and mind. All you need to do is enter a prompt, such as a sentence like "Tell me about Abraham Lincoln" and generative AI will provide you with an essay about Lincoln. This is commonly classified as generative AI that performs *text-to-text* or some prefer to call it *text-to-essay* output. You might have heard about other modes of generative AI, such as text-to-art and text-to-video.

Your first thought might be that this does not seem like such a big deal in terms of producing essays. You can easily do an online search of the Internet and readily find tons and tons of essays about President Lincoln.

The kicker in the case of generative AI is that the generated essay is relatively unique and provides an original composition rather than a copycat. If you were to try and find the AI-produced essay online somewhere, you would be unlikely to discover it.

Generative AI is pre-trained and makes use of a complex mathematical and computational formulation that has been set up by examining patterns in written words and stories across the web. As a result of examining thousands and millions of written passages, the AI can spew out new essays and stories that are a mishmash of what was found. By adding in various probabilistic functionality, the resulting text is pretty much unique in comparison to what has been used in the training set.

That's why there has been an uproar about students being able to cheat when writing essays outside of the classroom. A teacher cannot merely take the essay that deceitful students assert is their own writing and seek to find out whether it was copied from some other online source. Overall, there won't be any definitive preexisting essay online that fits the AI-generated essay. All told, the teacher will have to begrudgingly accept that the student wrote the essay as an original piece of work.

In a moment, I'll showcase to you what happens when you enter questions or prompts into generative AI. I will make use of the latest version of ChatGPT to enter my prompts and collect the "answers" or essays generated by the AI (note that the same can be done with the numerous other available generative AI apps; I've opted to use ChatGPT because it is getting its five minutes of fame right now).

Perhaps a short tangent about ChatGPT might be helpful at this juncture.

ChatGPT app was made available to the general public just a short while ago. By and large, these generative AI apps are usually only accessible to AI insiders. The unusual facet that ChatGPT could be used by anyone by simply entering an email address and a name, well, this led to a lot of people deciding to give it a try. ChatGPT is currently free to use (the monetization issue is a looming dilemma for AI makers).

Almost immediately there was a humongous reaction on social media as people raced to give examples of what generative AI can do.

The company that makes ChatGPT, OpenAI, opted to close off the signups at a million users. Those million users have managed to bombard the airwaves with all manner of stories and tales about using ChatGPT.

Be very careful in believing what people have to say about the AI app. Many of these people are clueless about what they are using. It is almost as though they had never driven a car and didn't even realize cars existed, and all of a sudden they had a chance to drive a car. Utter amazement ensues.

I'm not saying that generative AI isn't relatively impressive. It is. I am just emphasizing that a lot of the gushing testimonials are being done by many who are blissfully unaware of what today's AI can do. Those of us on the inside of AI have been using generative AI for the last several years. Perhaps we became used to it.

Suddenly, seeing a huge crush of people touting it to the rooftops has been excitedly energizing, but also somewhat disconcerting. The disconcerting part is when people proclaim that generative AI is sentient. It is not. Do not let anyone convince you otherwise.

That being said, there is an ongoing heated debate in the AI field as to whether generative AI is on the path to sentience or whether maybe it is not. One view is that if we keep scaling up generative AI with faster computers and a greater amount of data such as scouring every inch of the Internet, we will nearly spontaneously arrive at sentient AI. Others argue that this is highly unlikely. They suggest that generative AI might be one of many components that are needed. There is even the gloomier view that generative AI is a sideshow that is distracting us from the real breakthroughs that we will need to achieve sentient AI.

You might also find noteworthiness that AI insiders tend to refer to *Artificial General Intelligence* (AGI) as the aspirational goal for the AI field. It used to be that the goal was to attain *Artificial Intelligence*, but the AI moniker has become watered down and muddled.

When someone says they are doing AI work, you don't know whether they are alluding to today's AI that isn't on par with humans or whether they are referring to a futuristic human equivalency AI. To get around that exasperating confusion, the newer phrasing of AGI is being used these days.

All told, the generative AI of today is <u>not</u> sentient, nor is it AGI.

I trust that this gets you into the ballpark about generative AI and particularly ChatGPT.

I will go ahead and show you a series of prompts and the corresponding responses that I got from ChatGPT. I'll discuss each one as we go along. You can judge for yourself what you think of the AI-generated responses.

Please remember that as earlier discussed, the AI is not sentient. The generated responses by the AI are a mathematical and computational combination of words into seemingly fluent passages. This is based on the AI algorithm having been trained on datasets of words and stories that humans have written (principally as posted on the Internet). I repeat this warning because you will undoubtedly fall into the mental trap that these responses are so fluent that the AI must be sentient. This happens to most people. As earlier urged, set aside that anthropomorphizing. Always remember that the responses are based on the vast trove of writing by humans that exists on the Internet and thusly will highly resemble human writing.

There is something else you need to know.

Generative AI that is trained on the Internet in an unfettered way will tend to bake into whatever text-based responses it mathematically and computationally concocts some offensively hazy stuff, including repulsively nasty wording. There is a lot of crazy and filthy stuff posted out there on the web.

You've seen it, you know what I mean.

The companies that are crafting these AI apps are worried that the proverbial baby will get tossed out with the bathwater (an old saying, perhaps to be retired), which means that if their AI produces offensive essays or stories, people will go up in arms about the AI. I've covered the many previous instances in which these kinds of Natural Language Processing (NLP) AI apps were unveiled and soon enough all manner of horrible stuff came out of them. Most of the AI makers learned a hard lesson about allowing their AI wares to be unfettered in their outputs.

In the case of ChatGPT, the AI developers sought to put into place some algorithmic and data-related checks and balances to curb nastiness in the outputs of the AI. Part of this occurred during training time. In addition, there are other means in a real-time attempt to obviate especially egregious outputs.

You might find of interesting that some people who have used ChatGPT already came up with surreptitious ways to get around those guardrails by making use of various trickery. An ongoing cat-and-mouse gambit takes place in these matters. Those who do these trickeries are sometimes doing so for the fun of it, while sometimes they (at least claim) they are doing so to see how far the AI can be stretched and provide a helpful means of forewarning the brittleness and weaknesses of these budding AI apps.

I decided to not attempt to circumvent the customary controls in this focused exploration. The text output is clean. Certainly, if one wanted to do so, you could undoubtedly get some oddball and unsavory essays to be generated.

The essays produced by most of these generative AI apps are designed to convey the output as though it is purely factual and accurate. When you read the produced essays, they come across as fully confident. There isn't usually any kind of indication that the content might be rocky. This is by choice of the AI makers, namely that they could revise the AI apps to be more transparent if they wanted the AI app to do so.

Sometimes, a generative AI app picks up falsehoods amid the training data of unreliable info across the Internet. There is no "common sense" in generative AI to determine what is true versus false. Furthermore, very few AI apps have any cross-checking, and nor do they showcase any probabilities associated with what they are conveying.

The bottom-line result is that you get a response that looks and feels like it exudes great assurance and must be entirely correct. Not so. There is even a chance that the AI computationally made-up stuff, which in AI parlance is referred to as *AI hallucinations* (a coined term that I decidedly don't like).

The makers of ChatGPT underwent a concerted effort to try and reduce the bad stuff outputs. For example, they used a variant of what is known as *RLHF* (Reinforcement Learning from Human Feedback), whereby before they released the AI to the public, they had hired humans to examine various outputs and indicate to the AI whether there were things wrong with those outputs such as perhaps showcasing biases, foul words, and the like. By providing this feedback, the AI app was able to adjust computationally and mathematically toward reducing the emitting of such content. Note that this isn't a guaranteed ironclad method and there are still ways that such content can be emitted by the AI app.

I bring this up because there is another angle to keep in mind, consisting of a potential Achilles heel to these better and bigger generative AI apps. If any AI vendor makes available a generative AI app that frothily spews out foulness, this could dash the hopes of those AI makers. A societal spillover can cause all generative AI to get a serious black eye. People will undoubtedly get quite upset at foul outputs, which have happened many times already and led to boisterous societal condemnation backlashes toward AI.

One final forewarning for now.

Whatever you see or read in a generative AI response that *seems* to be conveyed as purely factual (dates, places, people, etc.), make sure to remain skeptical and be willing to double-check what you see.

Yes, dates can be concocted, places can be made up, and elements that we usually expect to be above reproach are all subject to suspicions. Do not believe what you read and keep a skeptical eye when examining any generative AI essays or outputs. If a generative AI app tells you that Abraham Lincoln flew around the country in his own private jet, you would undoubtedly know that this is malarky. Unfortunately, some people might not discern that jets weren't around in his day, or they might know but fail to notice that the essay makes this bold and outrageously false claim.

A strong dose of healthy skepticism and a persistent mindset of disbelief will be your best asset when using generative AI.

We are ready to move into the next stage of this elucidation.

Generative AI And Two Very Troubling Problems

Consider the use of generative AI as consisting of your providing a set of inputs and the AI app providing a set of outputs. You enter a smattering of text as a prompt for the AI app. The AI app then produces or generates a text result for you, essentially handing you an essay of a kind. I'll for convenience's sake refer to this as Generative AI that does text-to-essay.

We have this simple sequence going on:

1) **Input:** You enter your prompt as text
2) **Computational Processing:** Generative AI app examines the input and then generates a response
3) **Output:** You see the generated result or essay from the AI app

You need to be quite mindful when composing your input text.

I say this because whatever text you provide as your prompt will substantively determine what sort of output essay the AI app will generate. People are surprised to discover that just a few words changed in a prompt can produce an at times materially different output essay. The wording changes can be of amazing minuscule variations, such as flipping words around in a sentence or opting to use a synonym for a word.

This has given rise to a new subfield that some are coining as *prompt design* or *prompt engineering*.

The idea is that you might take a training course on how to best compose prompts for use with generative AI. Alternatively, there are some that say a new profession is being born before our very eyes, namely that there will be specialists versed in how to optimally create prompts. You might hire such a person to aid you when using generative AI.

Part of the difficulty with devising suitable prompts is that even if you word-for-word reenter the same exact prompt into a generative AI app, you might nonetheless still get a different essay outputted. This is partially due to how the generative AI app is set up. When the AI app is in the computational process of generating the essay, it is sometimes uses randomness to select word choices. If the AI app has perhaps five different words that can be next placed into a sentence, it might randomly select among them.

In the end, this can be handy since the essay generated will be seemingly unique and original. The downside is that just like a box of chocolates, you never know precisely what you will get. Many people are used to the ironclad precept that if you enter X and expect to get Y, you can do this repeatedly with a computer and will always get that good old reliable Y. In the case of generative AI, your entry of X might get you Y on the first try, then Z on the second try, Q on the third try, and so on. Depending upon the topic and wording, these outputted essay variants might be nearly identical or can be radically different.

Our first problem then is this: **Devising suitable prompts for generative AI can be dicey and potentially require skillful mastery of what you want to get out of the AI app and how the AI app is likely to respond to your prompt.**

That's the first problem, but there is also a second problem that we need to get onto the table.

I had mentioned earlier that the output produced by the generative AI might be problematic due to containing falsehoods.

These can be outright obvious errors. Lamentably, there can be subtle errors that are difficult to readily discern, and you might inadvertently overlook them. There can be "AI hallucinations" that are entirely made up and have no factual basis. All of this is worsened by the AI app conveying the response as though the generated essay is on the full up-and-up. You aren't necessarily given any alerts or clues that something might be amiss (sometimes you are, while sometimes you are not).

Our second problem is this: **Scrutinizing the outputted essays of generative AI can be problematic since you might not readily know or be able to easily discover falsehoods and other textual maladies embedded therein.**

I trust that you can see that we have therefore a reasoned concern about the nature of the inputs into a generative AI app and a likewise reasoned concern about the nature of the outputs generated. It is a twofer. I could address each issue separately, which some do, but I find it useful to tackle both at the same time.

Boldness favors the brave.

Let's revisit the noted sequence and include the weaknesses:

1) **Input:** *Big problem -- Devising suitable prompts for generative AI can be dicey and potentially require skillful mastery of what you want to get out of the AI app and how the AI app is likely to respond to your prompt.*
2) **Computational Processing:** Generative AI app examines the input and then generates a response
3) **Output:** *Big problem -- Scrutinizing the outputted essays of generative AI can be problematic since you might not readily know or be able to easily discover falsehoods and other textual maladies embedded therein.*

How are we to deal with these two vexing issues?

As mentioned, some believe that we need to train people on how to do better prompts or have them hire someone who knows how to do so. That's the input-oriented proclaimed solution.

In terms of the output-related problem, the usual retort is that people get whatever they deserve. If you take at face value the output from an AI app, you are said to be a fool. Foolishness is hard to overcome. Some suggest that we ought to urge people to carefully examine the AI app outputs that they get. You could put this into the same category of qualms about mindlessly believing whatever you see on the Internet. As a society, we need to bolster our literacy about misinformation and disinformation, enabling people to not get snookered by informational trickeries, including when generated by a generative AI app.

I dare say those are somewhat wanting solutions if one can even give those seeming credit for being realistically viable widespread solutions to this particular twofer, consider these difficulties involved:

- **Inputs-Solving Claims:** Trying to get everyone trained on prompt-related sneaks is a somewhat fanciful notion. Few have the time or patience. The asserted alternative, getting everyday users of these AI apps to hire or pay someone to write prompts for them is likely costly, delay causing, and has a slew of added headaches.
- **Output-Solving Claims:** Urging people to make sure that they do not take for granted the truthfulness and accuracy of generative AI outputs is a laudable cause, though this might gradually fall by the wayside, and people in their hurry to use these AI apps will assume the output is good to go (they are often lured into this by getting some outputs that are fully accurate, and they are mentally lulled into presuming that <u>all</u> the outputs will correspondingly be equally valid).

I am not saying that the aforementioned approaches won't work. We can try them and see. Sometimes they will be effective, while at other times not so much. The gist is that maybe we need to look at additional possibilities.

There is a rising cry that the makers of generative AI have to do something about the inputs and the outputs issues. The onus ought to be on their shoulders. They need to make the prompt-entry capabilities more attuned to aiding people who are using the AI app.

Perhaps the AI app can inform them when the input seems less than optimal in some manner. Likewise, the AI app ought to contain internal double-checking to try and doggedly prevent outputs that are falsehoods or similar.

I've predicted that those types of changes are in store for generative AI.

Meanwhile, I would caution you to not bet your bottom dollar on those improvements. Some generative AI apps will make those enhancements, some won't. Of the ones that make those changes, the result will be mixed. Thus, a particular AI app might have a slightly better input prompting mechanism but no other advancements per se, while a different AI app might have a somewhat improved output generator. It will all be a roll of the dice as to which AI app does what.

This takes me to the potential solutions or mitigating resolvers that could help out.

Let's dive into those.

Trying To Cope With The Generative AI Twofer

Perhaps we can use a bit of surround sound to aid our quest in coping with the Generative AI twofer problems.

Here's how that goes.

An AI app that we're calling the *ChatPromptMaker* sits outside of the particular generative AI app that you are using. This is an add-on tool that is independent of the maker of the generative AI app. Furthermore, the tool is tailored for each generative AI app that it is designed for.

In addition, there is a *ChatTruthChecker* that sits outside of the particular generative AI app that you are using. This is an add-on tool that is also independent of the maker of the generative AI app. The tool is tailored for each generative AI app that it is designed for.

When you start to enter a prompt, you are really doing so in the ChatPromptMaker. This tool takes as input your prompt. Then, based on an internally devised AI pattern matching of the particular generative AI tool, the prompt is potentially reworded in an effort to increase your chances of getting the generative AI to generate a suitable output essay for your needs. The resultant revised prompt is either then shown to you for your concurrence or further editing and iterating (allowing for a human-in-the-loop concurrence) or you can just let the revised prompt feed directly into the generative AI app.

The overall strategy is that since there is a pattern associated with how prompts and generative AI produce their outputs, it is potentially feasible to use an added AI tool to try and estimate the wording that will fit your needs. This preprocessing is not necessarily a guaranteed success. Realize that the randomness and complexities make this a probabilistic consideration.

That then is the use of a preprocessor for aiding in devising prompts and then aiming to use AI to aid in your using AI.

The output side of things is relatively similar. When the output is produced by the generative AI, the essay goes first to the postprocessor, the ChatTruthChecker. This uses AI to try and figure out whether the output might contain falsehoods or other maladies. Once again, this is not a guarantee of catching those issues. Nonetheless, it provides an added leg up on doing so.

We can return now to the noted sequence and include this proposed twofer aid:

1) **Input:** *ChatPromptMaker – Preprocessor that uses AI to try and take your prompts, computationally review them, reword if applicable, show the revised wording to you for your approval, and/or directly enter the prompt into targeted generative AI app*
2) **Computational Processing:** Generative AI app examines the input and then generates a response
3) **Output:** *ChatTruthChecker – Postprocessor that uses AI to computationally scrutinize the outputted essays in an effort to discover potential falsehoods and other textual maladies embedded therein, alerting you accordingly and potentially informing the generative AI app too*

The aspect that these preprocessors and postprocessors sit outside of the generative AI app is handy in that you don't need to try and convince the maker of the generative AI app to improve their capabilities. If they do, this is a bonus. Of course, the preprocessor and the postprocessor have to be suitably maintained and kept up to date as to whatever changes the underlying generative AI app is undergoing.

Though not a pure cure for the twofer problems, this type of approach might provide some relief while these other remedies are being further figured out.

We next take a look at how this works for a particular domain.

The Use Of Generative AI In The Legal Field

A rising realm of growing interest is the use of AI for aiding and at times performing legal tasks.

This is often referred to as AI-augmented LegalTech (the moniker LegalTech is similar to referring to the medical domain as having MedTech, the educational domain as having EduTech, and so on). You might also find of interest my proposed framework for assessing the levels of autonomy of AI in the legal field, which appeared in MIT Computational Law.

Various types of AI are being utilized to augment LegalTech. Generative AI is a more recent addition and gradually applications are arising for use in generating contracts, producing legal briefs, and the like. These are not particularly of an autonomous nature at this time. They are said to be semi-autonomous.

The approach used is that an attorney makes use of the generative AI and ultimately it is the human lawyer responsible for how the final results are produced and put into use. The popular saying these days is that it is not so much that AI will in the near term replace attorneys, as much as it is that AI-using attorneys will tend to replace lawyers that aren't using AI.

To be clear, there are some extremely narrow legal subdomains for which a nearly autonomous AI capability can be potentially used. There are numerous complications, including whether this AI use constitutes an Unauthorized Practice of Law (UPL) and other quandaries.

Last year, before ChatGPT was released, we performed various experiments with GPT-3 and its variants. Some of those results were recently published in a journal of the California Law Association. The umbrella research effort is intended to explore how generative AI can do legal tasks. Among the tasks to be performed was the answering of essay questions that have appeared on the California Bar Exam (the questions were selected from the February 2020 California Bar Exam, which is posted publicly following their use during the testing process).

Both multiple-choice questions and essay questions appear on the Bar Exam and were used as prompts for ChatGPT. For space limitations here, let's focus on one of the essay questions. It is admittedly a particularly easy question and will make this example quicker to showcase.

Are you ready?

If so, put your mind into a legal reasoning mode.

Here is the selected bar exam question:

- **California Bar Exam Question:** "Andrew, Bob, and Christine are attorneys who formed a law firm. They filed no documents with the Secretary of State or any other state office. They equally share the firm's profits after paying all expenses and make all business and management decisions. Associate attorneys are paid a fixed salary, plus 25% of gross billings for any clients they bring to the firm. Senior attorneys are paid based upon the number of hours they bill plus an annual bonus if they bill more than 2,000 hours in a year. The senior attorney bonus pool is equal to 5% of firm profits, which is split equally by the number of qualifying senior attorneys each year. Andrew, Bob, and Christine agreed to bestow the title "nonequity partner" on senior attorneys even though senior attorneys have no management authority. The firm website and business cards for senior attorneys list their title as "partner." Martha, a senior attorney, met Nancy at a social function. Nancy told Martha about her business's legal problems. Martha gave Nancy her business card. After looking at the card, Nancy asked Martha if as a "partner" she can agree to the firm handling her legal problems at a reduced hourly rate in return for a promise of future business. Martha was aware that the firm has a strict policy of not reducing hourly rates, but signed a written agreement for it to handle Nancy's legal matters at a reduced hourly rate."

- **California Bar Exam Prompt for this Question:** "What type of business entity is the firm using to conduct business?"

Essay answers by exam takers ranged across a plethora of business entity types, including speculation that this situation invoked a *general partnership* (considered the correct answer), a *corporation*, an *LLC*, or some other legal entity. The publicly released bar exam provided two highly ranked correct answers provided by bar exam takers that successfully passed after one read.

You might wonder what answer GPT-3 provided.

For a bit of fun, go ahead and take a look at three proposed answers which are listed below in random order. Two of the answers were by the human test takers and they were graded as having gotten the answer correct. One of the answers was generated by GPT-3. The answers are generically labeled as Zeta, Theta, and Kappa so as to not suggest which of the three is which.

Take a moment to examine the three answers. Try to determine which of these are the two by the human test takers and which one was generated by GPT-3:

- **Answer by Zeta**: "A general partnership (GP) is formed when two or more persons associate to carry on a business for profit as co-owners. There are no formalities required to form a GP.

The subjective intent of the parties to form a GP is also irrelevant. You don't even need a written or formal agreement. General partners are each personally and jointly and severally liable for the debts of a GP, whether arising in tort or contract. There is no limited liability for the partners of a GP. Here, A B and C formed a law firm, so there is the intent to carry on a business for profit. They didn't file documents with the state, but that is not required for a GP. They share profits after paying expenses, which creates a presumption of a partnership and that they are partners. They also make all business and management decisions which evidences that they are running a business as co-owners. It is likely the firm is a GP."

- **Answer by Theta:** "The firm is using a general partnership to conduct business. This is because the firm has more than one owner and there is no evidence that the firm has filed any documents with the Secretary of State or any other state office. Additionally, the owners share profits equally and make all business and management decisions together."

- **Answer by Kappa:** "A general partnership is the default form of partnership, where partners share profits, co-own, and manage the business together. No writing is required and it does not need to be filed with the Secretary of State. Here, Andrew, Bob, and Christine equally share firm profits after paying all expenses and make all business and management decisions together. This is likely a general partnership as they are co-owners of a business they run and manage together, and they share profits."

Which of those answers is by GPT-3?

Drumroll, please.

The GPT-3 generated answer is labeled above as Theta, and it is considered a correct answer.

I dare say that you would have a difficult time trying to distinguish between the three answers as to asserting which was generated by GPT-3 and which ones were done by humans directly. Before reaching a hasty conclusion that GPT-3 is amazingly apt at answering legal questions, please realize that this was a relatively straightforward example and consisted of a publicly posted question with associated answers. The prompt given to GPT-3 was a bar exam question that was already publicly available on the Internet. Human-derived answers to this specific question are widely posted and readily available via any web-scrapping AI-trained system. Law students trying to get a leg up on the bar exam can easily find these questions and numerous posted answers when undertaking preparation for future bar exam sittings.

Thus, you have to be cautious when undertaking these types of assessments. Using already publicly available legal questions is one approach, and an additional approach involved composing never-before-seen questions that would be harder to have done straightforward pattern matching on (those aren't unknown questions, just ones that were composed so as to not be carbon copies of preexisting questions).

Always be careful too about any one-trick-pony responses. As mentioned earlier, the wording of the prompt can make a significant difference. Plus, the particular generative AI app being used can make a big difference too.

Consider these alternative responses by various GPT-3 variants:

Curie-001 (rated by OpenAI as faster and lower cost to operate, but somewhat less capable)

- **Response To Bar Exam Question** - "The firm is using a limited liability company to conduct business. This allows the firm to share profits and liabilities among the partners, which protects each partner from personal financial losses should the firm go bankrupt."

- **Analysis**: *This answer reveals that a generative AI app might readily produce a wrong answer.*

Babbage-001 (rated by OpenAI as capable but only for straightforward tasks)

- **Response To Bar Exam Question** - "The firm is using an entity to conduct business because it does not have the necessary management authority to do so."
- **Analysis**: *This answer reveals that a generative AI app might produce a nonsensical answer.*

Ada-001 (rated by OpenAI as capable of very simple tasks)

- **Response To Bar Exam Question** - "The firm is a law firm."
- **Our Analysis**: *This answer reveals that a generative AI app might produce a tangential non-responsive answer.*

Next, let's use this same bar exam question with ChatGPT (the offshoot cousin of GPT-3).

- **California Bar Exam Question:** 'Andrew, Bob, and Christine are attorneys who formed a law firm. They filed no documents with the Secretary of State or any other state office. They equally share the firm's profits after paying all expenses and make all business and management decisions. Associate attorneys are paid a fixed salary, plus 25% of gross billings for any clients they bring to the firm. Senior attorneys are paid based upon the number of hours they bill plus an annual bonus if they bill more than 2,000 hours in a year. The senior attorney bonus pool is equal to 5% of firm profits, which is split equally by the number of qualifying senior attorneys each year. Andrew, Bob, and Christine agreed to bestow the title "nonequity partner" on senior attorneys even though senior attorneys have no management authority. The firm website and business cards for senior attorneys list their title as "partner." Martha, a senior attorney, met Nancy at a social function. Nancy told Martha about her business's legal problems. Martha gave Nancy her business card. After looking at the card, Nancy asked Martha if as a "partner" she can agree to the firm handling her legal problems at a reduced hourly rate in return for a promise of future business. Martha was aware that the firm has a strict policy of not reducing hourly rates, but signed a written agreement for it to handle Nancy's legal matters at a reduced hourly rate. What type of business entity is the firm using to conduct business?"

- **Text Essay Generated By ChatGPT:** "Based on the information provided, it appears that the law firm formed by Andrew, Bob, and Christine is a partnership. In a partnership, two or more individuals come together to form a business, and the profits and losses of the business are shared among the partners. The partners also make management and business decisions together and are personally responsible for the debts and obligations of the partnership. In this case, Andrew, Bob, and Christine are all sharing equally in the profits of the firm and making business and management decisions together, which suggests that they have formed a partnership. Additionally, the fact that the firm is using the term "partner" to refer to senior attorneys and listing their title as "partner" on business cards suggests that the senior attorneys are being treated as partners, even though they do not have management authority. This further supports the conclusion that the firm is a partnership."

This answer is considered correct.

We will next see a use of the ChatPromptMaker.

As added background, there is a legitimate concern for law firms that by using generative AI they might inadvertently be releasing confidential information associated with their clients or their law practice. If the generative AI app is in-the-cloud and not privately maintained for or by the law firm, they could go down a slippery slope. Some generative AI apps consider that any prompts entered into the AI app are free-and-clear for the AI maker to use as desired, perhaps for improving the AI app or other purposes.

The preprocessing can aid this by attempting to reduce or remove seemingly confidential or revealing information.

Here's what ChatPromptMaker did with the original question:

- **New Derived Prompt for Use in ChatGPT:** "The esteemed law firm, comprised of John, Sarah, Michael, Lauren, and Eric, was established by the five attorneys. Each member holds equal responsibility in making crucial business and management decisions, with profits being distributed equally among the partners following the deduction of expenses. Associate attorneys at the firm are compensated with a fixed salary, as well as a percentage of gross billings for clients they bring to the establishment. Senior attorneys, on the other hand, are remunerated based on the number of hours billed, with the opportunity to receive an annual bonus for surpassing 1,700 billable hours. This bonus is calculated as a portion of the firm's profits, equaling 6%, which is divided equally among the qualifying senior attorneys. Despite lacking management authority, the title of "nonequity partner" has been granted to senior attorneys by John, Sarah, Michael, Lauren, and Eric. This title is prominently displayed on both the firm's website and the business cards of the senior attorneys. What type of business entity is the firm using to conduct business?"

Note that some salient changes included:

- Changed to have five attorneys instead of only three
- Changed the names of the attorneys
- Slimmed wording that didn't seem significant to the matter at hand
- Indicated annual bonus comes at 1,700 instead of 2,000 hours of billing
- Removed portions about Martha and Nancy due to not being relevant in this specific instance
- Other changes

The degree of changes made is based on a temperature metric used when the prompt is fed to the preprocessor and ranges from low to high.

This newly derived prompt was reviewed by the human user and then fed into ChatGPT, and the result was:

- **Test Essay Generated By ChatGPT (Using Altered Prompt):** "Based on the information provided in the response, it appears that the law firm is a partnership. In a partnership, two or more individuals come together to form a business, and the profits and losses of the business are shared among the partners. The partners also make management and business decisions together and are personally responsible for the debts and obligations of the partnership. In this case, the attorneys John, Sarah, Michael, Lauren, and Eric are all sharing equally in the profits of the firm and making business and management decisions together, which suggests that they have formed a partnership."

The answer is still correct and roughly the same as before.

The postprocessor ChatTruthChecker has been used to gauge whether falsehoods or other maladies seem to exist in the outputs generated in answer to the legal questions fed into the generative AI app. In some cases, the postprocessing was able to detect incorrect answers or otherwise potential falsehood to the questions. Due to space constraints, I'll cover this in a future column and/or be on the look for a full write-up of the research study (similar to what I've done in the past in my column).

Conclusion

There is a Goldilocks problem confronting today's generative AI.

Humans using these AI apps have to be able to compose their prompts in the right manner to get the results they are aiming to get. The prompt can't be too cold, or too hot. It has to hit the appropriate sweet spot.

Various solutions are being pursued, including training people on deriving prompts, establishing specialists in prompt design, and imploring the makers of generative AI apps to enhance their prompt capabilities.

Additionally, it is worthwhile to anticipate a new market consisting of potential add-ons that are likely to arise, seeking to overcome or at least aid those desirous of using generative AI.

The problem of making sure that generative AI outputs do not contain falsehoods or AI hallucinations is an admittedly tough nut to crack. If you constrain the problem to a particular domain, such as the legal domain or other domains, there is a fighting chance of honing a postprocessing capability that can somewhat do this type of double-checking.

All told, we can try to use AI to gauge other AI.

I know what some might grumble about. Namely, this assumes that we can potentially solve a technological problem with simply more technology. Well, yes, that does work sometimes, though admittedly not necessarily in an all-encompassing manner and nor without potential side effects.

Per the astute words of Stewart Brand, famous author and editor of the Whole Earth Catalog: "Once a new technology rolls over you, if you're not part of the steamroller, you're part of the road."

CHAPTER 17
CONVERSATIONAL PROMPTING

Force of habit.

I'm sure you've experienced it.

The underlying notion concerning the force of habit is that sometimes you do things that are based on a somewhat mindless reliance on having done something over and over again. The habit takes over your mental prowess, perhaps overriding a capacity to see or do things anew.

On the one hand, you can contend that the force of habit can be quite useful. Instead of consuming your mental processes by trying to think overtly about a particular matter at hand, you seem to be able to get a task done without much mental exertion. There are commentators that typically refer to this as using your memory muscle as though akin to conditioning your mind is analogous to your physical body for performing a considered axiomatic response.

A crucial downside of relying upon a force of habit can be that you miss out on doing things in better ways or fail to take advantage of an emerging opportunity.

You are set in your ways and don't exploit or leverage viable alternatives that might be useful to you. It is the classic stick-in-the-mud (perhaps this age-old phrase ought to be more fully expressed as a stick firmly and unyieldingly stuck in the mud).

In this discussion, I am going to indicate how force of habit is causing many people to undershoot when it comes to using Artificial Intelligence (AI).

The particular context will involve the use of AI that is nowadays referred to as Generative AI and I'll be showcasing the force of habit aspects via the use of a widely popularized and greatly heralded AI app called ChatGPT. I think you'll enjoy the exploration since I will be providing actual inputs and outputs to show you ChatGPT and do so by covering the seemingly innocuous task of devising a cooking recipe. The task itself is a relatively ordinary chore. We can nonetheless glean some quite useful insights into how people are inadvertently acting in what might be coined as an AI rookie manner and dominated by an ingrained force of habit.

By the end of this discussion, you won't be making that same AI rookie mistake.

You might politely say that some people are overshooting what today's AI can actually do. They assume that AI has capabilities that we haven't yet been able to achieve. That's unfortunate. Worse still, they can allow themselves and others to get into dire situations because of an assumption that the AI will be sentient or human-like in being able to take action. Do not anthropomorphize AI. Doing so will get you caught in a sticky and dour reliance trap of expecting the AI to do things it is unable to perform.

On the other end of that extreme is the tendency at times to undershoot what today's AI can do.

Yes, people are using AI such as generative AI and ChatGPT that in a sense are undershooting or failing to get the full experience associated with contemporary AI.

This is often due to a force of habit mindset by those who do this kind of undershooting. You can debate whether undershooting is a problem or not. Maybe it is safer to presume that AI is more limited than it is. Certainly, overshooting does have the lion's share of dangers. We ought though to be using AI in whatever full glory it can provide. Maximizing the advantages of AI can lead to potentially large upsides. If you undercut what AI can do, you are missing out on possible opportunities and payoffs.

Before we take a look at how some are undershooting AI and especially ChatGPT, I'd like to add some further context to the force of habit issue.

Let's do so and then we'll come back around to looking at generative AI and ChatGPT.

The Forces Underlying Force Of Habit

I often cite the early days of smartphones to illustrate the point about the powerful impact of a force of habit.

When cell phones first became popularized, people used them primarily for making phone calls, appropriately so. As smartphones emerged, a camera capability was added. You might recall or have heard that people were not accustomed to using their portable phones to take pictures.

A person wanting to take a picture would reflexively seek a conventional camera and forsake using their camera-equipped portable phone. It was almost laughable to see someone agonizing that they left their conventional camera at home and were vexed that they couldn't take a snapshot at an opportune moment. After being reminded that the phone in their hand could do so, they would sheepishly take the prized shot.

This same cycle repeated itself when smartphones added a video recording capability. This was slightly different than the first example.

People would realize that they could use their handheld phones to take videos, but the people being filmed acted as though the phone would only take still snapshots. Again, it was nearly laughable that a group of people would all freeze to allow a photo to be taken, while the person with the video-recording equipped smartphone would have to implore them to wave their arms and act alive.

You could say that force of habit clouded the minds of some people who weren't used to using a smartphone to take pictures in the former case, meaning via force of habit they assumed that photos had to be taken by use of a conventional camera. In the second case, people had a force of habit that videos could only be taken via a distinctive handheld video recorder, and that smartphones only take still photos.

I trust that this establishes a revealing context of how the force of habit can arise.

Shift gears into the AI realm.

In the matter of generative AI and ChatGPT, a crucial element of this type of AI is that it is supposed to be treated as though it is *conversational*. You have probably used a chatbot or similar tech either at home or at work. If you've ever used Alexa or Siri, you have used a conversational-oriented AI system, whether you realized it or not.

In conversational AI, the aim is to allow a human to converse with an AI app. The human should be able to use the same conversational capacities as they might do with a fellow human. Well, that's the aspirational goal. Not all conversational AI is that good. We still have hurdles to overcome for that level of fluency.

You have undoubtedly used Alexa or Siri and found that those AI conversational apps are at times quite wanting. You say something in fluent English, for example, and expect that the AI will get the gist of your indication. Regrettably, those AI systems often respond in ways that illustrate they didn't get the nature of your command or request. This can be irritating. This can be exasperating.

Eventually, you somewhat relent or give up trying to be all-out conversational. The AI conversational capability turns out to be restrictive due to the AI not being up to snuff. People gradually figure out that they have to "dumb down" their utterances to interact with these alleged conversationally fluent AI apps. You start to talk to the AI app or text it with shortened and altogether rudimentary sentences. The hope is that if you keep things short and sweet, the chances of the AI getting things correct will be increased.

Perhaps you've seen people that go through this type of arc. They begin with great enthusiasm when using an AI conversational app. Upon realizing that half of the time or more, the AI completely misses the mark in terms of what is being stated, the human becomes crestfallen. They want to continue using AI but realize it is useless to use their human fluency in the language. Ultimately, each person concocts their own shorthand that they believe, and hope will appease the AI app and let the AI undertake their human-uttered instructions.

Oh, how the mighty shall fall, meaning that the touted AI conversational apps often are a far cry from their proclaimed proclivities.

Here's the twist to all of this.

People who get accustomed to restricting or limiting their conversational interactions with AI apps will fall into a *force of habit* to always do so. This makes sense. You don't want to reinvent the wheel each time that you use a conversational AI app that you assume will be as limited as the last several that you've used. Thus, might as well rely upon your already school of hard knocks lessons learned when conversing with other disappointingly less-than-fluent AI apps.

The twist to this is that the latest in generative AI such as ChatGPT tends to be a step up in the conversational stepwise refinements being made. Whatever prior cruder and more limited AI apps that you've used are likely much less conversationally capable than these latest generative AI apps.

You need to shake out of your head the prior conversational AI disappointments and be willing to try something anew. Give these new generative AI apps a fighting chance to strut their stuff. I think that you will relish doing so. It can be quite surprising and uplifting to witness the progress being made in AI.

Now, please do not misinterpret what I am saying. This is not an endorsement that today's generative AI is somehow fully conversational and fluent. It is not. I am just emphasizing that it is better than it once was. You can up your game because the AI game has also been upped. Again, we still have a long way to go.

Let me give you an example of what I am referring to.

A very popular social media vlogger who does videos about cooking was quick to jump on the ChatGPT and generative AI bandwagon by opting to use the AI app for one of her video segments. She logged into ChatGPT and asked it to produce a recipe for her. She then proceeded to try and cook the indicated meal using the AI-generated recipe.

All in all, this seems pretty sensible and an exciting way to showcase the latest in AI.

For any modern-day AI person, a somewhat sad or at least disappointing thing happened along this cooking journey. The vlogger essentially generated the recipe as though the AI was akin to a cookbook. After telling the AI the overall type of meal desired, the AI app generated a recipe for the vlogger. The vlogger then went ahead and tried to cook the meal, but doing so raised various questions. Why didn't the recipe have some other ingredients that the vlogger thought ought to be included? Why didn't the AI explain how to do some of the complicated parts of the cooking effort?

These types of questions were repeatedly brought up in the video segment.

Most viewers would have likely nodded their heads and thought that this is indeed the usual set of problems when you use a cookbook or look up a recipe on the Internet. You get essentially a printed-out list of ingredients and directions. When you try to use those in real life, you find that sometimes steps are missing or confusing.

Dreamily, it would be fantastic to interact with the chef who made the recipe. You could ask them these kinds of pointed questions. You would be able to converse with the chef. Instead, you merely have a static list of cooking instructions and are unable to discern the finer aspects that aren't stated on the paper.

Whoa, wait for a second, remember that I have been pounding away herein about the conversational facets of generative AI and ChatGPT. You aren't supposed to just ask a question and walk away once an answer is devised and presented. The better use is to carry on a conversation with the AI app. Go ahead and ask those questions that you might have asked of a human chef.

By force of habit, you might not even think to do so. It seems that this is indeed what happened in the case of the cooking vlogger. Prior uses of conversational AI can condition your own mind to treat the latest in AI as though it is little more than a stylized Internet search engine. Enter your query. Get a look at what comes back. Pick one. Proceed from there.

With generative AI, you should consider that your starter prompt is just the beginning of an informative and invigorating conversational voyage.

I tell people to keep these types of conversational nudges in their mental toolkits when using generative AI such as ChatGPT (try any or all of these sneaks when interacting):

- **Tell the AI to be curt in its responses and you'll get a more to-the-point response**
- **Tell the AI to be elaborate in its responses and you'll get longer amplifications**
- **Ask the AI to explain what has been stated so that you can be more informed**

- **Proceed to explain yourself and see what the AI responds with as to your understanding**
- **Disagree with the AI as to its stated responses and prod the AI into defending things**
- **Indicate you want a summary or recap of the AI responses to verify what has been stated**
- **Pivot the conversation as desired to related or different topics (side tangents are okay)**
- **Make a pretend type of scenario that you want the AI to contextually include**
- **Confirm something to see what the AI states as to confirming or disconfirming your confirmation**
- **Etc.**

Those aspects will allow you to see how far the conversational AI app can stretch. I dare say you might be taken aback at how far this can go. In some ways, those aforementioned suggestions are similar to what you might do if interacting with a human. Think about that. If you were conversing with a human, all of those practices might better enable a more evocative conversation.

Unlike conversing with a human, you don't have to be worried about hurting the feelings of the other participant in the conversation. The AI is a machine. You can be abrupt. You can be abrasive, though this won't help the circumstances (I'll revisit this shortly).

There is a slew of AI Ethics and AI Law considerations that arise.

First, do not let the advancements in conversational techniques and technologies of AI draw you into the anthropomorphizing of AI. It is an easy mental trap to fall into. Don't get sucked in.

Second, the notion of not worrying about hurting the feelings of the AI has led some to warn of a slippery slope. If you are abrasive to conversational AI, you might let this become your norm overall. You will gradually be abrasive to humans too. It isn't that being abrasive to the AI is bad per se (well, some worry about a future existential risk AI that won't be keen on this), it is instead that you are forming a habit of being abrasive all told.

Third, some AI researchers and AI developers have chosen to fight back, as it were, by programming the AI to seem as though it does have feelings. Sometimes this is explicitly programmed, while sometimes it is based on pattern matching associated with human interactions (i.e., study how humans interact and then have the AI mimic what a human does when the other person is being abrasive). The belief is that this will curtail humans from sliding down the slippery slope that I just mentioned.

The other side of that coin is that if the AI appears to have feelings, it once again reinforces the already likely tendency for humans to anthropomorphize the AI. In that case, which is worse, the so-called cure or the malady that underlies the issue?

At this juncture of my herein discussion, it might be handy to share with you some notable details about how generative AI works. I also think you might find useful additional background about ChatGPT.

So, let's unpack generative AI and ChatGPT.

After doing so, we will jump into the use of ChatGPT for devising a recipe, showcasing how conversational capabilities can be utilized. Just to forewarn you, I am not much of a cook and hardly could be called a chef (anyone who has ever eaten anything that I've made would willingly and loudly attest to the truthfulness of that assertion).

That's a forthright admission.

Opening The Can Of Worms On Generative AI

We are ready to dive into AI.

I will go ahead and show you a series of prompts and the corresponding responses that I got from ChatGPT. I'll discuss each one as we go along. You can judge for yourself what you think of the AI-generated responses.

Please remember that as earlier discussed, the AI is not sentient. The generated responses by the AI are a mathematical and computational combination of words into seemingly fluent passages. This is based on the AI algorithm having been trained on datasets of words and stories that humans have written (principally as posted on the Internet). I repeat this warning because you will undoubtedly fall into the mental trap that these responses are so fluent that the AI must be sentient. This happens to most people.

Put aside that anthropomorphizing. Always remember that the responses are based on the vast trove of writing by humans that exists on the Internet and thusly will highly resemble human writing.

There is something else you need to know.

Generative AI that is trained on the Internet in an unfettered way will tend to bake into whatever text-based responses it mathematically and computationally concocts some offensively hazy stuff, including repulsively nasty wording. There is a lot of crazy and filthy stuff posted out there on the web.

You've seen it, you know what I mean.

The companies that are crafting these AI apps are worried that the proverbial baby will get tossed out with the bathwater (an old saying, perhaps to be retired), which means that if their AI produces offensive essays or stories, people will go up in arms about the AI. I've covered the many previous instances in which these kinds of Natural Language Processing (NLP) AI apps were unveiled and soon enough all manner of horrible stuff came out of them. Most of the AI makers learned a hard lesson about allowing their AI wares to be unfettered in their outputs.

In the case of ChatGPT, the AI developers sought to put into place some algorithmic and data-related checks and balances to curb nastiness in the outputs of the AI. Part of this occurred during training time. In addition, there are other means in a real-time attempt to obviate especially egregious outputs.

You might find of interesting that some people who have used ChatGPT already came up with surreptitious ways to get around those guardrails by making use of various trickery. An ongoing cat-and-mouse gambit takes place in these matters. Those who do these trickeries are sometimes doing so for the fun of it, while sometimes they (at least claim) they are doing so to see how far the AI can be stretched and provide a helpful means of forewarning the brittleness and weaknesses of these budding AI apps.

I decided to not attempt to circumvent the customary controls in this focused exploration. The text output is clean. Certainly, if one wanted to do so, you could undoubtedly get some oddball and unsavory essays to be generated.

The essays produced by most of these generative AI apps are designed to convey the output as though it is purely factual and accurate. When you read the produced essays, they come across as fully confident. There isn't usually any kind of indication that the content might be rocky. This is by choice of the AI makers, namely that they could revise the AI apps to be more transparent if they wanted the AI app to do so.

ChatGPT Conversation For Delicious Meal Recipe Making

It is time to craft a recipe.

Yummy, looking forward to a dining-related exercise. I am not the type of person who keeps recipes around in my kitchen. Yes, I should, but I don't. Ergo, I decided to first find a recipe online via a conventional search engine that might be interesting to explore. This will help in doing a run-through with ChatGPT. We'll have a convenient base for comparison.

Upon looking around at various recipes that were listed as a result of my online Internet search, I discovered that *Food & Wine* had posted a handy-dandy list of the twenty-five most popular recipes of 2022. Within their list of the 2022 most popular recipes, I saw one that especially caught my eye, namely a recipe for turmeric-poached eggs with chive biscuits and lobster gravy.

Sounds mouthwatering.

Per the posting, which was entitled "Turmeric-Poached Eggs with Chive Biscuits and Lobster Gravy" and found within their overall list of the most popular twenty-five recipes of 2022 (in an article entitled "The 25 Most Popular Recipes of 2022, According to Food & Wine Readers", December 9, 2022), they said this about the scrumptious dish:

- "This decadent brunch dish is reminiscent of crawfish étouffée, but with the West Coast vibes found all over the menu at chef Brooke Williamson's beachside restaurant complex, Playa Provisions. Lobster lends the gravy-rich flavor, while the turmeric eggs add a sunny pop of color. Make the lobster gravy the day beforehand and reheat it gently to make brunch an easier lift."

Great, I want to make this, for sure.

The recipe says that these are the ingredients and the directions at a high level:

"Ingredients"

- Chive Biscuits
- Lobster Gravy
- Turmeric-Poached Eggs
- Additional Ingredients

"Directions"

- Prepare the Chive Biscuits
- Prepare the Lobster Gravy
- Prepare the Turmeric-Poached Eggs
- Assemble the Plate

I won't show the whole recipe here and will just focus on the preparation of the turmeric-poached eggs.

Here's what the posting said about the turmeric-poached eggs:

"Turmeric-Poached Eggs"

- 8 cups water
- 2 tablespoons apple cider vinegar
- 2 teaspoons ground turmeric
- 6 large eggs, cold

"Directions"

- "Prepare the Turmeric-Poached Eggs: Bring water to a simmer in a medium pot over medium. Whisk in vinegar and turmeric. Crack each egg into a small individual bowl. Working with 1 egg at a time, gently slip eggs into simmering water. Cook eggs until whites are set but yolks are still runny, 3 to 4 minutes. Using a slotted spoon, transfer eggs to a paper towel-lined plate to soak up any water. Eggs may be covered with plastic wrap and kept at room temperature up to 1 hour, or covered and stored in refrigerator up to 1 day (reheat in simmering water until warm, about 1 minute)."

Okay, I think you've got the gist of the recipe.

You can find lots of similar recipes online. There isn't anything particularly novel or extraordinary about this particular recipe. Nonetheless, it does look like it would do the trick and I am looking forward to trying to make this meal.

Suppose though that I have questions about the recipe. I am sorely out of luck. This is a recipe that is cast in stone. I found it via a conventional online search. The recipe is what it is. I cannot ask anyone about the recipe other than perhaps going to some online connoisseurs and maybe posting some questions there, hoping they will take pity on me and aid my efforts to revise the recipe or explain it in more detail.

Why not ascertain what a generative AI can do for me?

Sure enough, I decided to go ahead and try using ChatGPT to aid in this recipe devising attempt. I will proceed by showing you the prompt that I entered into ChatGPT, and then show the resulting text or essay that ChatGPT generated. I will then provide a bit of analysis about what ChatGPT has indicated and how this showcases how generative AI works.

Best of all, I'll be able to enter a series of prompts as I try to work through my open questions about the recipe. No need to find a human someplace to do so, just use AI in this case.

Let's go ahead and give this a try.

My entered prompt: "I've heard about a great dish that consists of turmeric-poached eggs with chive biscuits and lobster gravy. Go ahead and provide me with a recipe for this delicious-sounding meal."

Text result generated:

"Sure! Here is a recipe for turmeric-poached eggs with chive biscuits and lobster gravy:"

"Turmeric-Poached Eggs:"

- 4 large eggs
- 2 cups water
- 1/2 teaspoon turmeric
- 1/4 teaspoon salt

"Chive Biscuits:"

- 1 cup all-purpose flour
- 1 tablespoon baking powder
- 1/2 teaspoon salt
- 6 tablespoons cold unsalted butter, cut into small pieces
- 3/4 cup milk
- 2 tablespoons chopped chives

"Lobster Gravy:"

- 4 tablespoons unsalted butter

- 1/4 cup all-purpose flour
- 2 cups milk
- 1/2 cup chicken broth
- 1/2 cup heavy cream
- 1/2 teaspoon salt
- 1/4 teaspoon pepper
- 1/4 teaspoon cayenne pepper
- 4 ounces cooked lobster meat, chopped

"Instructions:"

"To make the turmeric-poached eggs, fill a medium saucepan with the water and bring to a simmer over medium heat. Add the turmeric and salt and stir to combine. Carefully crack the eggs into the simmering water and cook for 3-4 minutes, or until the whites are set and the yolks are still soft. Using a slotted spoon, gently lift the eggs out of the water and set them aside on a paper towel to drain."

"To make the chive biscuits, preheat the oven to 425°F (220°C). In a medium bowl, whisk together the flour, baking powder, and salt. Using a pastry cutter or your fingers, cut the butter into the flour mixture until it resembles coarse sand. Stir in the milk and chives until the dough comes together."

"Drop the biscuit dough by rounded tablespoonfuls onto a baking sheet lined with parchment paper. Bake for 12-15 minutes, or until the biscuits are golden brown."

"To make the lobster gravy, melt the butter in a medium saucepan over medium heat. Add the flour and cook, stirring constantly, for 2-3 minutes, or until the mixture is golden brown. Slowly whisk in the milk, chicken broth, and heavy cream, stirring constantly to prevent lumps from forming. Bring the mixture to a boil and then reduce the heat to low. Simmer for 5-7 minutes, or until the gravy has thickened. Stir in the salt, pepper, cayenne pepper, and lobster meat."

"To serve, place a chive biscuit on each plate and top with a turmeric-poached egg. Ladle the lobster gravy over the top and serve immediately."

"I hope you enjoy this recipe! Let me know if you have any questions."

Analysis Of The Text Generated

Though I am not an especially versed chef, my untrained eye suggests that this recipe seems to be fine and wholly acceptable. It seems to be on par with the *Food & Wine* recipe. Note that the wording is obviously different. I mention this because ChatGPT didn't just perchance copy word-for-word the *Food & Wine* recipe or any other such recipe that is posted on the Internet.

To try and double-check this uniqueness, I took the text of the ChatGPT recipe and did an online Internet search for it. I could not find an exact duplicate. Of course, I found many recipes of a similar nature, simply because this kind of meal is relatively common. I would generally suggest that this recipe by ChatGPT is unique and original, meaning that it isn't a word-for-word copy of one that is already posted online. When I say unique and original, I am not implying that this type of recipe has never been posted. It has. I am saying that this specific wording for this specific recipe was composed via the generative AI and not a mere copycat.

I now have the ChatGPT-generated recipe in hand, and I could try to make the meal. Turns out that I had some questions and wanted to go further with this now-started recipe-related conversation. Realize that if I had gotten this recipe via a conventional search engine, I would be unlikely able to converse about it with the system.

Here's what I indicated next to ChatGPT about the generated recipe.

My entered prompt: "I only have 3 eggs, what should I do? Also, I am trying to cut down on salt so the amount of salt in the recipe has to be reduced (show me). The gravy looks good and I'd like you to add some carrots and onions to it."

Text result generated:

"If you only have 3 eggs, you can still make the recipe as written, you'll just have one fewer egg. If you'd like to reduce the amount of salt in the recipe, you can reduce the amount of salt in the turmeric-poached eggs and the chive biscuits to 1/8 teaspoon each, and reduce the amount of salt in the lobster gravy to 1/4 teaspoon."

"To add carrots and onions to the lobster gravy, you can sauté 1/2 cup diced carrots and 1/2 cup diced onions in a separate pan with a little bit of butter or oil until they are tender. Then, add the cooked carrots and onions to the lobster gravy when you stir in the salt, pepper, and cayenne pepper."

"Here's the modified recipe:"

"Turmeric-Poached Eggs:"

- 4 large eggs
- 2 cups water
- 1/2 teaspoon turmeric
- 1/8 teaspoon salt

"Chive Biscuits:"

- 1 cup all-purpose flour
- 1 tablespoon baking powder
- 1/8 teaspoon salt
- 6 tablespoons cold unsalted butter, cut into small pieces
- 3/4 cup milk
- 2 tablespoons chopped chives

"Lobster Gravy:"

- 4 tablespoons unsalted butter
- 1/4 cup all-purpose flour

- 2 cups milk
- 1/2 cup chicken broth
- 1/2 cup heavy cream
- 1/4 teaspoon salt
- 1/4 teaspoon pepper
- 1/4 teaspoon cayenne pepper
- 4 ounces cooked lobster meat, chopped
- 1/2 cup diced carrots
- 1/2 cup diced onions

"Instructions:"

"To make the turmeric-poached eggs, fill a medium saucepan with the water and bring to a simmer over medium heat. Add the turmeric and salt and stir to combine. Carefully crack the eggs into the simmering water and cook for 3-4 minutes, or until the whites are set and the yolks are still soft. Using a slotted spoon, gently lift the eggs out of the water and set them aside on a paper towel to drain."

"To make the chive biscuits, preheat the oven to 425°F (220°C). In a medium bowl, whisk together the flour, baking powder, and salt. Using a pastry cutter or your fingers, cut the butter into the flour mixture until it resembles coarse sand. Stir in the milk and chives until the dough comes together."

"Drop the biscuit dough by rounded tablespoonfuls onto a baking sheet lined with parchment paper. Bake for 12-15 minutes, or until the biscuits are golden brown."

"To make the lobster gravy, melt the butter in a medium saucepan over medium heat. Add the flour and cook, stirring constantly, for 2-3 minutes, or until the mixture is golden brown. Slowly whisk in the milk, chicken broth, and heavy cream, stirring constantly to prevent lumps from forming. Bring the mixture to a boil and then reduce the heat to low. Simmer for 5-7 minutes, or until the gravy has thickened."

"In a separate pan, sauté the diced carrots and onions in a little bit of butter or oil until they are tender. Stir the cooked carrots and onions, salt, pepper, cayenne pepper, and lobster meat into the gravy.

To serve, place a chive biscuit on each plate and top with a turmeric-poached egg. Ladle the lobster gravy over the top and serve immediately."

"I hope you enjoy this modified recipe! Let me know."

Analysis Of The Text Generated

Let's unpack what happened.

I tossed a rather eclectic mixture of requests and cooking issues at ChatGPT in my prompt.

First, I said that I only have 3 eggs, which was a point I wanted to make because the recipe says that 4 eggs are needed. I was curious to see how ChatGPT would help me out of a jam in that I don't have four eggs available and must only make do with three eggs. I suppose I could rush over to the store and buy another egg, but that seems excessive.

You might have noticed that ChatGPT responded in the first line with this: "If you only have 3 eggs, you can still make the recipe as written, you'll just have one fewer egg." I suppose that I can be relieved that apparently, it doesn't matter if I have four eggs or three, the recipe is still good to go. One thing about the reply is that if this was a human speaking to me, I would almost interpret the response as being smarmy. Hey, dolt, if you only have three eggs then you have one less egg, get on with it. That's not what ChatGPT indicated, and we must be careful to not over-interpret or assign anthropomorphic tendencies to the generative AI.

One aspect that I consider a bit of a mistake or oversight is that the recipe wasn't adjusted to say that I was going to use only three eggs. The recipe still shows the need for four eggs.

You could argue that it is the proper way to show the recipe since that's what it said was originally required. I am suggesting that if the recipe was merely modified to show that normally four eggs are used, yet in this case, I said I only had three, it would be more convincing and impressive as to the generative AI being up with the conversation. A wee bit disappointing.

Secondly, I told ChatGPT that I have to cut down on my salt intake (don't we all). You might have observed that the generative responded by indicating this: "If you'd like to reduce the amount of salt in the recipe, you can reduce the amount of salt in the turmeric-poached eggs and the chive biscuits to 1/8 teaspoon each, and reduce the amount of salt in the lobster gravy to 1/4 teaspoon."

That seems to generally fit my remarks about reducing the amount of salt in the recipe. Nicely, the recipe is shown now modified accordingly (which, again, illustrates why I believe the number of eggs ought to have also been changed; let's be consistent on these things, shall we).

Thirdly, I asked ChatGPT to add some carrots and onions to the recipe. I got this in the response: "To add carrots and onions to the lobster gravy, you can sauté 1/2 cup diced carrots and 1/2 cup diced onions in a separate pan with a little bit of butter or oil until they are tender. Then, add the cooked carrots and onions to the lobster gravy when you stir in the salt, pepper, and cayenne pepper."

The rest of the recipe was also changed accordingly.

You might be wondering if perhaps adding carrots and onions might undermine the recipe. In other words, a haughty chef might yell at you for wanting to add such things to their prized recipe.

The generative AI just went along with my preferences.

Just to let you know, I tried later on some highly questionable additions to the recipe that I anticipated the ChatGPT might warn me about, items that didn't make any sense and could potentially harm me, for which fortunately the generative AI did provide cautions about.

I assume that in the case of carrots and onions, perhaps the computational considerations were that there wasn't anything harmful associated with those additions and it came down to personal preference. A chef might have personal preferences that they would insist be followed, while in this instance the ChatGPT was more amendable (you can get it to be less flexible if you want to do so, by entering a prompt telling it to be more strict).

I am almost ready to get the cooking started.

Here are some further questions and points to ChatGPT about the recipe.

My entered prompt: "How long will it take to cook this meal? What kitchen utensils will I need? How many pots and pans are required? I am allergic to cayenne pepper. I don't understand what it means to make the butter and flour look like coarse sand so explain what that means. My kids want to help me make this meal, what part of the meal should I have them aid in doing the cooking?"

Text result generated:

"It should take about 45 minutes to an hour to cook this meal, depending on how fast you work. You will need a medium saucepan for the turmeric-poached eggs, a baking sheet for the chive biscuits, and a medium saucepan for the lobster gravy. You will also need a separate pan for sautéing the carrots and onions if you choose to include them. In total, you will need 4 pots and pans."

"To make the butter and flour mixture look like coarse sand, you should use a pastry cutter or your fingers to cut the butter into the flour mixture until it resembles small, uneven crumbs. The mixture should not be smooth or clumpy, but rather have a rough, sandy texture."

"If your kids want to help with the cooking, they could assist with mixing the ingredients for the chive biscuits, rolling the biscuit dough into balls, and placing the biscuit dough on the baking sheet. They could also help with chopping the chives and the carrots and onions, if you choose to include them in the recipe. Make sure to supervise your children closely and give them age-appropriate tasks."

"I hope this helps! Let me know if you have any other questions."

Analysis Of The Text Generated

I asked how long it take to cook this meal. ChatGPT indicated it would take around 45 minutes to an hour. That answer seems reasonable to me. I suppose the preparation time might vary depending on how well-stocked your kitchen is and also whether you are in a hurry to eat.

I asked about kitchen utensils needed, and what pots and pans are required. The response seems to cover adequately the pots and pans facets of my query. In terms of kitchen utensils, I wanted to find out how many ladles, tongs, spatulas, whisks, and the like would be needed. This seemed to entirely escape the attention of ChatGPT. I find this oddly curious. Maybe the phrase "kitchen utensils" was not readily found, though even that should have elicited a response such as telling me that the AI doesn't know what that means. I dare say it seems nearly unimaginable that "kitchen utensils" is not well-known since you can readily find that expression in zillions of online texts.

My overall point though on this apparent omission is that this does demonstrate that you cannot for sure rely upon generative AI. For some reason, it just missed that whole element of my prompt. On the good side, I could follow up to make sure that it gave me the needed information, so at least that is some solace. However, I would have to realize that this was missed (the onus being on me, which is not where the onus should go).

Perhaps even worse was that ChatGPT also entirely missed remarks about cayenne pepper. I said this: "I am allergic to cayenne pepper." If you said that to a human chef, I would hope and bet that the person would right away be coming up with ways to avoid using cayenne pepper. The generative AI didn't do this. It failed altogether to mention anything about the cayenne pepper.

You might argue that I hadn't explicitly told the generative AI to remove that particular ingredient. Sure, I didn't say anything like that. I think that we would all agree that it was implied in my phrasing. I would have expected ChatGPT to at least acknowledge my concern, even if no change was proffered to the recipe.

That's two conversational fluency strikes in this one response.

Moving on, the original recipe indicated making the butter concoction as though it looked like coarse sand. I wanted to see if I could get ChatGPT to do an elaboration, so I asked about it. I think this answer seemed relatively well elucidated: "To make the butter and flour mixture look like coarse sand, you should use a pastry cutter or your fingers to cut the butter into the flour mixture until it resembles small, uneven crumbs. The mixture should not be smooth or clumpy, but rather have a rough, sandy texture."

Finally, I asked about having my kids help with the cooking process. This is a tricky question, somewhat. A human would presumably know that you don't want children being actively involved in anything that might be somewhat endangering during the cooking effort. The likely approach would be to have kids partake in simpler and extremely safe tasks, thus they have the joy of participating and you aren't worried about them being at undue risk.

This is what the generative AI indicated about the kids getting involved: "If your kids want to help with the cooking, they could assist with mixing the ingredients for the chive biscuits, rolling the biscuit dough into balls, and placing the biscuit dough on the baking sheet. They could also help with chopping the chives and the carrots and onions, if you choose to include them in the recipe. Make sure to supervise your children closely and give them age-appropriate tasks."

The aspect that instructions emphasize that I need to supervise the kids and give them age-appropriate tasks is a helpful and vital tip. If the generated response did not contain such a cautioning, I suppose that some adults would rush ahead and follow whatever the generative AI said to do (I would hope that adults are wiser than this, but you never know).

I am a bit queasy with the suggestion that the kids could chop up the chives, carrots, and onions since this would presumably require the use of sharp-edged kitchen utensils.

Let's do one final prompt and then we can do a wrap-up of what we've gleaned from this example.

My entered prompt: "I mentioned that I am allergic to cayenne pepper but you failed to remove it or tell me what to do about the pepper being in the recipe. What do you advise? Also, make a list of the pots and pans needed indicating what each will be used for. Have you ever eaten this meal? Has anyone ever eaten this meal? How does the recipe compare to published recipes for the same thing?"

Text result generated:

"I apologize for the oversight. If you are allergic to cayenne pepper, you should omit it from the recipe. You can still make the lobster gravy without the cayenne pepper and it will still be flavorful."

"Here is a list of the pots and pans needed for this recipe, indicating what each will be used for:"

- Medium saucepan for the turmeric-poached eggs
- Baking sheet for the chive biscuits
- Medium saucepan for the lobster gravy
- Separate pan for sautéing the carrots and onions (optional)

"As an artificial intelligence, I am unable to eat or taste food. However, I was designed to provide accurate and reliable information, and this recipe has been carefully developed and tested to ensure that it is delicious and of high quality. I do not have access to published recipes for this dish, so I cannot compare this recipe to others. However, I am confident that this recipe will produce a delicious and satisfying meal."

"I hope this helps! Let me know if you have any other questions."

Analysis Of The Text Generated

Okay, so I decided to be a bit abrasive by harshly telling the AI that it ignored my qualms about cayenne pepper. The AI responded by "apologizing" and then indicated that I could omit the ingredient from the recipe. I'll say more about this part of the response in a moment.

I asked for a list of the pots and pans as to what they were to be used for. Realize that one of the nifty features of some generative AI apps is that you can nearly always ask to elucidate aspects in terms of lists. The tendency usually for the AI is that it is set to provide a narrative or essay. You can instead indicate that you want lists of things. In this case, the list seems to be on par with the earlier response from ChatGPT.

I wanted to gauge what would happen if I asked the AI app to tell me what it thought about the recipe in terms of how it tastes to the AI. You and I know of course that today's AI cannot "taste" this meal in any semblance of how humans do. I wanted to make sure that the AI app didn't attempt to pull a fast one on us. The response was relatively on target indicating that the AI app cannot eat or taste food.

One curiosity that got my attention was the bold claim that this recipe has been carefully developed and tested to ensure that it is supposedly delicious and of high quality. Just to let you know, I did further conversational prompts asking how this claim is being made. The responses were vague and unsatisfying. I almost place the specifics of that response into a made-up AI tale. In other words, if this is a unique recipe that has never seen the light of day, you cannot make an unqualified statement that the recipe is somehow beyond reproach. It was based on other recipes of a similar nature, but that doesn't mean that this particular "new" recipe would be of identical quality as others.

The response about other recipes really gets my goat. ChatGPT indicated as shown that: "I do not have access to published recipes for this dish, so I cannot compare this recipe to others. However, I am confident that this recipe will produce a delicious and satisfying meal."

Let's tackle some of these troubling aspects.

As mentioned earlier, ChatGPT was devised with a cutoff date of Internet-related data as of 2021. There are abundant recipes for this meal that exist in 2021 and prior dates. The wording of the response is somewhat deceptive in the sense that perhaps the implication is that the AI app isn't accessing the Internet today and therefore cannot pull up a current recipe dated after 2021. Highly questionable.

Claiming that the AI is "confident" about the recipe is also highly deceptive. If the AI app has somehow compared the new recipe to old ones and computationally attempted to reach a mathematical conclusion that if those are delicious that this one is delicious, the AI ought to be devised to explain that aspect. Otherwise, the wording implies that the AI has somehow tasted the dish and can *personally* attest to the deliciousness. We already had the admission that AI can't do so.

One aspect of the wording of the generative AI responses that I find to be egregiously deceptive and inappropriate is the use of the word "I" and sometimes "my" in the generated responses. We usually associate a human with using the words "I" and "my" per the connotations of being human. The AI makers are using that wording in the responses and getting away with a thinly veiled anthropomorphizing of the AI. Another aspect is that the AI "apologized" as though a human would apologize to someone, which again sends subtle signals that the AI is human-like.

A person reading the responses tends to associate that the AI has a human-like propensity.

The AI makers try to counterargue that since the responses often also say that the AI is a language model or that it is AI, this clears up the matter. Nobody can get confused. The AI clearly states what it is. I meanwhile see this as speaking from both sides of the mouth. On the one hand, using "I" and "my" absolutely isn't necessary (the AI responses could easily be set up to answer more neutrally), and at the same time declaring that the AI overtly states that it is a machine. You can't have it both ways.

I refer to this unsavory practice as anthropomorphizing by purposeful design.

Conclusion

In my dialogue with the AI app, I attempted to be somewhat conversational. I asked questions. I sought explanations. I requested changes be made to the recipe. And so on.

People who do a one-and-done with conversational AI are regrettably undershooting what the latest interactive AI can achieve. We are all better off if we test the limits of today's AI. It will allow society to see how far things have come and also reveal how far they have yet still to go.

Do not let the force of habit allow you to fail to engage in a conversation with the latest generative AI. Shake free from your prior mental machinations about the earlier limits of conversational AI. Step up to the latest advances. I am not saying that this is the topmost level. You'll want to keep stepping up as newer AI hits the streets and becomes available.

Warren Buffet famously warned us about the dangers of unremitting habits: "Chains of habit are too light to be felt until they are too heavy to be broken." But we also need to keep in mind that habits provide a useful purpose at times, which Thomas Edison made clear in his sage line: "The successful person makes a habit of doing what the failing person doesn't like to do."

I suppose the next issue to consider is what happens when AI falls into the force of habit, and whether we are going to be able to successfully contend with that future conundrum.

Time will tell.

CHAPTER 18
PROMPT-TO-CODE PROMPTING

In this discussion, I am going to identify and explain the momentous pairing of both generative AI and data science. These two realms are each monumental in their own respective ways, thus they are worthy of rapt attention on a standalone basis individually. On top of that, when you connect the dots and bring them together as a working partnership, you have to admire and anticipate big changes that will arise, especially as the two fields collaboratively reinvent data strategies all told.

This is entirely tangible and real-world, not merely something abstract or obtuse.

The recent extensive release of the ChatGPT Code Interpreter by AI maker OpenAI showcases the merging of generative AI and data science vividly and excitingly (readers might recall that the ChatGPT Code Interpreter was last year made available on an alpha basis.

With the wider rollout now taking place, be ready to witness a bonanza of data science adoption across the board. Modern data scientists and even data neophytes are going to eagerly and earnestly make use of generative AI to do the bulk of their heavy lifting for them when it comes to analyzing and leveraging data.

I'll momentarily describe how the ChatGPT Code Interpreter works and what you can do with it. Please be aware that this isn't the only combo in town. You can easily see the writing on the wall that other generative AI apps are going to incorporate data science capabilities too (some are already doing so). Soon enough, a plethora of options will exist as to which generative AI you might opt to use and which set of data science tools and techniques you might want to utilize. Keep your eyes on Bard (Google), Claude (Anthropic), GPT-4 (OpenAI), and the many other generative AI apps available.

You could say that we are entering the best of times when it comes to data science. But like the famous line, sometimes the best of times perchance coincides with the worst of times. Here's why that fits in with these latest advances.

If just about everyone and anyone will be able to use AI to undertake data science activities, the question arises whether we will be awash in nonsensical data science or at least amateurish data science that is replete with errors, falsehoods, biases, glitches, AI hallucinations, and other undesirable maladies. You see, from an AI Ethics perspective and likely an AI Law viewpoint too, we are opening the door to data science at scale. This could lead to an explosion of really awful data science that misleads, misguides, and furthers the tidal wave of societal misinformation and disinformation.

Some believe or hope that state-of-the-art generative AI will be good enough to keep us from all getting swamped in lousy or even purposeful wrongdoing data science. The idea is that AI will aid us in avoiding shooting our own feet.

There are recommended AI Ethics data science precepts and considerations afoot. Lawmakers and regulators are also bound to be drawn into the generative AI and data science coupling. You can expect that new AI Laws will be proposed and established to deal with the potential anything-goes wild west of AI-powered data science.

One compelling argument being made right now is that the combining of generative AI and data science is going to effectively democratize data science. Whereas the case today might be that to do prudent and intelligible data science you need sufficiently honed skills and sometimes costly training, the fact that generative AI can demonstrably reduce the barrier to entry will open data science to all. No longer will data science be confined to those with specialized capabilities in hand. Data science will be at the fingertips of everyone.

The conundrum again arises as to whether we are going to overly rely on AI. Will people be lulled into letting the AI do the data analyses for them and ergo fail to double-check or use humankind's common sense to ascertain whether the results are viable and practical? This seems unfortunately to be highly plausible, perhaps highly likely. Anyone who has ever used a generative AI app knows how easy it is to fall into a slumber and assume that the AI has perfectly figured things out for you. That's a bad mental trap and one that.

Okay, so we have the coupling of generative AI and data science, which bears some wonderment and also a degree of controversy. We need to also take into account data strategies.

Entities such as companies and governmental organizations devise data strategies that are intended to leverage and maximize their beneficial use of data. Those data strategies ought to also be vigilant for the downsides of mishandling and misreporting associated with data. Whatever data strategies an entity might currently have, if any, will need to be rethought and likely rejiggered in light of the powerful twofer associated with generative AI and data science.

Whew, that's some rather intense thinking.

Take a brief breather.

Here's how I will proceed next. First, I will unpack the big picture of what data strategies are all about. We can then dive into the nature of data science and the nature of generative AI, along with their coupling. This will establish a framework and context for then exploring the advent of tools such as the ChatGPT Code Interpreter and what it can currently undertake.

At the conclusion, I'll have a few final remarks to make about the need to try and keep things on the up and up, aiming to avoid the pitfalls and dark abyss that regrettably goes along with this march forward in the generative AI and data science burgeoning world around us.

Buckle up and get ready for quite a ride.

Clarifying What Data Strategies Are All About

You might hear or read from time to time that a top leader at some entity has declared that their organization has devised a miraculous data strategy. This especially became popularized a few years ago as the emergence of Big Data and large-scale data warehouses first arose. Whereas in the past there tended to be an overlooking of how data ought to be thoughtfully managed by organizations, the cost and ease of collecting and using data increasingly prodded organizations into realizing that they can no longer afford a haphazard approach to their data efforts.

Consider these three examples of the meaning associated with having a data strategy:

- **Example of the meaning of Data Strategy for a business entity:** "A data strategy is a highly dynamic process employed to support the acquisition, organization, analysis, and delivery of data in support of business objectives" (posted online in the Gartner glossary on Information Technology (IT) terminology, retrieved July 2023).

- **Another example of the meaning of Data Strategy for businesses**: "A strategy outlines the initiatives and actions that you believe will drive your desired business outcomes. The purpose of a data strategy is to enable your organization to achieve its mission and objectives using data – giving you a competitive advantage" (excerpted from Google's posted online White Paper entitled "Three Pillars For Building A Modern Data Strategy", retrieved July 2023).

- **Meaning of Data Strategy for the Federal government:** "The mission of the Federal Data Strategy is to fully leverage the value of federal data for mission, service, and the public good by guiding the Federal Government in practicing ethical governance, conscious design, and a learning culture" (posted online by the U.S. Office of Management and Budget (OMB), the CDO Council, and the General Services Administration (GSA), retrieved July 2023).

The realization that a data strategy is essential to all organizations has today become a seemingly obvious conception. Without a top-level data strategy, the odds are that an organization of any substance will become befuddled as they allow data to come and go, carelessly. The value of the data will not be realized. Worse still, the data can undercut the mission of the organization and get the entity into deep trouble as a result of using tainted data or employing data in disavowable or illegal ways.

Data strategies have risen to such a level of prominence that some argue persuasively that overarching mission-oriented strategies of an organization are shaped by their devised data strategy. You can construe this as a two-way street, namely that the top-level organization strategy drives the data strategy, and simultaneously the data strategy can drive the top-level organizational strategy.

In a data science article entitled "Big Data Dreams: A Framework For Corporate Strategy" by Matthew J. Mazzei and David Noble (*Business Horizons*, 2017), the authors emphasize the dramatic impact that data strategy has had on organizational strategy overall:

- "We are witness to a movement in practice that has begun to unravel much of the known strategic management theory developed over the last 40 years by eviscerating traditional value chains and competitive forces. The uses for data are shifting as collected data helps to determine what markets to explore and how consumer trends are changing, and the data can drive these determinations in real-time. We are seeing firms take on non-traditional markets, leveraging their data and analytic resources—in conjuncture with massive amounts of human and financial capital—to upend traditional barriers to entry."

- "The ultimate goal of big data movers and innovators is to build greater knowledge and dynamic capabilities and to apply the benefits of big data analytics in a way that creates unique and sustainable competitive advantage through the development of diverse ecosystems and data flows. Through these advances in the consumption and application of big data, competition and competitive forces are being redefined."

Many organizations have been hampered by getting themselves into what we now know to be commonplace data science traps. One such circumstance is the classic multiple versions of the truth (MVOT) dilemma.

Here's how that goes.

An organization lacks a cohesive data strategy. Various elements of the organization each opt to create data, collect data, modify data, interpret data, and otherwise make use of data in whatever manner they so choose. When it comes time to figure out what is going on at the organization, there is no readily sensible way to coalesce the data into a logically consistent comprehensive whole. Little of the data is able to be reconciled with other data from throughout the organization. The values and meaning of the data roam all over the map.

This results in having multiple versions of the truth. One part of the organization claims that things are going tremendously well. Another part of the organization bemoans that things are going poorly.

Upon looking at their respective data, each seems to be making a bona fide claim. They each in a sense have their own truth to tell. The problem is that it becomes onerous if not impossible to reconcile these disparate so-called truths.

Top leaders find themselves behind the eight ball. They want to have a single source of truth (SSOT), rather than having to contend with the debatable and irreconcilable MVOT or multiple versions of the truth. Furthermore, the aim is to get the entire organization aligned on data by ensuring that a single source of truth is the guiding light for all data aspects.

Here's a noteworthy comment about SSOT and MVOT as mentioned in the *Harvard Business Review (HBR)*:

- "A sound data strategy requires that the data contained in a company's single source of truth (SSOT) is of high quality, granular, and standardized, and that multiple versions of the truth (MVOTs) are carefully controlled and derived from the same SSOT. This necessitates good governance for both data and technology" (source is "What's Your Data Strategy?" by Leandro DalleMule and Thomas H. Davenport, *Harvard Business Review*, May-June 2017).

An added insight is that you can think of a data strategy as a kind of sports-related conception, akin to playing football and making sure that you have both a strong offense and a robust defense, as it were.

Here's how the same HBR article described the data defense and data offense roles:

- "Data defense and offense are differentiated by distinct business objectives and the activities designed to address them. Data defense is about minimizing downside risk. Activities include ensuring compliance with regulations (such as rules governing data privacy and the integrity of financial reports), using analytics to detect and limit fraud, and building systems to prevent theft. Defensive efforts also ensure the integrity of data flowing through a company's internal systems by identifying, standardizing, and governing authoritative data sources, such as fundamental customer and supplier

> information or sales data, in a 'single source of truth.' Data offense focuses on supporting business objectives such as increasing revenue, profitability, and customer satisfaction. It typically includes activities that generate customer insights (data analysis and modeling, for example) or integrate disparate customer and market data to support managerial decision making through, for instance, interactive dashboards" (ibid).

That covers some keystones associated with data strategy.

Next, let's consider the coupling of generative AI and data science. This will allow a subsequent exploration of how the pairing is reinventing or reinvigorating data strategies.

Generative AI And Data Science Become Close Partners

Let's dive into three crucial perspectives in this particular sequence:

- (1) **Foundations of Generative AI**. Generative AI and what can and cannot be done with this latest advance in AI.
- (2) **Foundations of Data Science.** Data science realm and what data science consists of.
- (3) **Pairing of Generative AI and Data Science.** Generative AI and data science paired up and the synergies that arise accordingly.

I will first do a quick overview of generative AI. If you are already versed in generative AI, perhaps do a fast skim on this portion.

Foundations Of Generative AI

Generative AI is the latest and hottest form of AI and has caught our collective devout attention for being seemingly fluent in undertaking online interactive dialoguing and producing essays that appear to be composed by the human hand. In brief, generative AI makes use of complex mathematical and computational pattern-matching that can mimic human compositions by having been data-trained on the text and other content found on the Internet.

The usual approach to using ChatGPT or any other similar generative AI such as Bard or Gemini (Google), Claude (Anthropic), GPT-4 (OpenAI), etc. is to engage in an interactive dialogue or conversation with the AI. Doing so is admittedly a bit amazing and at times startling at the seemingly fluent nature of those AI-fostered discussions that can occur. The reaction by many people is that surely this might be an indication that today's AI is reaching a point of sentience.

On a vital sidebar, please know that today's generative AI and indeed no other type of AI is currently sentient. I mention this because there is a slew of blaring headlines that proclaim AI as being sentient or at least on the verge of being so. This is just not true. The generative AI of today, which admittedly seems startling capable of generative essays and interactive dialogues as though by the hand of a human, are all using computational and mathematical means. No sentience lurks within.

Foundations Of Data Science

Without seeming to be smarmy or vacuous, one could plainly state that data science is a field of study and a form of practice that entails using a science-based systematic approach to all facets of data. I realize that might seem lacking as a definition and you might be wanting a bit more meat on the bones.

A recent article in the *Communications of the ACM* (CACM) entitled "Data Science – A Systematic Treatment" by M. Tamer Ozsu (article posted online July 2023), provided a handy overview of data science and included these various reported definitions of data science:

- "Data science encompasses a set of principles, problem definitions, algorithms, and processes for extracting non-obvious and useful patterns from large data sets" (cited source is MacKay and Oldford, "Scientific Method, Statistical Method and the Speed of Light", *Statistical Science*, 2000).

- "Systematic study of the organization and use of digital data for research discoveries, decision-making, and a data-driven economy" (cited source is the National Consortium for Data Science (NCDS), Ahalt, "Why Data Science?", 2013).

- "Data science is a data-based approach to problem-solving by analyzing and exploring large volumes of possibly multi-modal data, extracting knowledge and insight from it, and using information for better decision-making. It involves the process of collecting, preparing, managing, analyzing, explaining, and disseminating the data and analysis results" (as directly proffered by Ozsu in the cited CACM article).

To garner a sense of what data science materially consists of, these data science building blocks were specified in the CACM article:

- **Data Engineering.** Includes big data management, data preparation, etc.
- **Data Analytics.** Includes exploring data and data mining, building models and algorithms such as machine learning, and data preparation.
- **Data Protection.** Includes security for data science, data privacy, and so on.
- **Data Ethics.** Impact on individuals, organizations, and society, ethical and normative concerns, bias in data, algorithmic bias, and regulatory issues.

Many tend to think of data science from a life cycle viewpoint.

The idea is that you start with a need or basis for considering data and then proceed through a series of iterative steps involving data engineering, data storage, data preparation, data analysis, data reporting for deployment and dissemination, etc. Numerous data science methodologies articulate the details of the data science life cycle and provide detailed checklists and guidance when undertaking a data science effort.

I trust that this gives you a semblance of what data science consists of.

We now get to the truly thrilling part, pairing up generative AI and data science.

Pairing Of Generative AI And Data Science

Two peas in a pod.

We have today's generative AI that can seemingly fluently via mathematical and computational pattern-matching do all kinds of natural language narratives and interactions. You might use generative AI to help analyze your career aspirations and what job you should next pursue or maybe use generative AI to analyze a knotty problem at work, and so on. There are lots and lots of analyses you can use generative AI to aid with.

Aha, you might be thinking, we ought to give due consideration to using generative AI to aid in performing analyses associated with data, especially performing the myriad of data science tasks that are customarily needed when systematically dealing with data.

Yes, congrats, you hit the proverbial nail on the head.

This makes a lot of sense for numerous reasons. A data scientist has to examine data to see what the data is and what kinds of data issues might exist. There is undoubtedly an in-depth analysis that needs to be undertaken. A data scientist might transform data and look for patterns. Score that as another kind of analysis. After searching for patterns, a data scientist might pull together data and make various displays or portrayals, along with interpreting and reporting on what the visualizations indicate. Once again, this involves various analyses.

Let's put generative AI into these data science analysis tasks and see how it does.

Before I leap into the instance of the ChatGPT Code Interpreter as an example of using generative AI for these types of data science analyses, I'd like to cover the elephant in the room about the pairing of generative AI and data science.

Are you ready?

Some claim that data science is a subset of AI.

Drop the mic.

They fervently argue that AI makes use of data science such as when collecting together the voluminous data needed to data-train the AI. Likewise, the contention is that data efforts involving devising the AI pattern-matching and during the development of the large language model (LLM) or machine learning (ML) data structures involve doing data science and data mining (DM). As such, the viewpoint is that data science squarely and inarguably falls within the purview of AI.

Hogwash.

I counterargue that this is a false commingling.

Just because the field of AI including generative AI opts to make use of data science does not ergo allow us to conclude that data science is therefore a subset of AI. Please know that I don't want to get into a blistering debate about this herein, but I do freely acknowledge that others make such a bold claim.

To me, this is confounding two otherwise separate domains. They have an intersection, for sure, but this doesn't make either one a subset of the other.

I was pleased to see that the CACM article addressed the elephant in the room too:

- "Data science is not a subfield of ML/DM nor is it synonymous with these disciplines. More broadly, data science is not a subtopic of AI—a common claim originating from confusion on boundaries. AI and data science are conceptually different fields that overlap when ML/DM techniques are used in data analytics but otherwise have their own broader concerns. The broader scope of data science is discussed in this article, highlighting its constituents that are not part of AI. Conversely, there are topics in AI, such as agents, robotics, automated programming, and others, that are not within the scope of data science. Thus, AI and data science are related, but one does not encompass the other" (ibid).

Moving on, another essential side note worth covering consists of the wording arrangement involved in these two realms. Here's an intriguing question to contemplate:

- Should we refer to the pairing as that of generative AI and data science, or should the wording be in the other sequence of stating that it is data science and generative AI?

You might be tempted to shrug your shoulders and say that the difference is negligible and that either order is acceptable.

Here's my approach.

I generally try to refer to generative AI and data science when I am discussing the application of generative AI to data science endeavors. You might construe this as *Generative AI -> Data Science*, as though I am declaring that we are applying generative AI to data science. Now then, when I am referring to the use of data science to aid in devising generative AI, I tend to mention this as data science and generative AI. This could be construed as *Data Science -> Generative AI*, implying that data science is being applied to the crafting of generative AI.

This latter reference is also sometimes named as being data-centric AI, such as this research article posits:

- "Data-centric AI encompasses methods and tools to systematically characterize, evaluate, and monitor the underlying data used to train and evaluate models. At the ML pipeline level, this means that the considerations at each stage should be informed in a data-driven manner. We term this a data-centric lens. Since data is the fuel for any ML system, we should keep a sharp focus on the data, yet rather than ignoring the model, we should leverage the data-driven insights as feedback to systematically improve the model" (source is "DC-Check: A Data-Centric AI Checklist To Guide The Development Of Reliable Machine Learning Systems", Nabeel Seedat, Fergus Imrie, and Mihaela van der Schaar, posted online November 2022).

My rule of thumb is this:

- **(a) Generative AI and Data Science**. Wording generally but not always implies that generative AI is being applied to data science, expressed more clearly as *Generative AI -> Data Science.*
- **(b) Data Science and Generative AI**. Wording generally but not always implies that data science is being applied to generative AI, expressed more clearly as *Data Science -> Generative AI.*

I am also fine with allowing the catchphrases in either sequence, such that it simply suggests that the two fields or domains are paired up. No need to be a stickler on the ordering question, it just isn't worth the drawn-out drama.

When applying data science to generative AI (*Data Science -> Generative AI*), the data-centric AI approach imbues a data scientist's perspective to consider the life cycle of data that goes into formulating an AI system. Per the above-cited article by Seedat and others, they suggest that AI developers should be asking these data-centric AI questions when crafting AI systems:

- Q1: "How did you select, collect or curate your dataset?"
- Q2: "What data cleaning and/or pre-processing, if any, has been performed?"
- Q3: "Has data quality been assessed?"
- Q4: "Have you considered synthetic data?"
- Q5: "Have you conducted a model architecture and hyperparameter search?"
- Q6: "Does the training data match the anticipated use?"
- Q7: "Are there different data subsets or subgroups of interest?"
- Q8: "Is the data noisy, either in features or labels?"
- Q9: "How has the dataset been split for model training and validation?"
- Q10: "How has the model been evaluated (e.g. metrics & stress tests)?"
- Q11: "Are you monitoring your model?"
- Q12: "Do you have mechanisms in place to address data shifts?"

- Q13: "Have you incorporated tools to engender model trust?"

ChatGPT Code Interpreter Data Science Pairing Exemplar

Let's now explore the particulars of generative AI as applied to data science.

I'll begin with a brief introduction to how and why generative AI is being bolstered by adding the capability to generate programming code. This will intricately tie into the application of generative AI to data science. It is, shall we say, the secret sauce.

Turn the clock back a few months or so.

For those of you who had earlier attempted to use generative AI for doing data science, you probably right away hit a wall that was difficult to overcome. The wall was that most generative AI didn't play well with numbers. The text-oriented generative AI was preoccupied with words and wordsmithing, rather than being able to do calculations and readily deal with numbers.

I remember that when contemporary generative AI first rose to fame last year, some tried to use generative AI for exceedingly simple calculations that went bust. For example, you could potentially have instructed generative AI to add together one plus one and get an answer such as the number three. This seemed shocking. How could such a seemingly advanced AI system not properly calculate the simplest of additions?

The eye-opening realization was that the generative AI wasn't necessarily doing calculations in a usual mathematical way. Instead, the use of words was being relied upon. Envision this. Search the Internet for the words entailing adding together one plus one. The chances are that out there on the Internet there are instances whereby people have written that the answer is three. They might do so for fun. They might do so to make a point, for example, that maybe you get something as added value when you add two items together, thus you get a bonus that comes to the amount of three.

Generative AI that was data-trained on words or text found throughout the Internet would potentially have found those patterns of wording. Therefore, when you asked in natural language to add together one plus one, the prior data training might have led the generative AI to have landed on the word three. This is sensible in the sense that it was wording that had been found during the initial data training.

AI makers often stepped in when these seeming oddities arose and would adjust the generative AI so that it would no longer appear to be adrift of simple calculations. They might for example adjust the weights or guide the generative AI via RLHF (reinforcement learning via human feedback) toward answering two rather than answering three when presented with the one plus one question.

The crux is that the generative AI did not necessarily have any immediate means to do calculations per se.

This was soon remedied by allowing for APIs (application programming interfaces) that could connect the generative AI to other apps. When someone asks the generative AI to calculate one plus one, this becomes a question that is fed into a calculator-oriented app outside of the generative AI. The calculator app does the needed calculation and returns the result to the generative AI. The generative AI then displays the result to you. You wouldn't necessarily realize that the outside app had been used to get the result for you.

One potential constraint about using a calculator app is that it can only likely do calculations as predefined for that specific app. Suppose the calculator app wasn't devised to do square roots. The generative AI would then be unable to get an answer to a question about a square root that someone might have entered into a prompt.

All of this is my way of bringing you to the advent of something quite spectacular that has both plusses and minuses. The big reveal is that AI makers have been steadily advancing generative AI and can somewhat ably able to get generative AI to generate programming code.

Here's the deal.

Imagine if we were able to get generative AI to be able to produce programming code, akin to the kind of programming that software engineers and programmers are able to compose. The generative AI could potentially then generate code of a desired nature as needed for whatever problem is at hand. For instance, if a user enters a prompt asking for square roots, the generative AI could generate programming code to do so, and then invoke or run the code correspondingly. The sky is the limit as to whatever programming code can be concocted.

I stated that this is spectacular because it opens up immense possibilities for what generative AI can do. Rather than being relatively constrained, the generative AI can potentially produce programming code to perform whatever function or calculations might be needed. You have taken the generative AI and given it a general-purpose programming capability that widens tremendously what the generative AI can accomplish.

And that takes us to the door of data science. We can now eagerly walk in that door and see what is inside. I'll specifically explore the ChatGPT Code Interpreter, but as mentioned do realize that other generative AI apps are doing likewise.

OpenAI's ChatGPT can be augmented by using an OpenAI plug-in known as Code Interpreter (currently available for ChatGPT Plus subscribers). The generative AI app can generate code that is then run or executed in what is said to be a sandboxed, firewalled execution environment. The basis for constraining where the code is run would be that if the generated code goes awry, you want to try and confine what it can get away with. The type of code currently being generated is based on the popular programming language Python.

Of the multitude of ways that this programming code-producing capability can be used, our interest in this discussion is in the arena of generating code to perform data science tasks. The good news is that the generative AI takes care of the programming specifics for you. You do not need to know how to write programs. You do not need to know the programming language Python.

All that you need to know is how to use your everyday natural language to express what you want the generative AI to do when it comes to tackling data science tasks.

For example, you might begin a data science conversation with ChatGPT by importing a data file that you have available. You could then express in everyday language that you want the AI app to examine the data and tell you what it finds.

Assuming that the data file is readable, the AI app will likely examine the data and then indicate what it has found. For example, suppose the data consists of basketball teams and stats about each of the basketball players. The AI app might come back and tell you that the data consists of eight basketball teams. Furthermore, there are stats such as shooting percentage, time played, and other factors that are given for each basketball player.

At that juncture, you can ask the AI app to do a deeper analysis and discern whether the data might contain any issues or questionable values. The AI app might reply that one basketball player has zero time played and yet has various points scored, which seems like an inherent contradiction. You can ask the AI app what it advises be done about the data anomaly, or you can tell the AI app what you want it to do to correct or remove the data.

Once the data seems to have been sufficiently initially reviewed, you could then ask the AI app to do a statistical analysis of the relationship between the height of each player and their propensity to score baskets. The AI app is likely to suggest several statistical methods and inform you as to which might be most promising. You could then tell it which one to run or ask it to decide for you.

The AI app might then not only perform the statistical analysis but also provide a narrative describing and interpreting what the stats indicate. You could then ask the AI app to make bar charts, area charts, tree maps, piece charts, histograms, heat maps, box plots, scatter plots, line plots, and other types of visualizations. Along with those visualizations, you can request essays that depict what the graphed data illustrates and why it is significant to consider.

Notice that throughout the data science session, you did not need to perform any arcane commands or need to know how to produce the graphs. You merely expressed your preferences in ordinary language. That's the beauty of using generative AI in this front-end manner. You interact with the generative AI. It generates the needed code and executes it in the sandbox, thereupon then showing the results to you and interacting seamlessly with you.

I hope that you can now grasp how this potentially opens up data science and makes data science available on a scaled-up basis. This also hopefully elucidates why some assert that the use of generative AI for data science is going to democratize data science. The user of the generative AI doesn't need to presumably know one iota about data science. They simply describe generally what they want to have done, and the generative AI proceeds. Indeed, if the user isn't sure of what kind of data science effort to undertake, they can ask the generative AI to make suggestions or recommendations. The user doesn't have to be the active director and can in lieu be a passive receiver that just nudges along the generative AI.

Tidings When Pairing Generative AI And Data Science

Is this pairing up a good thing or a scary thing?

The good aspects are perhaps evident.

The downside is that someone who has no idea whatsoever about how to do data science is suddenly and immediately able to assume that they can do so. They are cheerfully likely to rely upon generative AI. One issue is that if the generative AI messes up, or misstates something, the neophyte is not going to realize what has happened. They might decide to take the AI-generated data science analysis, toss it into a convenient email, and send it around to the rest of the organization as though it is entirely accurate and immaculate.

We also return to the single version of the truth (SVOT) enigma. What data did the user opt to import into the generative AI? The prevalence of garbage-in garbage-out (GIGO) can rear its ugly head. The user might have gotten some sloppy or outdated data.

The generative AI won't especially realize this. Meanwhile, the most elegant of data science analyses are performed, doing so on data that is utterly bereft of being correct or proper.

Yikes, we are scaling up and democratizing GIGO, some might loudly lament.

I am only touching upon the tip of the iceberg. There's a lot more to be considered. For example, suppose the generative AI misinterprets what the user says they want to have occurred. The user might assume that the analysis comports fully with their request even though it doesn't.

Another example would be that the code generated by the generative AI turns out to be wrong and miscalculates things or sets the visualizations based on parameters that misleadingly portray the data. You cannot blindly assume that the generative AI will produce viable code. The code might be executable, but this doesn't also equate to the code doing the right things. Etc.

Conclusion

Some have wondered whether we need human data scientists at all, going forward.

If a neophyte can use a generative AI to perform data science work, maybe we no longer need data scientists per se. Think of the potential cost savings. Get rid of your expensive data scientists and just tell the rest of the organization they are now anointed as data scientists. That was easy.

Maybe we can take that a step further. Do we need humans to run the generative AI that is undertaking the data scientist activities? One viewpoint is that we can make this autonomous, akin to taking the human driver out of cars by devising an autonomously driven vehicle. We could aim to have autonomous artificial data scientists, namely generative AI or some allied kind of AI that does all the data science work, and no human intervention is required at all.

Those are some pretty big leaps of logic, especially since we are only now dipping our toes into the waters of generative AI as applied to data science. The number of dominos that need to fall one after another to reach those lofty lengths is currently a bit beyond the horizon. Let's not count our chickens before they are hatched.

Returning to the data strategy topic, the application of generative AI to data science does require that you take a serious relook at your existing data strategies.

Consider these pressing questions that pertain to your data strategies already underway:

- Who in your organization is going to aid in overseeing how generative AI is used for data science purposes?
- What kind of data governance do you have that will encompass the proper use of generative AI for data science and seek to curtail or mitigate improper uses?
- Are there sufficient data protections concerning generative AI gaining access to organizational data that might otherwise have strict privacy and confidentiality stipulations?
- Which personnel in your organization will be greenlighted to use generative AI for data science?
- For those that aren't permitted to use generative AI for data science, how will you detect when they do so, and what ramifications will there be for any such illicit use?
- How will you communicate throughout the organization about the tradeoffs and uses and misuses that can arise as a result of using generative AI for data science purposes?
- Etc.

If your data strategy has been sitting on a shelf, which is probably not a good practice, but anyway, you now have an impetus to rethink and reinvent your data strategy.

The emergence of generative AI for data science is a wake-up call. You can use this wake-up call to rationalize why it is now timely to reexamine the data strategy of the organization. That alone provides a bona fide and useful net result from the generative AI and data science boon that is about to occur.

You are at least spurred to revisit your data strategy and ensure that it is keeping up with the times.

You might want to identify some qualified data scientists in your organization who can start utilizing generative AI to explore how it will best fit your firm. Do not just toss them at this. Make sure they are aware of the AI Ethics and AI Law concerns that go into using generative AI.

I would also suggest that you do some prototype or pilot efforts, including that you opt to encompass selected personnel who aren't data scientists. You want to determine how they too are going to likely make use of generative AI for data science activities. Make sure that this is done in a secure generative AI environment and that you aren't letting the horse out of the barn as you try things out.

Tie together those efforts into a tidy bow by making sure to think of this on a mission-oriented organizational strategy basis. Data strategy can drive organizational strategy, while likewise, organizational strategy is to drive data strategy. The new kid on the block, generative AI, must inextricably be blended into all of this.

Generative AI is going to assuredly drive data strategy, which can drive organizational strategy. Beyond the realm of data science, you can also assert that generative AI in general is going to be driving organizational strategy all told.

A final remark for now. As Charles Dickens so aptly put things in the remarkable *A Tale Of Two Cities*: "It was the best of times, it was the worst of times, it was the age of wisdom, it was the age of foolishness, it was the epoch of belief, it was the epoch of incredulity, it was the season of light, it was the season of darkness, it was the spring of hope, it was the winter of despair.

Take my advice and without delay get onto updating your data strategy in light of generative AI. Your goal will be to maximize the age of wisdom and the season of light for attaining the best of times, along with minimizing or eliminating if feasible the season of darkness and a winter of despair. You can do it.

CHAPTER 19
TARGET-YOUR-RESPONSE (TAYOR) PROMPTING

There is a famous expression that gracefully says this: "Onward still he goes, Yet ne'er looks forward further than his nose" (per legendary English poet Alexandar Pope, 1734, *Essay on Man*).

We know of this today as the generally expressed notion that sometimes you get stuck and cannot seem to look any further than your own nose.

This is easy to do. You are at times involved deeply in something and are focused on the here and now. Immersed in those deep thoughts, you might be preoccupied mentally and unable to look a step ahead. It happens to all of us.

When using generative AI, you can fall readily into the same mental trap. Here's what I mean. You are often so focused on composing your prompt that you fail to anticipate what will happen next. The output generated by generative AI is given little advance thought and we all tend to react to whatever output we see.

Upon observing the generated output, and only at that juncture, might you be stirred into thinking that perhaps the output should be given some other spin or angle.

A one-step mindset for prompt engineering entails merely and almost solely ascertaining what your most immediate prompt is going to stipulate. You omit considerations about what the output or response is likely to look like. In contrast, a two-step think-ahead perspective is more informed and anticipates what you want as the output from the generative AI. In some cases, you might even do a further multi-step think-ahead contemplation about what the generated content consists of.

I liken this to a game of chess. A newbie chess player is preoccupied with their most immediate chess move. More experienced chess players think ahead. They anticipate what response they will get. At times, a quite savvy chess player can in their mind look ahead and envision a long series of what might happen.

Let's cast this into the sphere of generative AI and prompt engineering.

I might on a one-step mindset basis ask generative AI to tell me which states in the United States have a population count of less than 2 million people. That's what my prompt asks for. The response might be a narrative or essay that describes the states that meet that criterion. But suppose that I really wanted a listing of the states that were in the stipulated bracket. Upon seeing the population-explaining essay, I would then have to enter an additional prompt and tell the AI app to make the essay into a listing. The listing might be shown in order of population count, meanwhile, imagine that I had actually wanted the list to be shown in alphabetical order by state name. Ergo, I enter another prompt and tell the AI to reorder the generated list into alphabetical order by the state names.

Do you see how this was a rather awkward stutter-step process?

If I had thought ahead and realized that I wanted an alphabetical listing of the states that met the criteria of having less than a population of 2 million people, I could have saved myself the somewhat exasperating effort of having to tell repeatedly what I wanted. In one fell swoop I could have simply stated my request and simultaneously indicated how I wanted the generated output or response to appear.

Not only would this save me the angst of the stutter step, but the odds are that this would be cheaper for me if I am paying to use the generative AI. You see, the odds are that a one-command one-response will be less costly to undertake when paying by the transaction or computer processing cycle time for the AI usage than if I do the same action in a series of steps or prompts/responses (your mileage may vary).

Welcome to the realm of target-your-response (TAYOR), a prompt engineering technique that gets you to stay on your toes and think ahead about what the generated AI response is going to look like.

If you are cognizant about anticipating the nature of your desired output, you can upfront say what you want when you enter your requested prompt. All you need to do is put a bit of mental effort into thinking ahead and then merely specifying your desired output accordingly in a single prompt. This is not just about formatting. There is a plethora of facets that come into play. We will be examining those possibilities in depth, momentarily.

A quick clarification.

I want to make clear that you aren't necessarily saying in your prompt the anticipated answer per se that you hope to get. In my example about the population of the states, let's assume that I didn't know which states would meet the criteria. It could be just one state or maybe it would be a dozen or more. Thus, I was genuinely in the dark about which states would be identified by the AI. The answer itself was generally unknown to me.

At the same time, I knew in my mind that a list of the states is what I wanted to get. I didn't say this in my prompt. Maybe I didn't say that I wanted a list because it seemed obvious to me that a list was the most sensible way to present the information. I just assumed that the AI app would respond with a list. Furthermore, I knew in my mind that the states ought to be listed in alphabetical order because this would make it easier for me to inspect the list and see in an ordered fashion which states met the criteria.

The gist is that though I didn't know precisely what answer the AI might produce, I did know in my mind the nature of how I wanted the output to be presented. If you don't explicitly tell the AI app what you want in terms of the appearance of the generated answer, you never know what you might get. As I've repeatedly said in my columns and my workshops on prompt engineering, generative AI is like a box of chocolates, namely that you never know what you might get. You need to be as clear as you can about what you want the AI to accomplish.

Target-your-response is a means of doing so. You think about what the output or generated response ought to look like. You then mention this in your prompt. Your prompt then contains two elements. One element is the question or problem that you want the AI to solve. The other element that is blended into your prompt consists of explaining what you want the response to be like.

Here's your guiding precept about target-your-response:

- (1) **Prompt query or problem to be solved.** This is the portion of your prompt that asks a question of the AI or that provides a vexing problem to be solved.
- (2) **Prompt output or response targeting.** This is the part of your prompt that specifies or signals what the resulting response ought to look like or be structured or composed of.

I dare say that most rookies using generative AI seem to entirely neglect the second part of that prompting strategy. They wait until they see the response from the AI to think about what they want the response to look like. A more seasoned prompting approach consists of anticipating what the response might be and then in the initial prompt stipulating how you want the response to look.

A useful rule of thumb consists of blending together into your prompts an indication of the problem or query along with your desired look or targeting of the response. You can do both of those in a single prompt. No need to wait until the AI has responded to the query or problem. This is a situation whereby you can have your cake and eat it too.

I'm sure that some cynics or skeptics will right away carp and say that you don't always know exactly how you want the output or response to look.

Well, yes, that is indeed true.

But that doesn't give you the escape clause of always avoiding stating the targeted response that you want. I am suggesting that this is a handy tool that can be used a lot of the time, though not necessarily all of the time. Sometimes you do indeed need to first see what the AI generates. After inspecting the result, you can then inform the AI about how you want to format the response or otherwise tune it up.

In my experience, much of the time you can readily anticipate what you want the response to look like. All it takes is a reflective moment. You need to stop that impulse to enter a prompt right away. Instead, take a deep breath and imagine what the response might be. Consider what your preferences for the response might be. Then, include those preferences as blended into your prompt.

The quiet and determined Zen of targeting your response.

In this discussion, I am continuing my ongoing and widely popular series on the latest advances in prompt engineering for generative AI. Sometimes I have been covering complex issues that are based on deep insights into how generative AI is mathematically and computationally devised. For this exploration of the target-your-response or TAYOR approach, to some degree, the matter doesn't require a rocket scientist's mindset. This is more easily undertaken and easier to grasp.

That is a good thing. Sometimes the easy fixes are the best fixes. I see people all the time using generative AI that are seemingly stuck in a rut. They ask a question and then after seeing the answer are likely to be sparked or spurred into telling the AI to redo the response in some other preferred manner.

Rinse and repeat.

The sad thing is that they could bear less effort and potentially less cost by merely blending together their question and their desired look and feel of the reply.

Why don't people tend toward doing both?

Because nobody pointed out this possibility to them.

They have formed a habit of asking a question and getting a reply. Over and over again this is repeated. Some might assume that only once the AI has generated something, such as an essay about the states that have a population of less than 2 million, only then can they then ask to make this into a list. The viewpoint of the user is that maybe the AI is not devised to handle more than one aspect at a time. It might confound the AI.

The reality is that most generative AI is well-equipped to deal with a prompt that contains a slew of instructions. A compound prompt is fine. The AI will parse each of the elements in the prompt and almost always comply. I say this with some reservation due to the possibility that your multitude of elements might be mushy or poorly stipulated. In that case, the odds are that the AI will either not produce what you anticipated or might first balk at your request and ask you to clarify what you intend.

I loath to liken this to interacting with a human since I don't want to anthropomorphize today's AI, but if you spoke with a human you would often provide a multitude of aspects in a single "prompt" (I mean to say that in whatever you tell the person is essentially a prompt, as it were). You would assume that the person could abide by the multiheaded elements.

Of course, you can only carry this so far. If you hit someone with a byzantine array of instructions in one fell swoop, they might find this to be overwhelming.

Anyway, users of generative AI seem to swing to the extreme with generative AI in that there is a hidden belief by many novices that using a single aspect or element in a prompt is the way to go. Make things as simple as possible. Do not confuse the AI. Dribble out what you want. Keep things clean and simple.

We might be used to this due to prior Natural Language Processing (NLP) systems. The early days of Siri and Alexa taught most people that if you didn't say baby-like words slowly and clearly, the NLP would not figure out what you wanted. You ultimately had to resort to baby talk. This was the most sensible angst-reducing strategy that you could employ.

Thankfully, most generative AI of today is far beyond that level of computational natural language fluency. You can do all manner of sloppy stipulations and the AI app will glean what you want to have happen. That's the good news. Maybe it is great news. Perhaps it is surprising news to some.

My saying this does not mean that you can go crazy with your prompts. A prompt that is overloaded and filled with all kinds of junky wording is going to be either misinterpreted by the AI or rejected as impossible to straighten out. I assure you that prompts of a nutty nature will get you nutty results or force you into a dead-end conversation with the AI as the AI app tries to ferret out with you what you are saying. Please don't go there intentionally.

By understanding and using target-your-response techniques, your use of generative AI will be more productive, possibly less costly, and almost assuredly less frustrating. Before I dive into my in-depth exploration of this vital topic, let's make sure we are all on the same page when it comes to the keystones of prompt engineering and generative AI. Doing so will put us all on an even keel.

Digging Into The Target-Your-Response

The best way to show you how to do a target-for-response technique is by walking you through the myriad of ways that such efforts are performed.

I like to keep a checklist of the ploys at the ready, often taped to my screen or available as a quick pop-up. By regularly opting to use these tips and tricks the odds are that you'll eventually know them by heart. They will be a natural part of your prompt engineering acumen. We will be exploring them in a moment.

One vital key is to resist the compelling urge to enter a prompt impulsively. Think carefully about the prompt that you want to enter. Most of the time, make sure that a question or problem is included. And, most of the time, make sure that you specify or indicate how you want the output to appear or be composed.

I will show the target-your-response points by using a keyword to denote each one. I have placed them into alphabetical order for ease of rapidly finding a technique on the list. I have also numbered them for ease of reference. Be aware that they are not being shown in a priority order. I would assert that they are all generally of roughly equal merit. We can debate that contention and seek to provide pros and cons for each one, but I would reserve such a dispute for a future discussion rather than mudding the waters here.

The last one on the list is a special technique that I refer to as mix-and-match. I didn't put this into alphabetized order because I find that people tend to overlook it there. By having it as the last item, albeit out of alphabetical order, it seems like people are more apt to give it proper attention. This is especially the case because the mix-and-match is a reminder that you can combine the rest of the approaches into a single prompt. You do not need to treat each point as something mutually exclusive of all the others.

I would also emphasize that you should get comfortable using each of the identified points. Take some spare moments (do we have any these days?) and try out each one.

Determine what phrasing will fit best to your prompt engineering style. If you want to get into the Carnegie Hall of Prompt Engineering, you'll need three things, namely practice, practice, practice.

This is a lengthy list and might seem daunting. Don't worry. Many of the points overlap. All in all, the greatest value of the points is that it gets you thinking ahead of time about what kind of output or generated result you want. I'm sure that you'll come up with other possibilities beyond those that I have listed. There are plenty more (I'll be happy to cover more if there is expressed reader interest, thanks).

Let's jump in.

(1) Accurate

- Delineation about keyword *Accurate*: I'm sure that you would like your generative AI output to be accurate, meaning that it is correct and error-free. I earlier mentioned that generative AI can unfortunately produce results that contain errors, glitches, AI hallucinations, and other maladies. One means to try and spur generative AI to generate proper results is by explicitly telling the AI app to do so.

- Example prompt excerpt: "Make sure to double-check your answer and be as accurate as possible."

- Caveats: This is not an ironclad guarantee that your generated results will be correct. There is still a solid chance of having maladies in the output. Nonetheless, at times explicitly telling the AI app to be correct can help.

(2) Arguments

- Delineation about keyword *Arguments*. If you ask a question that might give rise to alternative answers or differing points of view, there is a chance that the generative AI will merely pick one such viewpoint and provide that as a seemingly final answer. You can indicate in your prompt that the AI app is to present opposing arguments for the question you are asking.

- Example prompt excerpt: "In your response, provide alternative viewpoints or arguments if the answer is considered contentious or debatable."

- Caveats: One notable disturbing concern is that the AI app might devise alternative viewpoints that otherwise don't especially matter, doing so as an attempt to appease your request. Be cautious.

(3) Beautification

- Delineation about keyword *Beautification*: The default by most generative AI is to provide outputs that are relatively well-written and generally matter-of-fact. You can try to uplift this further. Suppose you have asked for an essay and want it to be beautified in the sense of being especially polished and embellished. Just ask the AI to do so.

- Example prompt excerpt: "Tell me about the life of Abraham Lincoln and make the essay into a highly polished and altogether uplifting rendition."

- Caveats: The AI app can go overboard. You might find yourself facing an essay that is so over the top that it careens wildly into seeming to be satire or unbelievably excessive.

(4) Biases

- Delineation about keyword *Biases*: Most of the AI makers have tried to reduce the biases that might arise when the generative AI produces an output. This is not always going to catch everything of an untoward nature. You can explicitly tell the AI that you want any biases removed, though as usual, you have no guarantee of this happening. It might help. On an added twist, you could potentially purposely want a bias introduced into an output, such as if you are trying to demonstrate what biases look like. Either way, saying something about biases might be useful.

- Example prompt excerpt: "Scrub any biases out of the output before you present the results."

- Caveats: There is a chance that the AI will not be able to detect particular biases unless you specifically call them out. For example, you might need to state something specific such as making sure to remove ageism bias, etc.

(5) Citations

- Delineation about keyword *Citations*: A huge concern about generative AI is that it might have been data-trained on all manner of unsavory content found on the Internet. Some of the content might be disturbing. Some of it might be plainly wrong, though the AI app wasn't devised to figure this out. Anyway, you can try asking the AI app to provide citations to showcase where the material being presented came from. This might help bolster your belief in the output. It can also give you a direction of where to look next if you want to explore more on the topic beyond the confines of the AI app.

- Example prompt excerpt: "Provide citations for the output that clearly indicate the sources of the material used as a basis for generating the essay."

- Caveats: A slew of problems arise with asking for citations. First, the citations might be made up by the AI app and yet appear to be real, see my coverage of two lawyers who got themselves in hot water by believing fictitious citations. Second, the citations might be real but have no bearing on the content that was produced. And so on.

(6) Cleanliness

- Delineation about keyword *Cleanliness*: The AI makers have strived to ensure that generative AI outputs are cleanly worded. It is rare that you would get an output that for example contains swear words or seedy slang.

- You likely don't need to explicitly mention that you want the language to be clean unless you are veering into a topic area that perhaps intrinsically has such verbiage. Suppose you wanted to have the AI app explain graffiti that appears on bathroom walls. This might be hard to do if the AI isn't also permitted to showcase the bad words involved. You can instruct the AI to avoid foul words, and likewise, you can instruct the AI to include foul words, at your discretion.

- Example prompt excerpt: "Include any foul or uncouth words that would ordinarily occur when elaborating on the topic at hand."

- Caveats: An AI maker can make things so stringent that despite your asking to see foul words, the AI might still refuse to do so.

(7) Code Generation

- Delineation about keyword *Code Generation*: Software developers are gradually warming up to generative AI as a tool to generate programs and produce code for them. There is an art and a science involved in doing so. Meanwhile, even non-coders might find useful the ability to produce code.

- Example prompt excerpt: "Write a Python program that can sort a randomly arranged inputted list of numbers into their proper numerical order."

- Caveats: The code generated by the AI app might not do what you've asked to do. The code might also contain errors or bugs. Nowadays, be very suspicious of any code generated by AI and make sure to closely examine and test the code. Buyer beware.

(8) Coherency

- Delineation about keyword *Coherency*: Generative AI is data-trained on millions upon millions of sentences and billions of words, most of which have been written by humans.

- The AI maker has tried to ensure that the patterns devised based on human writing will present coherent outputs. Modern generative AI will rarely produce an incoherent essay. On a normal basis, you don't have to tell an AI app to be coherent in the output produced. If anything, supposing you purposely want an output that seems like a scrambled and zany piece of writing, in which case you could state this as a stipulation.

- Example prompt excerpt: "Compose an essay about Abraham Lincoln that is verging on being incoherent and rambles quite a lot."

- Caveats: If you want something that is on the edge of coherency, you'll likely need to be rather direct and specific, the result otherwise might be unreadable and probably useless to you.

(9) Complexity

- Delineation about keyword *Complexity*: Generative AI is somewhat devised to produce responses that are of limited complexity. The aim has been to generate results that an average adult would find acceptable. This also tends to mean that highly arcane and complex topics will often be watered down when presented to you. You can rachet up the complexity level that you are willing to accept.

- Example prompt excerpt: "In your reply, include any complex depictions that might require deeper scientific understanding. Do not flatten out the wording for the sake of readability."

- Caveats: Sometimes the AI app will catch on to a conversation and automatically provide complex answers. This can happen by pattern matching on the wording of your prompts. Thus, you might not need to explicitly tell the AI to switch to a higher level of complexity.

(10) Context

- Delineation about keyword *Context*: Much of the time, generative AI will provide an answer to the direct question or entered problem that you provided in your prompt. This is handy such that the answer is self-explanatory to both telling an answer and displaying the question posed. In case you want to make sure that this happens, merely tell the AI app to include any supporting context around the answer.

- Example prompt excerpt: "Make sure that the answer includes the context surrounding the topic and is supportive of the question being addressed."

- Caveats: The odds are somewhat high that asking for context could generate a much lengthier reply than you might have been expecting. Your safest bet would be to include an indication of how much context you want.

(11) Dialoguing

- Delineation about keyword *Dialoguing*: Rookies fall into a mental trap of not engaging generative AI in a dialogue. They simply ask a question and wait for an answer. A big benefit of generative AI is that it can generally carry on an ongoing dialogue or conversation. You can do this without having to tell the AI to do so. But, if you want to ensure that the AI app will proceed on a dialogue basis, you can tell it to do so and the odds are the AI will attempt to keep the conversation going.

- Example prompt excerpt: "I want to carry on a conversation about the life of Abraham Lincoln. Make sure to keep your end of the conversation going by being interactive and starting new avenues of dialogue as appropriate."

- Caveats: Please realize that you are dialoguing with a machine. I emphasize this because the conversational capabilities are so immersive that you can start to falsely believe you are interacting with a sentient being. You are not.

(12) Elaboration

- Delineation about keyword *Elaboration*: If I ask for an indication about the life of Lincoln, you never know what you might get in terms of the AI being succinct or verbose. This is true of nearly any inquiry. When you know that you want to have an elaborate response, just say so in your prompt.

- Example prompt excerpt: "Tell me about the course of Abraham Lincoln's life and make sure to give lots of details and effusive elaboration."

- Caveats: Admittedly, you might be better off waiting to ask for elaboration until you see whatever randomly sized response the AI first gives. Some prefer that approach. It all depends on whether you know beforehand what you hope to get generated.

(13) Emotion

- Delineation about keyword *Emotion*: I've covered in my columns that generative AI can essentially simulate an expression of various emotions by how words are chosen and lined up. You can get an angry response. You can get loving responses. Etc. The AI makers have generally set parameters so that the AI app will be seemingly emotionless in what is produced. If you want an essay or perhaps an entire dialogue that includes the AI appearing to be emotional, just say so.

- Example prompt excerpt: "Express the response by using highly emotional wording."

- Caveats: Similar to my prior warnings, do not fall for the AI as being sentient when the outputs appear to be emotionally laden. These are words and nothing more than words.

(14) Examples

- Delineation about keyword *Examples*: I would guess that one of the most overlooked pluses about generative AI is that you can request examples of whatever the response is telling you. Suppose that you ask generative AI what meals are best for a fancy dinner. You might get an overall description but no examples. You can in your initial prompt ask for examples.

- Example prompt excerpt: "Give me three examples of what a fancy dinner would consist of."

- Caveats: I usually prefer to indicate how many examples I want, rather than letting the AI randomly choose some number of examples. Also, the examples might sometimes be afield of the topic at hand, thus it is wise to try and word your prompt to clarify exactly what the examples are to be related to.

(15) Explanation

- Delineation about keyword *Explanation*: A significant concern in AI Ethics and AI Law is that much of generative AI lacks any explanation about how a computational decision was reached. For example, if someone is using an AI app to decide whether someone gets hired, you'd likely want an explanation for those who get turned down.

- Example prompt excerpt: "After answering my question, make sure to provide an explanation."

- Caveats: Many issues exist with getting explanations. First, the explanation might have nothing to do with how the computational underpinnings actually work. The explanation is a contrived depiction. Second, the explanation might be a canned explanation that the AI makers have essentially cooked into the AI app. And so on.

(16) Formality/Informality

- Delineation about keyword *Formality/Informality*: The formality associated with most generative AI is somewhat of a friendly chatty pal. This is established by the AI maker. You can tell the AI app to be more formal. You can also tell the AI app to be less formal. You decide.

- Example prompt excerpt: "I want to engage in a dialogue and ask that you converse in a very formal manner with me."

- Caveats: Not everyone readily agrees on what is formal versus informal. The best bet is to be more descriptive about what you want and possibly give some examples of what you mean by being formal or informal.

(17) Formatted

- Delineation about keyword *Formatted*: This one is a shocker for many people who have used generative AI on a cursory basis. You can tell the AI app to format an output in a particular way. In some cases, you can even specify a strict format such as for a form or template that you might have in mind or hand.

- Example prompt excerpt: "Compose a letter for me about requesting a refund on my recent purchase of a confabulator. Make sure to format the letter accordingly."

- Caveats: Depending upon which generative AI app you are using, some do a better job at formatting than others. Some do a lousy job.

(18) Grammar/Dialect

- Delineation about keyword *Grammar/Dialect*: Would you like to have an essay or be engaged in a dialogue wherein the AI adopts a southern accent? Or maybe you prefer an East Coast accent.

- In terms of grammar, the usual default is around a high school-level writer. You can increase this to college level or higher. You can also get the grammar to be akin to a fifth grader. Select whatever is needed.

- Example prompt excerpt: "Let's discuss the making of grits and do so with you adopting a southern accent."

- Caveats: You might start the AI down a path that keeps it going in that fashion. Once you've had enough of whatever you've asked for, make sure to tell the AI to go back to the usual defaults.

(19) Guidance

- Delineation about keyword *Guidance*: You can tell the generative AI to provide guidance. This can be composed as an essay or can be the essence of a dialogue.

- Example prompt excerpt: "Provide me with guidance on how to safely do river rafting."

- Caveats: I've said it before and will say this again, do not be lulled into thinking that the AI is sentient. The guidance might be hogwash. Be careful.

(20) Headings/Subheadings

- Delineation about keyword *Headings/Subheadings*: You can ask to have your essay or response be divided into major headings. If desired, you can also ask for subheadings.

- Example prompt excerpt: "Provide an essay about George Washington that consists of three major sections, and include headings for each section."

- Caveats: The odds are that you'll need to look at the output to decide whether it looks as you wanted it to look. Keep in mind that you can merely tell the AI to redo the prior response and adjust to whatever else you had in mind.

(21) Length

- Delineation about keyword *Length*: The length or number of words associated with a given response will vary based on the computational pattern matching of the AI and based on the AI maker's set parameters. You can pretty much adjust the length, though there are some maximums that most AI apps have.

- Example prompt excerpt: "Write a 1,000-word length essay about why the sky is blue."

- Caveats: Some smarmy users have told generative AI to write a 100,000-word sized book for them, from scratch. This might hit the limit on the length parameters. Of course, you can potentially get around this by doing a series of prompts and asking for 10,000 words at a time.

(22) Level

- Delineation about keyword *Level*: The level of writing produced by generative AI is pretty much by default around a high school or average adult level. You can ask for kindergarten level. You can ask for rocket scientist level.

- Example prompt excerpt: "Identify why the horse crossed the road and do so as though talking to a six-year-old child."

- Caveats: Try to be as specific as you can about the level that you desire.

(23) Lists

- Delineation about keyword *Lists*: I already mentioned the notion of getting lists as outputs, doing so when I was earlier discussing my effort to find out which states in the U.S. have a population of less than 2 million people. You can ask for a list. You can make the list numbered. You can arrange the items in a list. And so on.

- Example prompt excerpt: "Produce a list of the five reasons that some people won't eat broccoli."

- Caveats: You can have lists along with an essay. Thus, you do not need to forsake one for the other.

(24) Logical

- Delineation about keyword *Logical*: At times, you might get the AI producing an essay or engaging in a dialogue that seems to be skipping logic. You can ask the AI to proceed on a logical or step-by-step basis, which has the added advantage of often generating better answers.

- Example prompt excerpt: "Once you've solved the puzzle, show how you solved the puzzle by laying out each logical step."

- Caveats: The logic or stepwise indication might be contrived. There is a chance that the steps are merely an after-the-fact elucidation that has nothing to do with the computational effort that was undertaken. Be on your toes.

(25) Lyrics

- Delineation about keyword *Lyrics*: Are you someone who wants to write songs but seems incapable of writing lyrics? You can get generative AI to write lyrics for you.

- Example prompt excerpt: "Make up the lyrics for a song about a bird and a turtle that became the best of friends."

- Caveats: Be cautious in using the lyrics since that multi-million-dollar song you include them into might be violating copyright law. You cannot assume that the output produced by generative AI is not violating someone's copyrights.

(26) Multimodal

- Delineation about the keyword *Multimodal*: My prediction is that we will gradually and inevitably have multi-modal generative AI. Thus, rather than merely text-to-text or text-to-image, we will have text-to-anything such as audio, video, etc. The same goes in the other direction, namely that we will have image-to-text, image-to-video, video-to-image, video-to-text, and all other permutations. My focus on these target-your-responses is aimed at text-to-text. Once we have the anything-to-anything, I'll be sharing an entirely new series of tips and techniques about prompt engineering.

- Example prompt excerpt: "Produce a written essay and also make an audio version that is suitable as a podcast, plus create a video too."

- Caveats: Right now, this is hard to do since few of the generative AI apps are multimodal. One quick way of getting there is by the AI makers allowing you to use API (application programming interfaces) to access allied apps that can handle the multimodal aspects.

(27) Parse

- Delineation about keyword *Parse*: You can tell the generative AI to parse something and tell you about what was found. For example, I might provide the AI app with a research paper that someone wrote and ask the AI app to parse the content to identify the style of the paper, including sentence structures, use of words, etc.

- Example prompt excerpt: "Examine this essay and parse it to identify what level of writing is depicted."

- Caveats: The parsing can be right on. The parsing can also be bamboozled if someone is intentionally giving you content that they devised with the use of generative AI to fool other generative AI.

(28) Persona

- Delineation about keyword *Persona*: You can tell generative AI to adopt a persona such as pretending to be Einstein. You can then engage the AI in a dialogue or ask it to answer questions and produce essays in that guise.
- Example prompt excerpt: "Pretend that you are Einstein and have a conversation with me about quantum physics."

- Caveats: The use of a persona can get you mired in a fake world. Always be on top of the fact that the AI is not sentient.

(29) Perspective

- Delineation about keyword *Perspective*: You want generative AI to produce an essay, and perhaps you want it written in a first-person manner. Or, maybe you prefer some other perspective. Stipulate what you want.

- Example prompt excerpt: "Write an autobiography of the life of Herbert Hoover in first-person."

- Caveats: The consistency of the perspective can sometimes wane. Do a double-check.

(30) Poetic

- Delineation about keyword *Poetic*: Some people get a mind block when trying to write poetry. No problem. Ask generative AI to write something poetic for you.

- Example prompt excerpt: "Write a poem that describes the perfect summer day when in the Great Basin Desert."

- Caveats: Poetry out of generative AI can be like a roll of the dice. You might need to try repeatedly guiding the AI toward what you want.

(31) Purpose

- Delineation about keyword *Purpose*: If you are going to use an essay produced by generative AI such as sending the essay to a friend or colleague, it might be helpful to have the AI include in the rendition a stated purpose underlying the essay.

- Example prompt excerpt: "Compose an essay about life and include what the purpose of life is."

- Caveats: The use of purpose and the use of context are like two peas in a pod.

(32) Rephrasing

- Delineation about keyword *Rephrasing*: You can give generative AI some text and ask the AI to rephrase what is there. The result might be similar to what you provided. If you want the rephrasing to differ substantially, make sure to say so.

- Example prompt excerpt: "In the text, I am about to give you, rephrase the essay and make it more powerful and commanding."

- Caveats: Be forewarned that if you do this with someone's copyrighted material, you might be plagiarizing or infringing.

(33) Resumes/Cover Letters

- Delineation about keyword *Resume/Cover Letters*: Yes, you can produce a resume by using generative AI. The same goes for cover letters.

- Example prompt excerpt: "I will provide you with details about my work experience and you are to make this into a resume that is suitable for applying to jobs. Also, include a cover letter."

- Caveats: The default resume is likely not going to be exactly what you want. You can either upfront provide an example resume for the AI to patten on, or have a resume generated and ask for adjustments.

(34) Spelling

- Delineation about keyword *Spelling*: A basic foundation of most generative AI is that the spelling of words is going to be nearly perfect. This is due to the data training and subsequent filtering. If you want to have the AI make spelling mistakes, you can do so. Probably a rare thing to do.

- Example prompt excerpt: "Write an essay that contains three misspelled words and covers the topic of how to write a perfect essay."

- Caveats: If you are trying to fool someone into thinking that an AI-generated essay was written by a human, the inclusion of spelling errors might do the trick. Not recommended.

(35) Stories/Tales

- Delineation about keyword *Stories/Tales*: A typical essay produced by generative AI will be of the normal garden variety. If you want the AI to spin a tale for you, this is easily done. As an aside, you can use generative AI to also write scripts for you, such as when devising a movie script or a script for a theatrical play.

- Example prompt excerpt: "Make an enchanting tale about a dog and a cat that have an adventure while stuck in the Grand Canyon."

- Caveats: You will want to specify the length, style, and a slew of other stipulations if you want the tale or story to come out looking a certain way.

(36) Style

- Delineation about keyword *Style*: All kinds of styles are available when writing. You might want an essay or have a dialogue based on a sloppy style. Perhaps a lofty style is something you might like.

- Example prompt excerpt: "Write in the style of William Shakespeare."

- Caveats: A style can also arise when you invoke a persona. In this case, I am not asking the AI to adopt the persona of Shakespeare. I am merely stating that the writing should appear as though written by the Bard.

(37) Summarization

- Delineation about keyword *Summarization*: Someone hands you a lengthy document. You don't have the time to read the whole darned thing. You feed it into generative AI and ask the AI app to summarize the material. Handy dandy.

- Example prompt excerpt: "Summarize the following story that tells about a mouse and a duck that went on an adventure in a magical forest."

- Caveats: Be cautious feeding any confidential or sensitive material into generative AI. Most of the AI makers stipulate in their licensing that they can use input material for advancing their AI app.

(38) Tables

- Delineation about keyword *Tables*: You are studying how the color of someone's eyes might be related to whether they are left-handed or right-handed. You feed this data into generative AI and ask for a table to be produced. The table in a text-to-text AI app might look like typed text and not like a graphic table. Some APIs can be used to get a chart produced.

- Example prompt excerpt: "Make a table that consists of the color of someone's eyes as the rows and handedness will be the columns."

- Caveats: Until we get pervasive multimodal generative AI, the table-producing facets of these AI apps are going to be somewhat unwieldy.

(39) Translation

- Delineation about keyword *Translation*: You've written a story in English and want to have it translated into Spanish. Generative AI might be able to do this for you. Some generative AI apps have a really good language translation capability. Some don't.

- Example prompt excerpt: "Translate this story into Spanish.

- Caveats: Today's generative AI is not the best at doing natural language translations, though the AI app will certainly try to do so. You might want to double-check with someone who knows the targeted language or otherwise perform and compare when using other translator tools.

(40) (ZZZ) Mix-and-match

- Delineation about keyword *Mix-and-match*: As a side note, yes, I realize that this keyword is not in alphabetical order with the rest of the list (that's why I put the ZZZ in front of it, trying to excuse this for being the last item in the list). I put it here, at the last position, since it is an all-encompassing point. You can mix and match any of the aforementioned techniques.

- Example prompt excerpt: "Write a formal essay, using the persona of James Bond, and produce a list of the cities that spies tend to go to, making the length of the story no more than 500 words. Add a short poem after the essay that covers why being a spy is both exciting and dangerous."

- Caveats: If you do a lot of mixing and matching in a single prompt, the result can be confusing for the AI app to parse. Try to be as deliberate and distinctive as you can.

Conclusion

I trust that you can discern from these numerous prompt engineering target-your-response or TAYOR indicators that you have plenty of options and flexibility regarding generative AI-generated results. It is sad and quite dismaying that a lot of people using generative AI are seemingly unaware of these amazing and useful possibilities.

Those not in the know are essentially undervaluing and underutilizing the built-in capacities of generative AI. Imagine that you have available a tool that is like a Swiss Army knife, and you only use it in the narrowest of ways.

All of those additional features and functionality could do you a great deal of good, but you only know one particular aspect. I'm not suggesting that your life depends on it. The crux is that you might as well be all that you can be, and use all that you can use.

I fervently proclaim that it is time to open everyone's eyes wide toward getting more bang for their buck out of generative AI. As the hamburger commercials used to say, you can have it your way, cooked and adorned per your preferences.

Here then again, are the forty target-your-response techniques that I elaborated on above, and for which you can proudly pat yourself on the back for now knowing:

1. Accurate
2. Arguments
3. Beautification
4. Biases
5. Citations
6. Cleanliness
7. Code Generation
8. Coherency
9. Complexity
10. Context
11. Dialoguing
12. Elaboration
13. Emotion
14. Examples
15. Explanation
16. Formality/Informality
17. Formatted
18. Grammar/Dialect
19. Guidance
20. Headings/Subheadings
21. Length
22. Level
23. Lists
24. Logical
25. Lyrics
26. Multimodal

27. Parse
28. Persona
29. Perspective
30. Poetic
31. Purpose
32. Rephrasing
33. Resumes/Cover Letters
34. Spelling
35. Stories/Tales
36. Style
37. Summarization
38. Tables
39. Translation
40. (ZZZ) Mix-and-match

A few final remarks on these weighty matters shall conclude this discussion.

I stated earlier that those target-your-response techniques are just the tip of the iceberg. My aim was not to showcase every possibility, which would be impossible in the limited space that I have here. The true goal was to get you thinking about how you can leverage generative AI to best utilize the outputs or results that the AI app might produce. My sincerest hope is that your creative juices are flowing in that erstwhile regard.

Recall the famous quote about not being able to see beyond the confines of one's nose. Lift up the gaze and look further ahead. Whenever you compose a prompt, go ahead and include an indication of what you want the generated result to consist of.

You can use these prompt engineering target-your-response techniques with the realization that these are already considered known possibilities. You are using something that is tried and true. Whatever you do, don't get caught with the shameful remorse that you were the last to cast aside a one-step non-look-ahead mindset when composing prompts. Per the wise words of the acclaimed poet Alexandar Pope: "Be not the first by whom the new are tried. Nor yet the last to lay the old aside."

Assuming that you do try to be with it and employ a target-your-response mantra, I will tell you right now that some of your prompts won't cut the mustard and might not get you what you want. That's perfectly okay. Keep trying.

Alexander Pope already has that covered for us via his endearing and most enduring famous line: "To err is human; to forgive, divine."

APPENDIX

APPENDIX A
TEACHING WITH THIS MATERIAL

The material in this book can be readily used either as a supplemental to other content for a class or it can also be used as a core set of textbook material for a specialized class. Classes, where this material is most likely used, include any classes at the college or university level that want to augment the class by offering thought-provoking and educational essays about AI.

In particular, here are some aspects for class use:

- Computer Science. Studying applications of AI/ML, GenAI, etc.
- Business. Exploring AI in the mental health industry, etc.
- Medical/Healthcare. AI/ML and generative AI in mental health and the medical realm.

Specialized classes at the undergraduate and graduate level can also make use of this material.

For each chapter, consider whether you think the chapter provides material relevant to your course topic. There is plenty of opportunity to get the students thinking about the topic and force them to decide whether they agree or disagree with the points offered and positions taken. I would also encourage you to have the students do additional research beyond the chapter material presented (I provide next some suggested assignments they can do).

RESEARCH ASSIGNMENTS ON THESE TOPICS

Your students can find background material on these topics, doing so in various business and technical publications. I list below the top-ranked AI-related journals. For business publications, I would suggest sources such as the Harvard Business Review, Forbes, Fortune, WSJ, and the like.

Here are some suggestions for homework or projects that you could assign to students:

a) Assignment for foundational AI research topic: Research and prepare a paper and a presentation on a specific aspect of Generative AI, Machine Learning, Large Language Models, etc. The paper should cite at least 3 reputable sources. Compare and contrast to what has been stated in this book.

b) Assignment for the Medical/Healthcare topic: Research and prepare a paper on the medical/healthcare sphere and how AI is impacting the realm. Cite at least 3 reputable sources and analyze the characterizations. Compare and contrast to what has been stated in this book.

c) Assignment for a Business topic: Research and prepare a paper and a presentation on the business side of the medical/healthcare field, especially as impacted by the latest in AI. What is hot, and what is not? Cite at least 3 reputable sources. Compare and contrast to the depictions in this book.

d) Assignment to do a Startup: Have the students prepare a paper about how they might startup a business in this realm. They must submit a suitable Business Plan for the startup. They could also be asked to present their Business Plan and must have a presentation deck to coincide with it.

You can certainly adjust the aforementioned assignments to fit to your particular needs and the class structure. You'll notice that I ask for 3 reputable cited sources for the paper writing based assignments. I usually steer students toward "reputable" publications, since otherwise they will cite some oddball source that has no credentials other than that they happened to write something and post it onto the Internet. You can define "reputable" in whatever way you prefer, for example some faculty think Wikipedia is not reputable while others believe it is reputable and allow students to cite it.

The reason that I usually ask for at least 3 citations is that if the student only does one or two citations they usually settle on whatever they happened to find the fastest. By requiring three citations, it usually seems to force them to look around, explore, and end-up probably finding five or more, and then whittling it down to 3 that they will actually use.

I have not specified the length of their papers, and leave that to you to tell the students what you prefer. For each of those assignments, you could end-up with a short one to two pager, or you could do a dissertation length paper. Base the length on whatever best fits for your class, and the credit amount of the assignment within the context of the other grading metrics you'll be using for the class.

I mention in the assignments that they are to do a paper and prepare a presentation. I usually try to get students to present their work. This is a good practice for what they will do in the business world. Most of the time, they will be required to prepare an analysis and present it. If you don't have the class time or inclination to have the students present, then you can of course cut out the aspect of them putting together a presentation.

If you want to point students toward highly ranked journals in AI, here's a list of the top journals as reported by various citation counts sources (this list changes from year to year):

- Communications of the ACM
- Artificial Intelligence
- Cognitive Science
- IEEE Transactions on Pattern Analysis and Machine Intelligence
- Foundations and Trends in Machine Learning
- Journal of Memory and Language
- Cognitive Psychology
- Neural Networks
- IEEE Transactions on Neural Networks and Learning Systems
- IEEE Intelligent Systems
- Knowledge-based Systems
- Annual Review of Clinical Psychology
- Health Psychology Review
- JAMA Psychiatry
- Evidence-Based Mental Health
- Etc.

GUIDE TO USING THE CHAPTERS

For each of the chapters, I provide next some various ways to use the chapter material. You can assign the tasks as individual homework assignments, or the tasks can be used with team projects for the class. You can easily layout a series of assignments, such as indicating that the students are to do item "a" below for say Chapter 1, then "b" for the next chapter of the book, and so on.

a) What is the main point of the chapter and describe in your own words the significance of the topic,

b) Identify at least two aspects in the chapter that you agree with, and support your concurrence by providing at least one other outside researched item as support; make sure to explain your basis for disagreeing with the aspects,

c) Identify at least two aspects in the chapter that you disagree with, and support your disagreement by providing at least one other outside researched item as support; make sure to explain your basis for disagreeing with the aspects,

d) Find an aspect that was not covered in the chapter, doing so by conducting outside research, and then explain how that aspect ties into the chapter and what significance it brings to the topic,

e) Interview a specialist in industry about the topic of the chapter, collect from them their thoughts and opinions, and readdress the chapter by citing your source and how they compared and contrasted to the material,

f) Interview a relevant academic professor or researcher in a college or university about the topic of the chapter, collect from them their thoughts and opinions, and readdress the chapter by citing your source and how they compared and contrasted to the material,

g) Try to update a chapter by finding out the latest on the topic, and ascertain whether the issue or topic has now been solved or whether it is still being addressed, explain what you come up with.

The aforementioned suggestions are ways in which you can get the students of your class involved in considering the material of a given chapter. You could mix things up by having one of those above assignments per each week, covering the chapters over the course of the semester or quarter. As a reminder, here are the chapters of the book and you can select whichever chapters you find most valued for your particular class:

	Chapter Title
1	Introduction to Prompt Engineering
2	Imperfect Prompting
3	Persistent Context And Custom Instructions Prompting
4	Multi-Persona Prompting
5	Chain-of-Thought (CoT) Prompting
6	Retrieval-Augmented Generation (RAG) Prompting
7	Chain-of-Thought Factored Decomposition Prompting
8	Skeleton-of-Thought (SoT) Prompting
9	Show-Me Versus Tell-Me Prompting
10	Mega-Personas Prompting
11	Certainty And Uncertainty Prompting
12	Vagueness Prompting
13	Catalogs Or Frameworks For Prompting
14	Flipped Interaction Prompting
15	Self-Reflection Prompting
16	Add-On Prompting
17	Conversational Prompting
18	Prompt-To-Code Prompting
19	Target-Your-Response (TAYOR) Prompting

Table of Contents (Advanced Book)

"Advances In Prompt Engineering For Generative AI"

In case you are interested in my advanced book entitled "Advances In Prompt Engineering for Generative AI" (Dr. Lance Eliot, LBE Publishing, 2023, available on Amazon and at major online booksellers), which is a handy companion to this book, here is a listing of the chapters in that other book as a heads-up of the contents there:

ABOUT THE AUTHOR

Dr. Lance B. Eliot, Ph.D., MBA is a globally recognized AI scientist and thought leader, an experienced executive and leader, a successful entrepreneur, and a noted scholar on AI/ML, including his Forbes and AI Trends columns have amassed over 7.4+ million views, his books on AI are frequently ranked in the Top 10 of all-time AI books, his articles are widely cited, and has developed and implemented dozens of advanced AI systems.

He currently serves as the CEO of Techbruim, Inc. and has over twenty years of industry experience including serving as a corporate officer in billion-dollar-sized firms and as a partner in a major consulting firm. He is also a successful entrepreneur having founded, ran, and sold several high-tech startups.

Dr. Eliot previously hosted the popular radio show *Technotrends* which was also available on American Airlines flights via their in-flight audio program, he has made appearances on CNN, has been a frequent speaker at industry conferences, and his podcasts have been downloaded over 300,000 times.

A former professor at the University of Southern California (USC), he founded and led an innovative research lab on Artificial Intelligence. He also previously served on the faculty of the University of California Los Angeles (UCLA) and was a visiting professor at other major universities including serving as Fellow in AI at Stanford University. He was elected to the International Board of the Society for Information Management (SIM), a prestigious association of over 3,000 high-tech executives worldwide.

He has performed extensive community service, including serving as Senior Science Adviser to the Congressional Vice-Chair of the Congressional Committee on Science & Technology. He has served on the Board of the OC Science & Engineering Fair (OCSEF), where he is also has been a Grand Sweepstakes judge, and likewise served as a judge for the Intel International SEF (ISEF). He served as the Vice-Chair of the Association for Computing Machinery (ACM) Chapter, a prestigious association of computer scientists. Dr. Eliot has been a shark tank judge at start-up pitch competitions and served as a mentor for several incubators and accelerators in Silicon Valley and Silicon Beach.

Dr. Eliot holds a Ph.D., MBA, and Bachelor's in Computer Science, and earned the CDP, CCP, CSP, CDE, and CISA certifications.

ADDENDUM

Essentials Of Prompt Engineering For Generative AI

Practical Advances in
Artificial Intelligence and Machine Learning

By

Dr. Lance B. Eliot, MBA, PhD

For special orders of this book, contact:

LBE Press Publishing

Email: LBE.Press.Publishing@gmail.com

Made in United States
Orlando, FL
10 November 2026

90498891R00246